Reflections on

Indian Wisdom

— Philosophical Perspectives —

Reflections on

Indian Wisdom

— Philosophical Perspectives —

Essays in Honour of

Prof. G.C. Nayak

Edited by

Bijayananda Kar

Aryan Books International
New Delhi

REFLECTIONS ON INDIAN WISDOM

ISBN-81-7305-332-4

First Published in **2007** by
ARYAN BOOKS INTERNATIONAL
Pooja Apartments, 4B, Ansari Road, New Delhi - 110 002 (India)
Tel.: 23287589, 23255799; Fax: 91-11-23270385
E-mail: aryanbooks@vsnl.com

Computer Typeset and Printed in India at
ABI Prints & Publishing Co., New Delhi.

Prof. G.C. Nayak

Preface

Here, out of the essays collected in the volume, most are new and unpublished. Few of the essays are either published or presented before the learned philosophical audience. The essay on Wittgenstein and Kant was originally published in the Gauhati University's *Journal of Arts*, XXXIV (pp. 134-43). The essay on Reason and Revelation in Śaṅkara was presented as Pratap Seth Endowment Vedānta Lecture in the sixty-fourth session of the Indian Philosophical Congress, held at Gujrat University in October 1989. The essay on Rethinking the Two Faces of Svarāja : Pre-independence and Post-independence appeared first in the *Indian Philosophical Quarterly*, Volume XXVIII, No. 2, April 2001. The essay on Commonism was first published in the *Visva-Bharati Journal of Philosophy*, Santiniketan, Volume XXVII, No. 2, February 1991.

The very idea of bringing out a festschrift volume (dedicated to Professor G.C. Nayak) originated as early as 1998 and the essays were collected from the learned scholars at different phases. I am extremely thankful to the contributors who are good enough to respond to my request for presenting their essays for the volume. Their contribution has not only helped me to bring out the volume, but that is also a good token for expressing their tribute to and honouring Professor Nayak.

The collection of essays, editing those and finally sending the same to the press have taken considerable amount of time. Even if it is somewhat delayed, the publisher has been able to bring out the volume and that too in an appreciable manner. I, therefore, express my thanks to Mr. Vikas Arya who has brought out the volume on behalf of Aryan Books International, New Delhi.

I hope that the essays, printed in the volume, will stimulate the interested readers to re-look at the issues on which thought-provoking discussions have been undertaken by the learned scholars. I also thank my dear students: Dr. (Mrs.) Madhumita Dash, Dr. (Mrs.) S. Mohapatra and Dr. Bibhuti Bhusan Nayak for helping me in preparation of the Index and checking the page-proofs. I am grateful to my wife, Dr. Namita Kar for all the assistance she ungrudgingly has given for the completion of the work.

AM-26, VSS Nagar **Bijayananda Kar**
Bhubaneswar - 751 007

Contents

Prof. G.C. Nayak
A Profile

I

Professor G.C. Nayak (Goranga Charana Nayak) was born at Cuttack on 14th February 1935. He originally hails from a respectable family of Jajpur. His parents were social, kind-hearted and above all greatly spiritual. He has one brother and three sisters. All of them are now well settled and his brother (Manmatha) is now in Chicago and is a Professor of Mathematics. Professor Nayak is married and is blessed with three sons and one daughter.

I had the good occasion of having close relation with both the brothers in their childhood days as we were neighbours at Cuttack (Deewan Bazar) for a long time. Manmatha is almost my contemporary but three of us used to play together and quite often listened to the stories from the epics and the purāṇas, narrated by the elderly people of our families. Being influenced by such dharmic stories, we used to play the roles of Viṣṇu, Mahāviṣṇu, etc. during light moments. Because of dharmic cultural background of our parentage, we were instructed by our elders to recite Sanskrit and Oriya devotional hymns (*stotraṃ*) and that had influenced us. Of course we were interested in such mythological narrations, not exactly of identical motive or intention. Because of the strong religio-spiritual family background, Nayak used to ponder about life, its origin and final destination. The theistic world-view, found in the traditional sources, used to have deep impact in his mind since then and he was more interested in going through the classical sources in original. That, perhaps, propelled him to read ancient literature particularly Sanskrit most sincerely.

Not only he had Sanskrit during his school career, he continued to have it in his college-days upto the degree level. The most important event that took place during that time was Nayak's being best Graduate, having Sanskrit Hons. (securing first position in First Class) with holding Distinction in other subjects from the Utkal University in 1954. It is notable that his interest in Sanskrit was not simply limited to know the traditional heritage, but also to critically study and evaluate it by the canons of reflective thinking. That is the ground because of which, he had logic and philosophy during his college-days.

His rational inquisitiveness encouraged him to take up philosophy at the M.A. stage and he went to Allahabad University wherefrom he obtained the first position in First Class of M.A. examination in 1956. During his student-days at the undergraduate and postgraduate stages, he got prestigious awards like Woodburn prize for being the best graduate, Pandit Jagannath Mishra Memorial prize for obtaining highest marks in Sanskrit in B.A. examination and Nandarani Medal for obtaining highest marks in Indian philosophy in M.A. examination.

He joined the P.G. Dept. of Philosophy of Utkal University in 1958 as a Lecturer and during that time he got the opportunity of having renewed contact with his teacher : Ganeswar Misra as his senior colleague (Head of the Dept.). This contact was found to be a significant turning point for Nayak at least in reviewing the classical Indian philosophy at the background of conceptual analysis. With Misra, he prepared a paper "Doctrine of Self in Absolute Idealism" which he presented in the Cuttack session of the Indian Philosophical Congress (henceforth referred to as IPC) in 1959 and that was subsequently published. The paper contains critical analysis of Śaṅkarite arguments for the concept of ātman and the paper did create a sensation in the philosophical circle during that time.

After few years, Nayak was awarded Commonwealth Fellowship and went to U.K. After his going abroad, I joined in his post in the same Dept. Nayak continued his research in the Bristol University under the supervision of Professor S. Körner and was awarded the degree of Ph.D. on the thesis "Evil, Karma and Reincarnation" which was subsequently published in India (Visva-Bharti, Santiniketan) in 1973. Dr. Nayak, after his return from U.K., joined back in the same Dept. of Utkal University and I got the scope of having him as my senior colleague along with our common teacher : Ganeswar Misra. Dr. Nayak had a long career in Utkal University (from 1958 to 1994). During that period, he became Reader in 1966, Professor and Head of the same Dept. in 1978. He was the Vice-Chancellor of Shri Jagannatha Sanskrit University, Puri (on being deputed from Utkal University) during 1989-92, was a visiting Professor in the Dept. of Buddhist Studies and Philosophy in Nagarjuna University (on deputation) during 1992-94. After retirement from Utkal University in 1994, Prof. Nayak got the honour of being a visiting Professor in the Dept. of Religious Studies at the University of Saskatchewasn, Canada in 1995. During 1996-98, he became a Senior Fellow of the Indian Council of Philosophical Research (henceforth referred to as ICPR), UGC Emeritus Fellow at BHU during 1999-2000 and, on being selected, he was a Fellow in the Indian Institute of Advanced Study at Shimla from 2001-2004.

Prof. Nayak has the rare distinction of having proficiency in four prominent languages (English, Hindi, Bengali and Sanskrit), besides his mother-tongue (Oriya).

His knowledge in Hindi is quite profound and he has passed Kovida examination in Hindi, conducted by the Rastrabhasa Prachar Samiti, Wardha. Because of his erudite scholarship in Sanskrit, he was honoured by the Rāṣṭriya Sanskrit Saṁsthān, Govt. of India on 28th March 2000 as an eminent Sanskrit Scholar.

Prof. Nayak proved himself as an efficient organizer. He organized number of UGC, ICPR National Seminars, Conferences, Workshops, Refresher Courses during his tenure at Utkal University. He was the Local Secretary of the 56th session of IPC held at Bhubaneswar, 1984. While he was the Vice-Chancellor of Shri Jagannatha Sanskrit University, he organized National Seminar on Nehru and Indian Culture.

He has the credit of delivering Endowment Memorial Lectures in several Universities and Academic Bodies on different occasions. To name a few: he gave the K.C. Bhattacharya Memorial Lecture on Vedānta in Calcutta University and delivered Raja Ram Mohun Roy Memorial Lecture at Bangalore in 2001. Prof. Nayak gave the Buddha Jayanti Lecture twice in IPC, once in its Gauhati session in 1983 and another in its Platinum Jubilee session held at Delhi in 2000. He has delivered Shri B.V.S.S. Mani Endowment Lecture at S.V. University, Tirupati, Dharma Endowment Lecture at Dharmaram College, Bangalore and Swami Narayan Sesvara Vedānta Lecture in the 37th session of Akhil Bharatiya Darshan Parishad at Nalanda, Rajagriha, 1993.

He has visited abroad several times and participated in number of international seminars and conferences. He has presented papers in the 29th International Oriental Conference at Paris in 1973, in the World Hindu Conference at Colombo in 1982, in the International Conferences on Vedānta at the University of Miami, Oxford, Ohio, USA in 1985 and 2000, in the International Conference of Waves in USA in 2000 and he has delivered series of lectures in the University of Sophia, Bulgaria (being nominated as a Visiting Fellow under Cultural Exchange Programme) in 1983 and in the University of Calgary and Saskatchewan, Candada in 2000.

Besides being a Life-member of IPC, he was a nominated member of the Executive Body of ICPR, nominated member (by HRD Ministry, Govt. of India) of Senate of the Rastriya Sanskrit Vidyapith, Tirupati, a panel-member of UGC, National Lecturer of UGC during 1984-85, Academic Consultant of *Encyclopaedia of Hinduism* and has acted as an expert in several Academic Committees of UPSC. He was the General President of the Tiruchirapalli session of IPC in 1992 and also the General President of the 46th session of the Akhil Bharatiya Darshan Parishad in 2001.

II

As indicated earlier, Prof. Nayak's interest in philosophical studies grew originally from his solid foundation in Sanskrit reading. On account of that, he developed strong inclination to probe into the Indian philosophical tradition and to expose as well as explore its originality and distinctiveness. During his postgraduate studies in the University of Allahabad, he came in contact with teachers, having good background in Indian philosophy. By that time, the Dept. of Philosophy of Allahabad University had been quite conspicuous in the whole country by developing a specialized interest for Indian Idealism (grounded mainly on Advaita Vedānta of Śaṅkara) under the leadership of the well-known figure : Professor A.C. Mukherji. The department had reputed teachers like Prof. R.N. Kaul, Dr. S.S. Roy, Dr. S.C. Biswas and Dr. S.L. Pandey. The younger Nayak had the good opportunity of having personal contact with all the teachers. Consequently he became thorough in his reading of Indian philosophy, specially Vedānta.

With the affectionate patronage of his teacher-cum-senior colleague Prof. Ganeswar Misra at the Utkal University, Dr. Nayak became serious in going through the dominant analytical trends, specially advanced in some British and American Universities. He got inspiration from Prof. G. Misra to review classical Indian philosophy from the analytical point of view. This is not necessarily to graft or even superimpose the foreign analytical technique on the Indian dārshanic reflection. But, it is primarily undertaken with the aim of studying as well as evaluating the Indian point of view afresh so that its uniqueness and distinctive features can be better exposed and it can be placed as a serious and challenging approach in philosophical discussion. As a consequence, Dr. Nayak became successful in pointing out the significance of logico-linguistic analysis (*vākyārtha-vicāraṇa*) in Śaṅkara Vedānta. This important point has been well figured in his book : *Essays in Analytical Philosophy* (1978). Besides Śaṅkara Vedānta, Dr. Nayak has developed interest also on Buddhism. In later years he went through the original texts of Nāgārjuna and Candrakīrti primarily which are usually considered as the basic source of Mādhyamika stand of Bauddha darśana. Seeing the whole Mādhyamika position *(dṛṣṭi)* from new and refreshing perspective, Dr. Nayak could establish that Mādhyamika Buddhism is a typical form of analytical philosophy, having nothing to do with absolutism, nihilism and mystical transcendentalism. This is well presented in his later writings like : *Philosophical Reflections* (1987/2002) and *Mādhyamika Śūnyatā* (2001).

There is another important facet which is notable in Prof. Nayak's philosophical reading of analytical trend. Though in general, he is inclined to some form of conceptual analysis in his philosophic pursuit, he is found to be distinctly critical about the logical positivistic programme of outright rejection of metaphysics. The

classical Indian dharmic tradition in which he was bo and brought up is found to have deep impression in h mental set up and he was, therefore, not inclined to g with the logical positivistic move for outright eliminatio of religion and theology. This is well reflected in hi symposium-article "Can Metaphysics Survive?" presente at the B.H.U. session of IPC in 1967. Of course, he i all through influenced by the trend of philosophica analysis and is quite sharp about certain misconceptions caused due to the adoption of non-analytic procedure But, none the less, he is equally cautious for any radical step towards either unguarded rejection or unreflective acceptance of any stand, however popular-based it might be.

In his matured philosophical writings, Prof. Nayak has developed his distinctive philosophical position which he identifies as philosophy of Commonism. This position has been primarily designed to reveal the significant point that philosopher has to take due cognisance of the need and requirement of the common deprived mass and it should not be merely confined to the elites, neglecting the ordinary folk. It goes without saying that this stand of Prof. Nayak puts him on the solid ground of humanism with spiritual foundation.

Prof. Nayak is now very much philosophically alive, despite his numerous problems at the advanced age. Regularly he brings out books, monographs, essays and papers and those are referred to and discussed in the philosophical circle. I am personally happy to have him as a teacher-cum-senior colleague and, above all, a genuine friend in my philosophic studies and research. I wish him a long and prosperous life. Let me lovingly dedicate this volume : *Reflections on Indian Wisdom (Philosophical Perspectives)* as a token of my sincere appreciation of his reflective pursuit.

Bijayananda Kar

Publications by Prof. G.C. Nayak

Section – A: English

(I) Books

1. *Philosophical Reflections* (second enlarged and revised edn.), New Delhi: Indian Council of Philosophical Research (I.C.P.R.), 2002 (first edn., 1987). (This book is awarded with Pranavananda prize in 1988 session of the Indian Philosophical Congress).
2. *Mādhyamika Śūnyatā*, New Delhi: I.C.P.R., 2001.
3. *Understanding Religious Phenomenon*, Bangalore: Dharmaram Publications, 1997.
4. *Philosophical Enterprise and the Scientific Spirit*, Delhi: Ajanta Books International, 1994.
5. *Evil and the Retributive Hypothesis*, Delhi: Motilal Banarasidass, 1993.
   (It has been honoured with Pranavananda Book Prize in 1988 session of Indian Philosophical Congress.)
6. *Essays in Analytical Philosophy*, Cuttack: Santosh Publications, 1978.
7. *Evil, Karma and Reincarnation*, Visva-Bharati, Santiniketan, 1973.
8. *The Concept of Nirvāṇa in Candrakirti's Prasannapadā* (to be published in IIAS, Shimla-171005).

(II) Edited Books

1. *Nehru and Indian Culture,* Puri: Śrī Jagannātha Sanskrit Viśvavidyālaya (SJSV), 1991.
2. *Jagannātha Jyotiḥ,* Puri: SJSV, 1990.
3. *Prajñā,* Bhubaneswar: Dept. of Philosophy, Utkal University, 1978-89.
4. *Analytical Studies in Buddhist Philosophy,* Bhubaneswar: Dept. of Philosophy, Utkal University, 1984.
5. *Abstract of Papers,* Indian Philosophical Congress, 1980-82.

(III) Articles/Papers/Essays/Review Articles/Critical Notes

(A) In Foreign Sources

1. "Plotinus and Śaṁkara: Significant Affinities and Divergences" in *Neo-Platonism and Indian Philosophy,* Ed.: Prof. Paulos Mar Gregon, State University of New York: 2002.
2. "Śaṁkara's Māyā – A Fresh Look" in *Contemporary Views in Indian Civilisation* (Third Biennial International Conference of World Association of Vedic Studies, Ed.: Prof. Bhudev Sharma), USA: July 2000.
3. "Vedāntic Morality – A Critical Approach", *Religious Studies and Theology,* Canada: December 1996.
4. "Scientific Temper, Religion and Secularism", *Do,* Canada: June 1996.
5. "Religious Language and Religion: the Periphery and the Core" in *Do,* Ed.: Prof. David W. Atkinson, Canada: December 1995.
6. "Dharma: An Analytical Retrospect" in *Freedom, Dharma and Religion,* Eds.: C. Peden, Y. Hudson, USA: 1993.

7. "Does Śaṁkara Advocate Enlightenment through Analysis?: A Reappraisal of the Vedāntic Conception of Enlightenment vis-à-vis the Mādhyamika" in *Perspectives on Vedānta,* Ed.: Prof. S.S. Rama Rao Pappu, New York: E.J. Brill, Leiden, 1988.
8. "A Study in Hindu Secularism" in World Hindu Conference, *Souvenir*, Sri Lanka: 1982.
9. "The Mādhyamika Attack on Essentialism: A Critical Appraisal", *Philosophy East and West*, Honolulu, USA: October 1979.
10. "The Vedānta Conception of Liberation – An Analysis of the Views of Śaṁkara and Yajñavalkya", Proceedings of 1973 Session of the International Orientalists Congress, Paris: 1976.
11. "Survival, Reincarnation and the Problem of Personal Identity" in *Philosophical Dimensions of Parapsychology*, Eds.: J.M.O. Wheatley and H.L. Edge, Illinois, USA: 1976.
12. "Spiritual Experience in the Vedic Corpus and the Vedāntic Tradition" in *Mysticism: Select Essays*, Ed.: Prof. M. Mbonimpa *et al.*, Canada (Essays in honour of Prof. John Sahadat, University of Sudbury).

(B) In Indian Sources

13. "Professor Balasubramanian on Philosophy for Liberation" in *Paramparā* (Prof. Balasubramanian's Festschrift Volume), Eds.: Prof. Srinivas Rao and Dr. Godavarish Mishra, New Delhi: ICPR, 2003.
14. "Relevance of Buddhism and Other Religions in Modern Society" in *Perspectives of Buddhist Studies*, Ed.: Prof. P. Jash, New Delhi: 2002.
15. "Sāṅkhya-Yoga" in *Life, Thought and Culture in India (c. AD 300-1000)*, Ed.: Prof. K.S. Murty, New Delhi: PHISPC/CSC, 2002.

16. "Some Reflections on *Mānasa Dūtaṃ* (by Pt. Prabodh Kumar Mishra), Cuttack: Cuttack Students' Store, 2002.
17. "Pandit Nilakantha Das", *Quarterly Journal of the Mythic Society (QJMS)*, Bangalore: July-October 2002.
18. "Philosophy for Value-Education" in *Teaching Philosophy in twenty-first Century*, Ed.: Prof. P.G. Victor, New Delhi: 2002.
19. "Viśuddhādvaita Brahmavāda of Viśwanatha Bābā – An Evaluation", *QJMS*, Bangalore: July-December 2001.
20. "Dharma and Mokṣa as Humanistic Values in Indian Thought", *Śrī Veṇkaṭeśwara University Oriental Journal (SVUOJ)*, Tirupati: 2001.
21. "Nāgārjuna, Candrakīrti, and Wittgenstein: A Critical Evaluation of Certain Significant Aspects", *Annals*, Bhandarkar Oriental Research Institute (BORI), Vol. LXXXI, Pune: 2001.
22. "The Advaita Philosophy of Value: A Review", *Jagannātha Jyotiḥ* (Jagannāth University Journal of Indology), Vol. VI, Puri: 2001.
23. "Indian Philosophy and Its Social Concern: With Special Reference to the Concept of Dharma", *Journal of Dharma*, Bangalore: April-June 2001.
24. "Śaṁkara's Formulation of Vedānta", *The Voice of Śaṁkara* (Śaṁkara-Bhārati), Ed.: Prof. R. Balasubramanian, Vol. 26, No. 2, 2001.
25. "The Concept of Sākṣhi Caitanya in Advaita Vedānta with Special Reference to the Upaniṣads", *The Philosophical Quarterly (IPQ)*, Amalner: January-April 2000.
26. "Dharma and its Transcendence – A Comparative Study of Hindu, Mādhyamika and Zen Views", *Souvenir*: World Philosophy Conference, Platinum Jubilee Celebration of Indian Philosophical Congress *(IPC)*, Delhi: December 2000.

27. "Dharma and its Transcendence as a Value in Indian Thought, and its Culmination in Mādhyamika and Chan Buddhism, *QJMS*, Bangalore: July-September 2000.
28. "Śaṁkara vis-à-vis other Systems – I" in *Advaita Vedānta*, Ed.: Prof. R. Balasubramanian, PHISPC/CSC, 2000.
29. "Nāgārjuna, Candrakīrti and Śūnyatā Philosophy: A Review" in *Spirituality, Science and Technology* (A Select Proceedings of the IPC), Ed.: Arun Mishra, New Delhi: 2000.
30. "Thakur's Concept of Dharma and Practical Philosophy of Existence", *Iṣṭa Tapa*, Birbhum: West Bengal, September 1999.
31. "The Unique Synthesis in Jagannātha as Lokāyata Brahman and Vaiṣṇavism – A Philosophical Approach", *QJMS*, Bangalore: July 1999.
32. "Jagannātha – A Study in the Unique Cult of Puruṣottama-Brahman", *Orissa Review*, Bhubaneswar: July 1999.
33. "Speculative Philosophical Reflections in Yajurveda and Atharvaveda", *Annals* (BORI), Vol. LXXIX, Pune: 1999.
34. "Secular Values in Hinduism", *Souvenir* (National Seminar on Perspectives in Values – Eastern and Western), Bhubaneswar: Utkal University, September 1999.
35. "Hinduism and Its Scriptures: An Analysis", *Tattvanidhi* (Prof. C. Ramaiah Felicitation Volume), Eds.: Prof. B. Sambasiva Prasad and Dr. G. Vedaparayana, Tirupati: 1999.
36. "Sītā in Vālmīki Rāmāyaṇa" in *Vālmīki Rāmāyaṇa – Adwitīya Mahākāvya*, Ed.: Dr. M. Sahdev, Patiala: Punjabi University, 1999.
37. "A Tribute" (to Prof. K.T. Pandurangi) in *Madhu Parka* (Prof. Pandurangi Felicitation Volume), Bangalore: 1999.

38. "Karma, Causation and Retributive Morality", *PQ*, Amalner: July-October 1998.
39. "Māyāvada – An Approach from Ācārya's Point of View", *SVUOJ*, Tirupati: 1998.
40. "Bairagi Misra and a New Dimension in the Understanding of the Gītā Concept Śaraṇāgati", *QJMS*, Bangalore: 1998.
41. "Sādhu Dharma, Critical Justice and Value – A Constructive Approach with a Social Perspective", *Do*, April-June 1998.
42. "A Plea for a Dynamic View of Things and Values: With Special Reference to the Spiritual Masters", *The See-Ence* (A Quarterly Journal), Vol. IV/98, Mumbai: October 1998.
43. "Some Aspects of the Philosophical Enterprise in the Mādhyamika Buddhist Thought and Ludwig Wittgenstein — A Comparativa and Critical Study", *Jadavpur Journal of Philosophy*, Vol. X, No. 1, 1998.
44. "Doctrine of Transmigration of Soul in the Upaniṣad" in *Reincarnation: Concept and Implication*, Ed.: Dr. G.N. Bhat, Mangalore: 1998.
45. "The Concept of Freedom in Sartre and Śaṁkara", *IPQ*, Pune: Jan. 1998.
46. "Assembling Reminders – to Myself", *The See-Ence* (A Quarterly Journal), Vol. I/98, Mumbai: January, 1998.
47. "Secularism and Scientific Temper", *The Hindustan Times*, New Delhi: 19-12-1998.
48. "Commitment to Faith is not Fanaticism", *Do*, 21-04-1998.
49. "Dharma and Social Justice", *Do*, 10-02-1998.
50. "A Sequel to Assembling Reminders", *The See-Ence* (A Quarterly Journal), Vol. II/98, April 1998.
51. "Pratītya Samutpāda and Anti-essentialism: Some Theoretical and Practical Implications" in *Homage to Tathāgata* (An Anthology of Studies in Buddhism), Saranath-Varanasi: 1998.

52. "Hinduism – Its Secular Values", *SVUOJ*, Tirupati: 1997.
53. "The Concept of Evil in Indian Religion" *Dva Suparna*, Ed.: Prof. K.T. Pandurangi, Oct. 1997.
54. "Āchārya Nāgārjuna's Philosophical Contribution – Some Salient Features", *Souvenir,* Contribution of Andhra Deśa to Buddhism, Hyderabad: Birla Archaeological and Cultural Research Institute, December 1997.
55. "Dharma – An Analytical Retrospect" in *Bhāratiya Vidyā,* Mumbai: Bharatiya Vidya Bhawan, 1997.
56. "Relevance of Buddhism and Other Relgions in Modern Society", Key-note address included in Relevance of Buddhism and Other Religions in Modern Society, Proceedings of the XXII, International Conference on Buddhist Studies in India, Nalanda: 1997.
57. "Freedom and Equality in Vedānta and Buddhist Tradition with Special Reference to Certain Asymmetry in the Jīvanmukta and Bodhisattva Ideal", *Annals* (BORI), Vol. XXVI, Pune: 1996.
58. "Approach of Hinduism to It's Scriptures", *Journal of Dharma,* Bangalore: Oct.-Dec. 1996.
59. "Understanding Religious Phenomenon – A Philosopher's View of Religious Language vis-à-vis Religious Experience", Proceedings of the IX Conference of All Orissa Philosophy Association *(AOPA),* Balugaon: June 1996.
60. "Jñāneshvara and His Integral Philosophy: Some Salient Features" in *In Quest of Universal Peace,* Published on the Occasion of World Philosophers Meet, Chief Editor: V.B. Karad, Pune: 1996.
61. "Ethical Consideration in Vedānta – A Scientific Approach", *Journal of Dharma,* April-June 1996.
62. "Scientific Pursuit and Philosophical Enterprise" in *Indian Philosophy and History,* Ed.: Prof. S.P. Dubey,

New Delhi: ICPR, 1996. (This was partially translated into Oriya by Sri B.N. Mohanty and was published under the title *Darasana O Vijñāna in Gaurava*, Ed.: S. Dash, Puri: 1992).

63. "Are Jīvanmukta and Bodhisattva Ideals Asymmetrical?", *IPQ*, July 1995.
64. "Understanding Śaṁkara Vedānta", *Journal of Indian Council of Philosophical Research (JICPR)*, New Delhi: ICPR, Sept.-Dec. 1995.
65. "A Note on R.D. Ranade's Contribution to the Study of Upaniṣadic Philosophy", *SVOUJ*, Tirupati: 1995.
66. "The Gītā in the Eyes of Bairagi Misra – An Evaluation" (Prof. Ratnakar Pati Memorial Lecture), Proceedings of the VIII Conference of AQPA, June 1995.
67. "A Study in Secularism and Varaṇāśama Dharma as Spiritual and Social Values in Hinduism" in *Philosophy of Swami Vivekananda*, Ed.: Prof. P.K. Sengupta, Calcutta: 1995.
68. "Pratītya Samutpāda and Anti-essentialism" in *Studies in Buddhism*, Ed. Dr. K.C. Mishra, Bhubaneswar: Institute of Orissa Culture, 1995.
69. "Pratītya Samutpāda and Anti-Essentialism: Some Theoretical and Practical Implications", *The Journal of Philosophical Studies*, Jodhpur: December 1994.
70. "Foreword" to the Book: *Īśā* (by Dr. K.C. Dash), Puri: Loka Bhāsā Prachāra–Samiti, 1992.
71. "Foreword" to a *Bibliography on Lord Jagannāth* (Compiled by Dr. G.N. Das and Dr. P.C. Mishra), Puri: Sri Jagannatha Sanskrit Visvavidyalaya (S.J. S.V.), 1992.
72. "Foreword" to the Book: *Inscriptions of the Temples of Puri and Origin of Sri Purusottama Jagannatha*, Vol. I (by Dr. S.N. Rajguru), Puri: S.J.S.V., 1992.
73. "Philosophy of Commonism: Some Implications", *Triveni*, Vol. 61, July-September and October-December in No. 3-4, 1992.

74. "Jagannātha, as I see Him", *Sreedham*, Cuttack: Bhubaneswar, 1991.
75. "Foreword" to the Book: *Mahāpuruṣavidyā* (Ed.: Dr. S. Mishra Pt. S. Dash), Puri: S.J.S.V., 1991.
76. "Social Justice and Dharma: A Philosophical Perspective", *The Journal of Philosophical Studies*, Jodhpur: February 1994.
77. "Religion and Secularism", *Prajñā* (Utkal Journal of Philosophy), Ed.: Prof. B. Kar, Bhubaneswar: March 1994.
78. "Varṇa Dharma and Sādhu Dharma – An Analysis" in *Sārasvata Kusumāñjalīḥ*, Darbhanga: Indira Prakashan, 1994.
79. "Reason: Its Nature, Function and Limits", *Ānvīkṣkī*, Dept. of Philosophy, B.H.U., Varanasi.
80. "The Problem of Suffering", *Do*, B.H.U.
81. "Some Reflections on Problems of Language, Computational Model and Sanskrit" in *Indian Semantics*, Ed.: Prof. K.C. Dash, Delhi: 1994.
82. "A Study in Secularism and Varṇāśarama Dharma as Spiritual and Social Values in Hinduism" in *Value Orientation*, Calcutta: December 1993.
83. "All Pervasive Delusion, Buddhism and World-Peace" in the *Souvenir* (on the occasion of the National Seminar on Buddhism and World-Peace), Nagarjuna University, December 1993.
84. "Kauṭilya and Gandhi – A Comparative and Critical Appraisal", *IPQ*, Pune: October 1993.
85. "Philosophical Enterprise and the Scientific Temper" in *Prajñā*, Ed.: Prof. P.K. Mohapatra, Bhubaneswar: March 1993.
86. "Problems of Religious Tolerance", *Indian Express*, Delhi: 22-12-1992.
87. "Tolerance in Advaita – A Study of the Unique Culture of Transcendence" in *Tolerance in Indian Culture*, Ed.: Prof. R. Balasubramaniam, New Delhi: ICPR, 1992.

88. "Social Justice and Dharma" in *Social Justice and Its Ancient Indian Base*, Ed.: Prof. K.C. Dash, Delhi: 1992.
89. "On Presidential Address, Scientific Pursuit and Philosophical Enterprise", *University News*, 03-08-1992.
90. "Indian Culture in the Eyes of Nehru", *Bhavan's Journal*, 31-05-1991.
91. "Salient Features of the Philosophy of Jagannātha and their Cantemporary Relevance" in *Studies in the Cult of Jagannātha*, Ed.: K.C. Mishra, Bhubaneswar: 1991.
92. "The Philosophy of Jagannātha and Its Contemporary Relevance", *Śrī Jagannātha Jyotiḥ* (Sri Jagannath University Journal of Indology), Puri: 1990.
93. "Scientific Pursuit and Philosophical Enterprise", *Do*, Vol. V, 1990.
94. "Some Reflections on Rakta Jhankāraṃ" in *Jhaṅkāraṃ*, Ed.: Pt. Probodh Mishra, Cuttack: Vidyapuri, 1990.
95. "On Teaching Philosophy and Comparative Religions in Value-Oriented Education, *Souvenir* (On the occasion of Silver Jublee of D.M. School and Religional College of Education), Bhubaneswar: 1989-90).
96. "Justification of Rational Enterprise", *The Visva-Bharati* (Journal of Philosophy), Shantiniketan: 1989.
97. "Śaṁkara's Formulation of Vedānta" in *Perspectives of Śaṁkara*, Eds.: Prof. R. Balsubramaniyan and Prof. S. Bhattacharya, New Delhi: Dept. of Culture, Min. of H.R.D., Govt. of India, 1989.
98. "Radhakrishnan on Institution – A Critical Apprisal" in *Prospectives on the Philosophy of Prof. S. Radhakrishnan*, Ed.: Prof. K. Bagchi, Shantiniketan: 1989.
99. "Bairagi Mishra & His Gītā" in *Essays on Religion*, Eds.: Dr. B. Misra and Dr. B. Panda, Bhubaneswar: 1989.

100. "Prajñā Pāramitā: A Unique Insight in the Mādhyamika Thought" in *Amalā Prajñā: Aspects of Buddhist Studies*, Ed.: Prof. N.H. Santani, Delhi: 1989.
101. "Reason Rationality and The Irrationals", *JICPR*, Sept.-Dec. 1988.
102. "Man and Religion on Tagore's Philosophy" in *Freedom, Transcendence and Identity*, Ed.: Prof. P.K. Sengupta New Delhi: *ICPR*, 1988.
103. "Does Advaita Vedānta Advocate Illumination through Analysis"?, *Viswabharati Journal of Philosophy*, Do, February 1987.
104. "Tagore's Spiritual Humanism: A Fresh Look", *Vision* (Journal of the Institute of Economic and Social Studies), Bhubaneswar: January-June 1987.
105. "Śaṁkara and Linguistic Analysis", *IPQ*, Oct.-Dec. 1986.
106. "The Philosophy of Śrī Aurobindo", *JICPR*, Spring 1986.
107. "Pratītya Samutpāda: The Mādhyamika Approach" in *Pratītya Samutpāda* (Institute of Tibetan Studies), Saranath: 1986.
108. "Paul Deussen's Contribution to Indian Thought" in Indo-German Seminar on German Thinkers and India, Cuttack: Society for German Studies and Relation, Maitri Sarani: 05-10-1986.
109. "Saptasati Chandi –A Fresh Look", *Orissa Review*, Bhubaneswar: October 1986.
110. "Philosophy of Śri Aurobinda", *Darshana Manjarī*, Burdwan: University of Burdwan, 1985.
111. "Analytic Philosophy of Nāgārjuna and Candrakīrti: Some Observations", *JICPR*, Spring 1985.
112. "Transcendental Secularism – A Study in one Characteristic Aspect of the Hindu System of Values" in *Reality, Knowledge and Value*, Ed. Prof. S.R. Bhatt, Delhi: Bhāratiya Vidyā Prakāshan, 1985.
113. "Jagannātha and the Philosophy of the Upaniṣads"

in *The Cult and Culture of Lord Jagannātha*, Eds.: Dr. D. Panda and Dr. S.C. Panigrahi, Cuttack: 1984.

114. "Jagannātha and Vedānta Philosophy: A Study in the Unique Cult of Brahman", *Unmana, Souvenir* of Akhil Bharat Jagannāth Consciousness Conference, December 1984.
115. "Sri Aurobindo and the Supramental Knowledge-claim", Proceedings of the 6th Conference of AOPA, Bhubaneswar: 1983.
116. "The Concept of Saraṇāgati" in *Gītā: News of the World*, Bhubaneswar: 27-2-1983.
117. "Gandhi, Spiritualism and the Problem of Have-nots" in *Multiverse* (Souvenir on the occasion of the Seminar – on Gandhiji and Modern Times), Cuttack: 1982.
118. "The Concept and Role of Tolerance in Indian Culture – A Study in Transcendental Monism and Transcendental Secularism", *Vision* (Do) July-Sept. & Oct.-Dec. 1982.
119. "The Role of Intellectual Elites in Modern India – A Philosopher's Point of View", *Vision* (Do), Vol. I, No. IV, April-June 1982.
120. "Maxmüller and Vedānta", Proceedings of the Society for German Studies and Relations, 1981-82.
121. "Religious Crisis, Hinduism and Commonism", *Philosophica*, Ed.: Shankar Basu, Vol. X, Nos. 1-4, Calcutta: 1981.
122. "Analytical Philosophy – It's Multiple Facets", *Souvenir* (On the occasion of 56th Session of the Indian Philosophical Congress), Bhubaneswar: 1981.
123. "Crisis in Indian Religion" in *Crisis in India*, Ed.: Dr. B. Sahoo, Cuttack: Santosh Publications, 1980-81.
124. "Dāru Brahma and the Spiritual Commonism", *Journal of the Comparative Literature and Aesthetics*, Orissa: Viswanath Kaviraj Institute, 1979-80.

125. "The Criterion of Personal Identity – Must it be Physical?" *IPQ,* July 1978.
126. "The Philosophy of Śaṅkarācārya – A Reappraisal", *IPQ,* Vol. I, No I, 1973.
127. "The Philosophy of Aruṇi and Yajñavalkya – An Analysis", The Indian Philosophical Congress, 46th Session (Addresses, Lectures and Symposia), Kanpur: I.I.T., 1972.
128. "Jagannātha and the Philosophy of the Upaniṣads", *Bharati,* Utkal University – Journal (Humanities), July 1972.
129. "Evil and the Karma Doctrine: An Analysis", Proceedings of the 2nd Conference of AOPA, August 1971.
130. "Zen Buddhism – An Exposition", *Pathway to God,* Belgaum: June 1971.
131. "Can there be any Indeterminate Perception?", *Darshana International,* Moradabad: April 1970.
132. "A Plea for Transcendental Secularism", *Do,* Moradabad (The Contemporary Indian Thinkers Issue).
133. "The Philosophy of Freedom and Absolute Surrender", *Pathway to God,* Belgaum: Nov. 1969.
134. "Satkāryavāda and Asatkāryavāda – The Doctrines of Causality", *The Journal of the Indian Academy of Philosophy,* Calcutta: 1969.
135. "Can Metaphysis Survive?", Proceedings of the Indian Philosophical Congress, B.H.U. Session, Varanasi: 1967 (also Published in the *Visva-Bharati Journal of Philosophy*).
136. "Theistic Description of God and the Death by a Thousand Qualifications – A Critical Appraisal", *Bharati,* Utkal Univ., 1967.
137. "Is Disembodied Existence after Death Logically Impossible?", *Journal of Indian Philosophical Association,* Vol. I, Nagpur: 38, 1967.

138. "The Doctrine of Karma and the Criterion of Falsifiability – A Critical Evaluation", *The Calcutta Review*, Calcutta: August 1966.
139. "Doctrine of Self in Absolute Idealism" (in Collaboration with Prof. G. Mishra), Published in the *Journal of Utkal University*, Dec. 1961, and also subsequently published in the *Journal of the Indian Philosophical Association*).
140. "An Exposition of the Philosophy of Baladeva Vidyābhūṣaṇa", *Philosophical Quarterly*, Ed.: G.R. Malkani, Amalner: 1960.
141. "Baladeva Vidyābhūṣaṇa" (A Philosopher of Orissa), *The Eastern Times*, Cuttack: 31-12-1959.
142. "The Ultimate Why?", *Philosophy Association Bulletin*, Allahabad: 1955-56.

(iv) Reviews of Prof. G.C. Nayak's Writings

(A) Foreign Sources/Scholars

1. His *Mādhyamika Śūnyatā* (ICPR, New Delhi: 2001).
(i) Prof. Bhikkhu Pasadika, *Hsi-Lai Journal of Humanistic Buddhism*, Vol. IV, U.S.A.: 2003.
(ii) Prof. Kari H. Potter, *The Journal of Indian Council of Philosophical Research (JICPR)*, Vol. XIX, No. 4, New Delhi: Oct.-Dec. 2002.
2. His *Philosophical Reflections* (ICPR, New Delhi: 1987).
(i) Timothy J. Madigan, *Free Inquiry*, New York: Summer 1993.
(ii) Prof. Kennith Liberman, *International Philosophical Quarterly*, New York: June 1992.
(iii) Prof. J.L. Brockington, *JICPR*, New Delhi: May-Aug. 1992.
(iv) Prof. K.N. Upadhyaya, *Philosophy East and West*, Honolulu: January 1991.
(v) Prof. J.N. Mohanty, *Journal of Indian Philosophy*, New York: 1991.

(vi) Prof. Miklos Vito, *Revue Philosophique*, Paris: 1990-92.

(vii) Prof. Frank Whaling, *The Scottish Journal of Religious Studies*, Vol. IX, No. 1, 1988.

3. His *Evil and the Retributive Hypothesis* (Delhi: Motilal Banarasidass, 1993).

(i) Prof. John Brockington, *Journal of the Royal Asiatic Society*, 1995.

4. His *Evil, Karma and Reincarnation* (Viva-Bharati, Shantiniketan, 1973).

(i) Karl H. Potter, *South Western Journal of Philosophy*, U.S.A.: Vol. XI, No. 1, July 1980.

(ii) Prof. John Hick, *Religion: Journal of Religion and Religions*, Journal of the University of Lancester, Vol. V/2, Autumn, 1975.

(B) Indian Sources/Scholars

1. His *Mādhyamika Śūnyatā* (ICCR, New Delhi: 2001).

(i) Prof. Bijayananda Kar, *The Philosophical Quarterly*, Amalner: Jan.-April 2002.

(ii) Dr. M.R. Chinchore, *Indian Philosophical Quarterly*, October 2002.

(iii) Dr. D.K. Mohanta, *The Journal of the Indian Academy of Philosophy*, Kolkata: 2001.

2. His *Philosophical Reflections* (ICPR, New Delhi: 1987 and 2002).

(i) Prof. Sachidananda Mohanty, *Sri Aurobindo's Action*, October 2003 (Reviewed the latest 2nd and Revised Edition).

(ii) Prof. R.C. Pradhan, *IPQ*, October 1988.

(iii) Prof. M.K. Bhadra, *Darshan Manjari*, Bardwan: 1989.

(iv) Prof. S.L. Pandey, *Review of Darshana*, July 1988.

(v) Do, *Darshana International*, 1987.

(vi) Mr. M.P. Pandit, *Triveṇī*, April-June 1989.

(vii) *The Heritage*, April 1989.

(viii) Dr. D.R. Jatava, *Review Projector*, 1988.

3. His *Evil and the Retributive Hypothesis* (Delhi: Motilal Banarasidass, 1993).
(i) Ms. Radha Burnier, *The Theosophist*, April 1995.
(ii) Prof. M.P. Marathe, *Indian Philosophical Quarterly*, July 1994.
4. His *Essays in Analytical Philosophy* (Cuttack: Santosh Publication 1978).
(i) Prof. S.K. Sen, *The Journal of the Indian Academy of Philosophy*, Calcutta: 1988.
(ii) Prof. S.L. Pandey, *Review of Darshana*, Allahabad: July 1987.
(iii) Prof. M.K. Bhadra, *Darshan Manjari*, Bardwan: 1987-88.
5. His *Understanding Religious Phenomenon* (Bangalore: Dharmaram Publication, 1997).
(i) Prof. D.K. Barua, *Prabuddha Jagat*, June 2000.
(ii) *Deccan Herald*, 26-07-1998.
(iii) *The Times of India*, Bangalore: 08-04-1988.
(iv) *The Hindu*, 17-02-1988.
(v) *Dva Suparna*, Jan-April 1999.
(vi) Prof. A. Rambachan, *IPQ*, July 1999.
6. His *Evil, Karma and Reincarnation* (Visva-Bharati, 1973).
(i) Prof. N.S.S. Raman, *IPQ*, Pune.
7. His *Philosophical Enterprises and the Scientific Spirit* (Ajanta Books International, Delhi: 1994).
(i) Prof. S.V. Bokil, *IPQ*, Pune.
(ii) Mr. Alok Tondan, *JICPR*, Jan-April 1996.

(C) Besides reviews made on Prof. Nayak's Books (as stated before), there are expression of views, critical discussions and appreciative notes by scholars on Prof. Nayak's Contributions made in his numerous articles and essays on different themes. Some of those are listed below:

1. Prof. Hoyt L. Edge has discussed the work of Prof. Nayak along with those of Flew and Penelhum in

his Introduction to Section IV of *Philosophical Dimensions and Parapsychology*, Eds., John Wheetley and Hoyt L. Edge, U.S.A. 1976.

2. His *Views on Personal Identity*, has been critically discussed by Dr. P.K. Mohapatra in *IPQ*, January 1982 and subsequently published in his book: *Concepts and Problems* (Cuttack: Santosh Publication, 1988).
3. His *Philosophy of Commonism*, has drawn attention of number of scholars as detailed below:

(i) Prof. B. Kar, "Commonism: An Analytical Review", *The Visva Bharati Journal of Philosophy*, Vol. XXVII, No. 2 January 1990 (also reprinted in Kar's book: *Value Perspectives in Indian Philosophy*).

(ii) Prof. K.P. Mishra, "Janatā Darshna", *Dharitrī*, 17-02-1985.

(iii) Prof. Bhupendra Nath in his article "Religious Crisis: Some Comments", *Philosophica*, Vol. II, No. 14, 1982-83.

4. His *Views on Advaita, Transcendental Secularism and Monism,* has been critically discussed in the following sources:

(i) Prof. Bijayananda Kar, "National Integration, Secularism and Advaita Philosophy of Value" in *Perspectives of Śaṁkara*, Eds.: R. Balasubramaniam and S. Bhattacharya, New Delhi: Department of Culture, Ministry of H.R.D., 1989.

(ii) The Current Trends in Indian Philosophy", *The Philosophical Quarterly*, July-October 2002.

(iii) "*Mokṣa* as Value and *Jñāna* as Method in Śaṁkara Vedānta", *The Visva Bharati Journal of Philosophy*, Vol. No. 1, August 1987.

5. Prof. Karl H. Potter has referred to Prof. Nayak's paper on "The Doctrine of Karma and the Criterion of Falsifiability" in his *Guide Resources for the Study of Asian Philosophy and Religions*. This paper has also been included in the *Bibliography of Karma and*

Rebirth in Classical Indian Traditions, Ed.: W.D.O. Flaherty, Univ. of Chicago, U.S.A. His *Analytic Approach to Śaṁkara Advaita* has been discussed in detail by Prof. Klive (vide *Perspectives on Śaṁkara*, Ed.: Prof. S.S. Rama Rao Pappu of U.S.A.).
Prof. Nayak is the founder of "Tathāgata Sansad", an organisation dedicated to the intellectual, spiritual and social elevation of the destitute children of the society.

Section – B: Hindi

Published Articles (In Hindi)

1. "Bhāratīya Sāhitya men Saundaryānubhūti Tathā Saundaryasādhanā: Ek Samīkṣātmak Adhyayan", *Dārshanik Traimāsik*, 49, 3 July-Sept. 2003.
2. "Brahmavād aur Śūnyavād – Ek Tulanātmak aur Tāttvik Samīkṣā" (The Presidential Address of Akhil Bhāratiya Darshan Parishad, 46th Session, January-March 2001).
3. "Meghdūt Kā Kālidās: Ek Nayā Diganta" in *Harihara Satadalam* (Āchārya Hari Har Jha Abhinandana Granthaḥ), Puri: 2000.
4. "Mādhyamik Śūnyatā Daraśan aur Nirguṇa Brahmavāda: Ek Tulanātmak Vivecan", *Dhīḥ*, Journal of Rare Buddhist Texts. Research Project, Tibetan Institute, Sarnath: 1999.
5. "Pūjya Swāmī Nārāyaṇji Kā Śeśwar Vedānta", *Bhāratīya Sikṣaṇa*, Mumbai: July-August 1993.
6. "Śūnyatā Darśan Tathā Brahmavād–Ek Punarmūlyāṅkan", *Parāmarsh*, June 1999. Also published in *Meghdūt*, Sept. 1992.
7. "Kālidas Ke Meghdūt – Ek Nayā Āyām", *Do*, May-June 1992.
8. "Meghdūt aur Mahākavi Kālidās", *Navneet* (Hindi Digest), August 1992. The article of Prof. Nayak on

Meghdūt in Original Hindi has been translated by Sri Kamalakanta Pati into Oriya and published in *Dharitrī* 29.11.1992 under the title – "Meghdūtare Sādhāraṇīkaraṇa".

9. "Meghdūt", *Parāmarsh,* September 1992.
10. "Kālidas Sāhitya me Vaidik Dhārā", *Himānjali,* IIAS, Shimla-171005.

Section – C: Oriya

(I) Books

1. *Tataḥ Kiṃ* (Prajna loka), 1990.
2. *Bulgariā Anubhūti,* Upagupta Pub. Berhampur: 1986.
3. *Dārshanika Cintana,* Do, 1984. (This book has been translated into English under the title: *In the Eyes of the Philosopher* by Dr. S.K. Mohanty, Meerut: Anu Books, 1988).
4. *Dārshanika Druṣṭire,* Rastrabhasa Samavaya Prakashan, 1979.
5. *Bhāratīya Darshana,* Orissa State Bureau of Text Book Preparation and Production, 1978.
6. *Upaniṣada Darshana,* Do, 1975.

(II) Articles/Essays/Papers/Review Articles Published in Oriya

1. "Chandra Sekhara Rath – Eka Ananya Pratibhā", *Chandra Sekhara 70,* Bhubaneswar (BBSR), 2003.
2. "Mahābhāgavata Chandra Sekhara – Koṭikoṭi Juhāra", *Pathaprānte Panchastari,* BBSR, 2003.
3. "Jātīya Sanghatira Ādarśa Sūtra Paripreksịre Tyāga Sikṣāra Prāsaṅgikatā", *Samaj,* Annual Issue, 2001.
4. "Jagannātha Sanskruti – Eka Digdarśana", *Bhāgya Lipi,* January 2001.
5. "Parijā Sāheb – Eka Vinamra Śradhānjali", *Sikṣāvit Prāṇa Krushna Parija,* Ed.: Prof. Gadadhara Mishra, Cuttack: June 2000.

6. Bhāratīya Jana Mānasare Kṛṣṇa, *Dharitri*, 25.8.1997.
7. "Thākura Anukula Chandra Jīvana Darśanare Dharmara Swarūpa", *Iṣṭatapī*, 19.09.1999.
8. "Subidhāvāda Rājanīti O Mulyabodha – Eka Samikṣā", *Sahakāra*, Cuttack: August 1999.
9. "Jagannātha Samskṛti O Cetanāra Vaiśiṣṭya", *Do*, January 1999.
10. "Gopabandhu, Samāja O Nirapekṣa Sāṁbādikatā", *Samaja* (Annual Issue) 1995.
11. "Vākyapuspahāra", *Śraddhānjali*, (Smaraṇikā on the occasion of the Completion of 75th year of Swami Narayanananda Saraswati), Puri: 1994.
12. "Gopabandhu Smaraṇe – Ādarśa O Vāstava Sthitira Eka Samikṣā", *Samaja* (Annual Issue), 1992.
13. "Jagannātha Saṁskruti", *Sambāda*, 02.07.1992.
14. "Semānaṅka Dṛṣṭire Sāhitya", *Sāgarikā* (31st Issue), Puri: S.C.S. College, 1991-92.
15. "Jātīya Sanghatira Kauṇasi Ādarśa Āchiki?", *Samāja*, 3.11.1991.
16. "Urvaśīra Kāvya – Eka Mugdha Anubhava", *Prajātantra*, 11.3.1991.
17. "Nīti, Anīti O Rājanīti", *Sambāda* (in two parts) 21.11.1991 & 23.11.1991.
18. "Mūlyabodha O Rājanīti", *Samāja* (Annual Issue), 1991.
19. "Mo Belara Kataka O Mu", *Utkala Prasanga*, BBSR, April 1991.
20. "Mūlyabodha Sacetanatā – Eka Samikṣā", *Samāj* (Annual Issue), 1990.
21. "Swargata Satyabadi Mishra", *Guru dakṣiṇā*, Puri: 17.3.1990.
22. "Mādhyamika Śūnyavāda", *Jhankāra*, Jan. 1990.
23. "Āma Sanskrutire Ādhyatmikatāra Sthāna", *Prajātanatra Prativā* and *Samaj*, 07.1.1990.
24. "Vijñāna Sammata Sāmbādikatā – Eka Digdarśana", *Smaranikā*, Puri Sāmbādika Sangha, Puri: 1990.

25. "Śraddahānjali – Eka Samikṣā, Samāja" (Two parts) 4.3.1990 & 11.3.1990.
26. "Bhāratīya Darśana", *Samaja*, 29.7.1990.
27. "Odiśāra Dharmadhārāre Śrī Chaitanya", *Samaja*, 1.4.1989.
28. "Viplabī Śri Aurobindo", *Prajātantra*, 10.11.1989.
29. "Kalpanā Vilāsa, Vastu Sthiti O Prajñā", *Samāja* (Four parts), 10.12.1989, 17.12.1989, 24.12.1989, & 31.12.89.
30. "Utkala Maṇi Upādhi O Gopabandhu", *Samaja* (Annual Issue), 1989.
31. "Tataḥ Kiṁ", *Sambāda*, 5th Special Issue, 1989.
32. "Āma Saṁskṛti Prakṛtare Ādhyātṁika Ki?", *Baula*, Cuttack: Oct. 1988.
33. "Ājira Gaṇatantraku Semāne Jepari Dekhīchanti", *Sambada*, 26.1.88.
34. "Sītā Kaṇa Abalā?", *Sanjaga*, January 1982.
35. "Ādhyātmikatāra Mūlyāyana – Eka Digdarśana", *Smaranikā* of Viswanath Kaviraja, BBSR, 1987.
36. "Advaita Vedānta, Bhāṣā Viśleṣaṇa O Dārśanika Ganeswar Mishra", *Darsanika Ganeswar Mishra*, Eds.: G.P. Das and S.C. Panigrahi, 1987.
37. "Bhakti Sāhitya, Sādhāraṇavādi Darśana O Jātiya Sanghati", *Paursha*, 7th and 8th Issue, February-March 1986.
38. "Saptaśatī Chaṇḍī – Sāmānyavādi Darśana O Gaṇatantra", *Swarajya*, 1986.
39. "Kṛṣṇa Tattva", *Prajātantra*, 27.8.1986 and Dharitrī, 27.8.1986.
40. "Gītā O Bhāgavatare Kṛṣṇa", *Sāmukā*, Oct. 1986.
41. "Bhakti Dharma, Sāhitya O Darśanara Keteka Diga", *Konārka*, 1985.
42. "Aśrula Śraddhānjali" (in honour of Late Prof. G. Mishra) *Dharitrī*, 5.12.1985.
43. "Bhāktika Mithyā, Akapaṭa Dharma O Bhakti", *Āndolana*, *Sambāda* 12.12.1985.

44. "Nūā Rajara Vicitra anubhūti", *Sāmukā,* Oct.-Dec. 1985.
45. "Mūlyabodhara Sāmpratika Samasyā O Tāra Pratikāra", *Paurusha,* 16th Year. 10th Issue, April 1984.
46. "Prācina Sāhitya Jīvana O Ādhunika Sikṣā", *Do,* 18th year, 3rd & 4th Issue, 1984.
47. "Mūlyabodha: Prācya O Pascātya Dṛṣṭikoṇa", *Dharitrī,* 14.3.1984.
48. "Thākura Anukula Chandra" in *Odiśāra Sādhu Santha,* Complied by B.M. Mohanty, Cuttack: 1983.
49. "Pavitra Viveka Buddhi", *Phālgunī,* Bhubaneswar: October 1983.
50. "Ādhyātmika Sāmyavāda O Jagannātha Cetanā – Eka Samikṣā", *Sri Jagannāth,* Orissa Sahitya Academy, BBSR, 1982.
51. "Jāhā Aṅge Nivāichi", *Tathāgata,* Eds.: R.C. Pradhan and R.M. Nanda, Balasore: June 1982.
52. "Jagannātha Dharma Darśanara Yugapojogī Vaiśiṣṭya", *Pānchajanya,* BBSR, 1981.
53. "Saptaśatī Chaṇḍī – Sāmānyavādi Darshana O Gaṇatantra", *Do,* 1981.
54. "Jagannātha Cetanā – Sāmānyare Asāmānya", *Nandighosha,* Cuttack: 1978.
55. "Jagannātha Tattva O Upaniṣadiya Darshan", *Nandi Ghosha,* Cuttack: 1977.
56. "Ādhyātmika Sāmyavāda O Jagannātha Cetanā – Eka Samikṣā", *Koṇārka,* Orissa Sahitya Academy, BBSR, 1977.
57. "Samudra Eka Cā Cupre", *Adhūnā,* Cuttack: 1976 (Some chapters of Roy Houserman's 'Ocean in a Tea Cup', translated by Prof. G.C. Nayak into Oriya).
58. "Kāṅgāli Se Sneha Tike Lode – *Nandi Ghosha",* Cuttack: 1978.
59. "Kaṇa Satare", *Sanu,* Koraput: D.A.V. College, 1974.
60. "Dharma Sabhā", *Jibana-ranga,* Cuttack: 1972.

61. "Mahāmuni Śuka" in *Mahāpuruṣa Paricaya O Vāṇi*, Compiled by N.C. Das, Cuttack: 1970.
62. Reviewed Mr. N.C. Rath's Book on *Śaṅkarāchārya* (in Oriya) Published by the Text Book Bureau of Preparation and Production (TBPP), BBSR.
63. Reviewed Dr. N.C. Padhi's Book on *Radhakrishanan* (in Oriya), Published by the TBPP, Bhubaneswar.
64. Reviewed Pt. Achutananda Kar's Book on *Yuge Yuge Dharma* (Pub. in the Book itself).
65. Reviewed Biswanath Baba's *Alakha Parama Brahma Darshanam* (Published in the Book itself).
66. "Bṛthā" in *Piṇḍa* (Eds. D.M. Praharaj and S. Pujari), Bhubaneswar.
67. "Nārī Śakti – Eka Digdarshana" in *Paurusha*, 20th year, 4th Issue.

(III) ORIYA REVIEWS OF BOOKS/ESSAYS OF PROF. G.C. NAYAK

1. His *Tatah Kiṁ* (Oriya: 1990) is reviewed:
(i) *Amṛtāyana*, BBSR, December 1991.
(ii) *Prajātantra*, Cuttack: 24.9.1991.
(iii) *Nityanūtan*, BBSR, 15-30 March 1991.
(iv) *Samāja*, Cuttack: 24.3.1991.
2. His *Bulgāria Anubhūti* (Oriya: 1986).
(i) *Samāja*, Cuttack: 16.4.1989.
(ii) *Sanjoga*, Bhubaneswar (Dr. R.C. Pradhan), Oct. 1986.
(iii) *Sambāda*, Bhubaneswar: September 1986.
(iv) *Dharitree*, Bhubaneswar: 20.4.1986.
3. His *Dārśanika Cintana* (Oriya: 1984).
(i) *Samaj*, Cuttack: 1.9.1984.
(ii) *Dharitrī*, (by Prof. K.P. Mishra under the title of Janata Darshan), 17.2.1985.
(iii) *Śāmukā*, Cuttack (by R.C. Pradhan), Sept. 1985.
(iv) *Sambāda*, Bhubaneswar: 3.10.1985.
(v) His article: "Saptaśatī Caṇḍi, Sāmānyavādi Darśana O Gaṇatantra" (in Oriya) is discussed with a critical

note by Dr. G.P. Das in his article "Jnanamasti Samastasya", *Sambāda*, Bhubaneswar: 5.1.1990.

4. His *Dārśanikara Dṛaṣṭire* (Oriya: 1979).
 (i) *Pāncajanya*, April-June 1980.
 (ii) *Istāhāra*, Bhubaneswar (by Dr. Kunja Behari Dash), July-September 1981.
5. His *Evil and Retributive Hypothesis* (Delhi: MLBD, 1983) is reviewed in Oriya: *Nitya Nūtan*, Bhubaneswar, August 15-30, 1995.
6. His Edited Volume: *Nehru and Indian Culture* (Puri: S.J.S.V. 1991) is reviewed in Oriya.
 (i) *Samāja*, Cuttack: 6.10.1991.
 (ii) *Amṛutāyana* (in Oriya), Bhubaneswar (by Gita Hota), July 92.
7. His Edited Journal: *Sri Jagannāth Jyotiḥ* (4th Issue), (Puri: S.J.S.V.) is reviewed in *Samāja*, Cuttack: 25.8.1991.
8. His *Philosophy of Life and Commonism* are reviewed:
 (i) *Sahakāra*, Cuttack (by Dr. R.C. Pradhan), June-July 1997.
 (ii) *Prajātantra*, Cuttack (by Pt. Prabodha Kumar Mishra), 27.9.92.
 (iii) *Nitya Nūtan*, Bhubaneswar (by Pt. Prabodha Kumar Mishra in his Editorial Writing), Sept.-Oct. 1992.

Section – D

(I) Articles – Forthcoming Publications

1. "A Descriptive and/or Prescriptive Appraisal of Other Religions in General, by Hinduism" included in the Volume, eds. Professors Gort, Jansen & Vroom, Amsterdan, The Netherlands (now published).
2. "Śaṁkara and World-Peace" in the Proceedings of International Conference on World-Peace at Ahmedabad during 29 December 2003 – 2 January 2004.

3. "Raja Rammohan Roy and Vedānta Philosophy", *Sri Venkateswar University Oriental Journal*, Vol. 46 (for the year 2003), in the Press.
4. 18 entries on different topics of Indian Philosophy to be published in *Dictionary of Indian Philosophy* to be edited by Professor D.P. Chattopadhyaya.
5. Article on Late Prof. Sangam Lal Pandey's contribution to be published in *the Commemoration Volume on Prof. S.L. Pandey*, edited by Prof. R.L. Singh (now published).
6. "The Idea of Justice in Buddhism" to be published in *the Commemoration Volume in Honour of Late Prof. U.N. Dhal*.
7. "Radhakrishnan's Philosophical Message" to be published in the Journal: *Philosophy and the Life – World*, edited by Prof. Prabhat Mishra, Vidya Sagar University, Midnapore.
8. "Sadhu Dharma, Justice, and Value – A Critical and Constructive Approach with a Social Perspective" to be published in *Dr. Satyavrata Shastri Felicitation Volume* (now published).
9. "Sītā in Vālmīki Rāmāyaṇa – A Reappraisal" to be published in *Prof. A.M. Shastri Commemoration Volume* (now published).
10. "Ṛta, Dharma and Sanātana Dharma in Indian Culture – A Critical Appraisal" to be published in the *Journal of IIAS*, Shimla, edited by Prof. R.N. Mishra (now published).
11. "Spiritual Experiences in the Vedic Corpus and Vedāntic Tradition" to be published in *Summer Hill*, edited by Prof. S. Bhattacharya, Shimla (now published).
12. "Religion without Dogma: A Philosophical Exploration with Special Reference to Indian Religious Literature" to be included in the Volume edited by Prof. D.A. Shankar containing the Proceedings of the

National Seminar held at Dhvanyaloka, Mysore during 22 to 24th Feb. 2000 on "Nationalism, Religion and Literatures".

13. "Hindutva – The Spirit of Hinduism" to be published in *The Journal of Dharma*, Bangalore (now published).
14. "Saṁkara and Nāgārjuna: Two Philosophical Perspectives with Reference to Modern Age" (now published in *Sandhān*, 2004).
15. "Hindu Tolerance – An Analytic Profile" (now published in *Research Bulletin*, VVRI, Hoshiarpur: 2004).
16. "Indian Philosophy and its Relevance for Man's Social Concern" (now published in *The Concept of Man:* Ed.: Dr. D.M. Praharaj, Meerut: 2004.

(II) REVIEWS TO BE PUBLISHED ON PROF. G.C. NAYAK'S BOOKS

1. "Philosophical Reflections" (2nd enlarged and revised edition) to be reviewed in the *Journal of the Indian Academy of Philosophy*, Kolkata (now published).
2. Do., to be reviewed in *Indian Philosophical Quarterly*, Pune.
3. Do., to be reviewed in the *Philosophical Quarterly*, Amalner (now published).
4. "Philosophical Reflections" (2nd enlarged and revised edition) to be reviewed in *Philosophy and the Life World*, Dept. of Philosophy, Vidya Sagar University, Midnapore (now published).
5. "Mādhyamika Śūnyatā" to be reviewed in *Philosophy East & West*, USA by Prof. Roy W. Perrett.
6. Do., to be reviewed by Prof. Gesh N. Samten, *Sarnath*.

Notes on the Contributors

John M. Koller : He is Professor of Philosophy (Rensselaer Polytechnic Institute, School of Humanities and Social Sciences, 110, 8th Street, Troy, New York - 12180-3590, USA). He has specialized in Indian philosophy and religion. On being invited, he has come to India several times and has delivered lectures at various academic centres and universities including Madras, Delhi and Utkal (Bhubaneswar). In America, he has been closely associated with Prof. Rama Rao Rappu at the University of Miami and has actively participated in the International Conferences on Vedānta on many occasions. His writings on Indian philosophy, specially on Vedānta are notable.

K.R. Sundararajan : He is Professor of Theology (St. Bonaventure University, St. Bonaventure, New York, 14778, USA). Though originally he hails from Tamil Nadu (India), he is now in USA. His special field of interest is theology with emphasis on Indian theological trends. He has several visits to India and has delivered lectures on classical Indian thought at several academic centres. He is also associated with the International Conferences on Vedānta and has participated in such Conferences in USA, India and West Indies.

John Brockington : He is the Chairperson of the Department of Sanskrit, University of Edinburgh (7 Buccleuch Place, Edinburgh EH8 9LW U.K.). He has his education from the university of Oxford. He is one of the top-ranking Indologists of the present-day. He has specialized on the *Rāmayaṇa*, particularly its linguistic and philological basis. He has come to India on several occasions and, on being invited, he has delivered lectures in notable academic centres including Delhi, Kolkata, Bhubaneswar and Puri. His originality is evidenced from his numerous writings, published in the International sources in UK, USA and India. He has widely travelled in different continents, including Europe, Asia and Australia.

Rabindra Raj Singh : He is the Chairperson in the Department of Philosophy (Brock University, St. Cathorines, Ontario, Canada L2S 3AI). Though originally, he hails from Panjab (India), he is now in Canada. His interest in philosophical research covers wide areas of both Eastern and Western origin with special emphasis on the philosophy of Martin Heidegger, Contemporary European philosophy, Gandhian thought, Vedānta and Bhakti tradition. Some of his research papers are published in the *International Journal of Applied Philosophy, Journal of Aesthetics and Art Criticism, Diogenes* and *Phenomenological Inquiry.* He has come several times and, on being invited, he has delivered lectures in number of reputed academic centres in India, including Delhi, Chandigarh and Bhubaneswar. He is also associated with the International Conferences on Vedānta held at the Univeisity of Miami, Ohio, Oxford (USA) and in Trinidad and Tobago.

Shashi Bhusan Prasad Sinha : He is retired Professor and Head of the Department of Philosophy, Bihar University. After his retirement, he became UGC Emeritus Fellow, Senior Research Fellow of the Indian Council of Philosophical Research. He was General President of the Indian Philosophical Congress held at Hardwar. He has actively participated, chaired in number of national and international Seminars, including World Congress of Philosophy, held at Boston, USA. His major field of interest is to explore the philosophy of spiritualistic humanism. He resides in Muzaffarpur (Majholia, Near Railway Crossing (Gumti) No. 5, Khabra, Muzaffarpur - 842001).

R.S. Bhatt : He is Professor in the Department of Philosophy, Delhi University (Residence : M/P-23, Maurya Enclave, Pitampura, Delhi-110034). He has the rare combination of having specialized study in both Sanskrit and Philosophy. As a result, he has intensive research in Viśiṣṭādvaita Vedānta, Buddhism and Pancarātra darśana. He was General President of the Jodhpur session of the Indian Philosophical Congress (IPC). He has widely travelled both in India and abroad. His major publications are from both India and USA. On several occasions, he has participated in World Congress of Philosophy and is now associated in its different working committees. He himself has organized number of national and international Seminars including the Platinum Jubilee session of the Indian Philosophical Congress held at Delhi. He has been a member of the Indian Council of Philosophical Research and has served in UGC panel of Philosophy and in several activities of UPSC.

Ripusudan Prasad Srivastava : He was Professor of Philosophy and also Pro-Vice Chancellor of Bihar University. After his retirement, he has become UGC Emeritus Fellow. He has doctoral research from I.I.T., Kanpur. His special field of interest is philosophy and its social relevance. In his writings, he usually adopts critical and analytical methodology. He has number of publications, in form of articles, books, monograph and anthology. He has delivered lectures in number of universities. He is settled in Muzaffarpur, Bihar.

Ramesh Chandra Pradhan : He is Professor of Philosophy in the Central University, Hyderabad- 500046. He has his doctoral research on the philosophy of Wittgenstein. He is a regular contributor to all the standard philosophical journals of the country. He has visited abroad on several occasions and he represented India at the International Seminar on Wittgenstein. He is now the Associate Editor of the *Journal of the Indian Council of Philosophical Research*. He was the Member-Secretary of the Council in recent past. His major publications are : *Language and Experiences, Recent Development in Analytic Philosophy, Truth, Meaning and Understanding,* and *Wittgenstein* (Ed.). Recently he has developed interest in Indian philosophy and has contributed number of articles to the philosophical sources. He has visited several universities and academic centres and has delivered lectures on several issues of philosophy. He is now settled in Hyderabad (93, Doyens Township, Seri Lingampally, Hyderabad - 500019).

S. Shyamkishore Singh : He is Professor of Philosophy (Manipur Univeristy, Imphal - 795003). His publications appear in standard journals. His major interest is in the philosophy of Wittgenstein and Kant. He has widely travelled and has delivered lectures in seminars, symposia and conferences. In recent past, he was a member of the Indian Council of Philosophical Research. He is settled in Imphal (Residence : Palace Compound, South of Sri Govindji Temple (near postal colony), Imphal - 795001).

R.L. Singh : He is a retired Professor of Philosophy, Allahabad University. He has specialized in Indian philosophy, specially on Vedānta. He has contributed articles to standard philosophical journals. He was nominated by the U.P. state government to the Indian Council of Philosophical Research. He has participated and organized number of national seminars in philosophy, including one on the philosophy of late Prof. Sangam Lal Pandey. He is settled in Tagore Town of Allahabad.

Sobha-jit Mishra : He was for a long time Professor and Head of the Department of Philosophy in the university of Gorakhpur. During his professional career he has to his credit number of research publications in standard philosophical sources. He has specialized in Indian philosophy with particular reference to Vedānta. He has participated and organized a number of seminars, symposia and conferences at the national level. He resides in Gorakhpur.

Kalyan Kumar Bagchi : He is a retired Professor and Head of the Department of Philosophy, Visva-Bharati. He has specialized in the philosophy of K.C. Bhattacharya. His comparative studies on Bhattacharya and Kant are notable. On the basis of his research output, he is considered as the most critical exponent of K.C. Bhattacharya. Besides this, Bagchi has also taken keen interest in phenomenology, conceptual analysis and Vedānta darśana. His writings appear in all the standard philosophical journals in India. Recently, he was the General President in the 80th session of IPC held at North Bengal University. He has visited abroad and has spent long time in the Oxford University. He is now settled in Santiniketan (Simantapalli, P.O. Santiniketan - 731235).

S. Panneerselvam : He is Professor of Philosophy in the Dr. S. Radhakrishnan Institute for Advanced Studies in Philosophy, University of Madras. He is one of the notable philosophers of the younger generation. He is one of the few Indian scholars who has developed special interest in continental philosophers like Heidegger, Gadmar and Ricoeur. Besides this, his interest is to review Indian philosophy from analytical standpoint. He is a regular contributor to all the standard philosophical journals in the country.

S.S. Rama Rao Pappu : He is Professor of Philosophy in the University of Miami, Oxford, Ohio (USA). Though originally he hails from Andhra (India), now he is settled in America. He is well known in popularizing classical

Indian philosophy, specially Vedānta, by way of organizing number of international conferences in USA, India and Trinidad & Tobago. His organizing capacity in arranging seminars and conferences has been well recognized in the international forum. His special interest is to revitalize the spirit of Indian thought and to present it in its proper perspective at the global level. His research findings are well noticed among the philosophical community.

Rajendra Prasad : He has, for long years, remained as Professor and Chairperson of the Department of Philosophy in I.I.T., Kanpur. He has been a Fulbright/ Smit-Mundt Fellow, a Rockefeller Foundation Fellow. He has been a National Lecturer of UGC on three occasions, a Senior Fellow and also National Lecturer of the Indian Council of Philosophical Research. He has been General President of IPC, also General President of Indian Philosophical Association and Akhil Bharatiya Darsan Parishad. He has published numerous scholarly papers in philosophical sources both in India and abroad. He has edited the journals : *Indian Review of Philosophy, Dārśanika Traimāsika* and is currently a co-editor of *Indian Philosophical Quarterly* and *Parāmarśa*. Some of his noted books are : *Regularity, Normativity and Rules of Language, Karma, Causation and Retributive Morality, Varṇa Dharma, Niṣkāma Karma and Practical Morality,* and *Dharmakīrti's Theory of Inference.* He is now in Patna (Opposite Stadium, Prem Chand Marg, Rajendra Nagar, Patna - 800016).

Arun K. Mookerjee : After completing his teaching profession at the Jadavpur University, Kolkata, he continues his research activities and is now Director of the Academy of Comparative Religion, India. He has special interest in the areas of socio-political philosophy and has number of publications in the standard philosophical sources. He was the General President of IPC and is now settled in Jadavpur, Kolkata.

Bijayananda Kar : He is the editor of the present volume.

Introduction

This festschrift volume comprises of number of essays by researchers who are well-established in their reflective pursuits. The essays, compiled here, are the outcome of deep study of various issues of philosophical interest. The issues are of wide coverage, comprising Indian as well as Western dimension. On certain occasions, there has been also a good comparative study of both the approaches. The points raised in the essays pertain to metaphysics, theology, philosophy of religion, philosophy of language, analytical philosophy, socio-political philosophy and applied philosophy of ethics and value. On account of this the volume has been given the title: *Reflections on Indian Wisdom (Philosophical Perspectives)*.

The first essay "Śaṅkara on Human Embodiment" is by Professor John M. Koller (Rensselaer Polytechnic Institute, Troy, New York) who has special interest in the classical Indian philosophy. He has, in the present essay, made a penetrative study of the problem of human embodiment in the philosophy of Śaṅkara. Even if the difficulty faced in the Sāṅkhya dualism of relating two different ontological realities : puruṣa and prakṛti is avoided in the non-dualism (advaita) advocated by Śaṅkara, there is, Koller asserts, still the persistence of the dilemma as to how *avyākṛte nāmarūpa* is both evolved from and also "is different in essence from Ātman". The analogy offered by Śaṅkara, in this connection, of relating dirty foam and clean water to explain the problem of embodiment does not become satisfactory. For, Koller argues, the water containing dirty foam is also dirty and impure. And, in that way, the purity of Ātman remains unclear. To him, Śaṅkara Advaita has no ontological status for *avidyā*. And, for that, the issue raised here continues to be problematic. Koller's view-point, of course, requires serious deliberation.

The second essay "The Spirituality of Līlā" is by Professor K.R. Sundararajan (St. Bonaventure University, U.S.A.). He deals with the Vaiṣṇava account of *līlā* with its distinctive mark on spirituality. He, by way of surveying the concept of *līlā* is far more positive in respect of the world than the māyic account of *līlā* as advanced by Śaṅkara. Even the goal of *niṣkāma* karma (as usually attributed to *Bh. Gītā*) is not found to be convincing in contrast to the view offered by the Vaiṣṇavas, asserts Sundararajan. In this context, he prefers the coinage of the expression "purposeless purpose" to explain the nature and scope of *līlā*. To him, the Vaiṣṇava theology provides scope for joyful participation of *līlā* in the world : while in Advaita, because of the introduction of *māyā*, the manifestation of the world of creation is not explained and, as such, it is less convincing from the theological point of view. Sundararajan's remark deserves due attention.

Usually the Mīmāṃsā darśana is pictured as exposing the theoretical background for specific forms of rites and rituals, found in certain passages of the Vedas. But, in addition to that, Mīmāṃsā definitely is more conspicuous in providing a philosophical foundation in respect of the relation between word and its meaning in the background of the study of language. In that way, the role of Mīmāṃsā, so far as philosophy of language is concerned, cannot be belittled.

Professor John Brockington (University of Edinburgh, U.K.), in his contribution "Early Mīmāṃsā on Language" has pointed out that the main aim of Mīmāṃsā is to elucidate the correct meaning of Vedic utterances and not to attain *mokṣa* or liberation. He has viewed Mīmāṃsā not as theology but as philosophy, as other classical darśanas are. Basing on Śabara's work (on I.I.27-31), he has expressed that *codanā* or Vedic commandments are *apauruṣeya* not because "name of any historical person is not found in the Veda" but because it is valid or true by itself. In other words, the truth of the Vedic expression is not person dependent (*puruṣa-vyāpāra-tantra*) but is true by itself, meaning thereby that it is universally true irrespective of having any allegiance to any theological dogmatic source whatsoever. To be more precise, for the primary meaning of *śabda* or word is its *ākṛti* or the universal (*jāti*). It is interesting to note that a similar view had also been held by Professor Ganeswar Misra (vide his book, *Vaidika Dharma-Cetanā, eka Dārśanika Vicāra* (in Oriya), Cuttack: Santosh Publications, 1986, p. 24). *Nityatā* of the Vedic utterance, therefore, means, in this context, proper and specific not necessarily eternal in a quixotic sense of flippant speculation. The word or *śabda* is thus viewed as unchanging in the sense that its meaning component remains unaffected even if the object that is denoted by the word is perished. It is rightly noted that the Mīmāṃsakas like Śabara do not differentiate between the Vedic *śabda* and the *śabda* used in ordinary language and that aptly justifies the point that the acceptance of *śabda* as authentic is not held in some transempirical mystical plane. It is something that too is ordinarily intelligible through the usual process of enquiry.

Brockington has drawn the attention of the reader to the Mīmāṃsaka's distinction between *yoga* and *ruḍhi*, while analysing the concept of meaning. In this regard, the Mīmāṃsaka's general attitude of putting more emphasis on *ruḍhi* than on *yoga* is very significant. Both Śabara and Kumārila, Brockington observes, duly acknowledge the meaning of certain words, conventionally used by the *mlecchas* and which are not known to the people of Āryavartta. This well reveals the non-dogmatic and liberal attitude in which the Vedic approach to language is established.

The essay "Plotinus and the Contemplative Life" by Professor Rabindra Raj Singh (Brock University, Canada) is an exposition of the philosophical outlook of Plotinus at the background of Plato's metaphysical position. Singh has tried to impress upon the reader the important point that Plotinus is not simply reiterating the Platonic standpoint but also is keen to restabilise the contemplative life in the human situation. Contemplation is not viewed here as full rejection of the world but only "turning away" from excessive worldliness. To Plotinus, the contemplative realization is "the best attainment of human life". Developing the Platonic message, as found in *Phaedo*, that "idea of philosophy as a rehearsal of death", Plotinus, as well exposed by Singh, appeals for "shut your eyes and change to and wake another way of seeing". The contemplative life to Plotinus is not viewed as full suppression of the body, not as embracing pre-mature death but only for "a death of excessive bodily involvements". Thus the world of sense and the higher world are not mutually exclusive. The rewards of contemplation is a "return to the worldly life with a new resoluteness and renewed inclination toward the contemplative life". Singh's presentation is clear and impressive.

The next essay "Humanism in Swami Vivekananda's Philosophy : Some Critical Observations" is by Professor S.B.P. Sinha (from Muzaffarpur, Bihar). He has first tried to impress upon the readers as to what he thinks as the typical feature of Indian philosophy where philosophy is not formal, technical and is divorced from life. It is deeply related with the practical problems and issues of living. The modern Indian philosophers like Vivekananda, Gandhi, etc. may not be philosophers in the technical sense but are notable thinkers having far-reaching philosophical view-points of practical concern. In that sense, Sinha remarks, "Vivekananda's humanistic outlook has profound impact on his philosophy of practical Vedānta". Sinha thinks that technical formalistic trend in recent philosophy has "divorced philosophy from life" and, as such, it is "one of the causes of the present value-crisis and other maladies". In this context, he views that Vivekananda's spiritualistic humanism is highly significant. Vivekananda's humanistic approach has been distinguished from the usual Western conception where humanism has taken mostly a non-spiritual, mundane, secular formulation. To Sinha, Vivekananda's approach is not fully opposed to mundance but it is aimed at harmonising between spiritual urge and material need in the human life-situation. It is "a synthesis of the transcendent and the immanent". Sinha's point of view needs a critical consideration.

In the essay "The Buddhist Theory of Two-faceted Knowledge" Professor S.R. Bhatt (Delhi University) discusses the theory of *dvairūpya jñāna* as advanced by Dignāga in his *Pramāṇavārtika*. According to this theory, every knowledge has a subject-form (*svākāra*) and object-form (*viṣayākāra*) and they all occur simultaneously in the same cognition. The theory of two-faceted knowledge has been, Bhatt indicates, interpreted differently by the Sautrāntika and the Yogācāra standpoints, as referred to by Dignāga. While for the Sautrāntikas, there is the admittance of external object, for the Yogācāras, the cognition itself appears as subject and object. Despite the discussion being somewhat concise, Bhatt's treatment of Dignāga's point of view is interesting and notable.

Professor R.P. Srivastava (from Muzaffarpur, Bihar) in his contribution "A Note on Contemporary Indian Philosophy" has raised certain issues regarding the very formulation of the expression "Contemporary Indian Philosophy" and prefers another expression "Contemporary Trends in Philosophy in India". By way of clarifying his point of view, Srivastava has identified two major trends and, accepting Karl H. Potter's classification, has named the trends as Progress philosophy and Leap philosophy. The Leap philosophical trend in contemporary India preaches theistic spiritualism with least regard for free rational enquiry. Srivastava is critical about this trend and he is inclined to take that as "pseudo-philosophy". So far as Progress philosophy is concerned, it has to take into consideration, Srivastava thinks, the contemporary situation in which philosophical investigation can be undertaken in tune with scientific progress and also social dynamics. Srivastava identifies three predicaments : Alienation, Futility of human endeavour and Pangs of mediocrity. Philosophical thinking in India, according to him, has to tackle these issues seriously and effectively. His suggestion is important and it deserves careful consideration.

The essay "On the Very Idea of Metaphysics" is by Professor R.C. Pradhan (Central University, Hyderabad). It is one well argued out essay in which metaphysics is regarded to be a vision of reality that is beyond language and scientific thought. He, in the beginning of his essay, has tried to clarify as to what metaphysics is not. In this connection, he has referred to the Aristotelian view of metaphysics as the science of being qua being. It is the first philosophy "that inquires into the fundamental principle of reality".

Pradhan has referred to Quine's criticism of Aristotle's view and he, in this connection, is critical about Quine's concept of philosophy as continuous with science.

He seems to have gone along with Heideggar to hold that metaphysics deals with "why-question" that "penetrates to the underlying realms". To Pradhan, "metaphysics is not a science", it "leaves everything as it is and transcends the limits of all description". He has referred to the Strawsonian distinction between descriptive and revisionary metaphysics; but has preferred to regard metaphysics as something deeper and more fundamental than the two types, as formulated by Strawson.

In this connection, Pradhan discussed both the metaphysics of the transcendent and the metaphysics of the immanent. He has concluded that metaphysics is a higher-order activity which "takes us back to the ultimate nature of things". The essay, presented by Pradhan, is original and highly thought-provoking.

In the philosophic world, Kant is regarded as the most important thinker in the later part of eighteenth century and is given credit for bringing a "Copernican revolution". So also Wittgenstein is held as the most original and revolutionary thinker in the twentieth century to bring to focus the importance of linguistic and conceptual analysis in matters of philosophizing. Both the philosophers are centuries apart. And, their philosophical methodologies and the conclusions they arrive at are strikingly different. Yet it is also noticed, as nicely brought forward by Professor S. Shyamkishore Singh (University of Manipur, Imphal), that these two great philosophers have shared "similar views on certain fundamental issues of philosophical inquiry". He has convincingly made the point that a "critique of thought" is in essence a "critique of language" and, in that way, the similarity between Kant and Wittgenstein becomes notable. Kant warns by remarking that the application of "ideas of Pure Reason" to the transempirical realism ends in contradiction and antinomies. So also Wittgenstein warns "where we cannot speak about we must pass over to silence". But, nevertheless, Kant tries to locate scope for ethics, religion and aesthetics in the domain of Critique of Practical Reason and Critique of Judgement. Wittgenstein too makes a venture of breaking the "silence" in his later writing by maintaining that a philosopher is bound to raise issues which are perplexing and puzzling. In his characteristic expression, philosophical problem has the form "I don't know my way about". But, even then, Wittgenstein concedes that philosopher's puzzlement is due to his misconception about language. So also, in this context, Kant's pointing at "transcendental illusion" is quite striking.

Singh has referred to the Western writers like Max Black, Quinton, Maslow who have also made good comparative studies between Kant and Wittgenstein. Singh's venture, in this regard, is laudable.

The next essay "Reason and Revelation in Śaṅkara" is by Professor R.L. Singh (from Allahabad). He points out that Śaṅkara has applied analogical reasoning to establish his philosophical point. It can, according to him, yield a highly probable conclusion. Reasoning, he says, "is the unfolding of a vision in the medium of intellectual understanding; but itself it cannot lead to the vision".

Revelation, to him, is not scriptural statement or dogma. It "is seeing or direct perception of reality". Scripture only bears testimony to direct perception (*sākṣāt pratyakṣa*). After the attainment of direct perception, it can be, to him, put to reasoning. And, in that way, he thinks that there is no antagonism between revelation and reason in Śaṅkara Advaita. Brahman, being realised through intuition, "cannot be the object of thought-knowledge". Reasoning is, therefore, said by Śaṅkara as *apratiṣṭhita*. Hence Brahman is translogical. *Śruti* or scriptural testimony is regarded as the most authoritative because it "is the direct expression in words of the vision of Brahman". But *śruti* itself does not give the knowledge of Brahman. The Brahman, to Singh, "is an insight into our being".

He, then, discusses the issue as to whether Śaṅkara can be held as a mystic, or a theologian or a philosopher. He concludes by maintaining that in Śaṅkara there is "a clear dovetailing of mysticism, theology and philosophy". It is held that these are not conflicting but complementary to each other in Śaṅkara Advaita. Singh's point of view deserves analytical treatment.

The next essay is "Logical Positivism and the Advaita Metaphysics". It is by Professor S. Mishra (from Gorakhpur, U.P.). He has, in the beginning, briefly touched upon the dominant trends of philosophy since Kant so far as metaphysics is concerned. He deals with Hegelianism, Logical Positivism, Phenomenology and Existentialism. While discussing all these at the background of Kantian philosophy, Mishra has come to the conclusion that Kant has actually rejected dogmatic metaphysics but not (what he terms) genuine metaphysics. In this context, he becomes critical about the logical positivistic programme of anti-metaphysics. The genuine philosophical questions relating to freedom, value, reality, truth and beauty are not tackled but rather are evaded by way of designating such questions as meaningless.

Mishra distinguishes between reflective and unreflective attitude. To him, the knowability of the Advaita Ātman is due to the reflective attitude. On the reflective plane, knowledge has to be "understood as an unmeant and unmeanable content". In this context, Mishra holds that the *mahāvākyas* like *Tattvamasi* are "meaningful for a man seeking knowledge and freedom". They are significant and their contents "mark on an advancement in knowledge". The Advaitic metaphysical knowledge, Mishra holds, "may be mysterious, unclear and inarticulate but in it lies a hope for a happy, harmonious and peaceful world". Mishra's presentation is interesting; however, it requires further critical study.

Professor Kalyan Kumar Bagchi's (Visva-Bharti, Santiniketan) essay "Two Competing Interpretations of Śaṅkara : G. Misra and G.C. Nayak" is important in view of the fact, that this is one of the few essays included in the present volume which directly deals with certain views held by Professor Nayak himself. Bagchi, of course, has compared as well as contrasted Nayak's view on Śaṅkara Advaita with his mentor's (Misra) view on the same subject. He has noted the point that for both Misra and Nayak the Śaṅkarite programme of philosophy is a "conceptual reordering of our knowledge or thought reordering in this that it revises our ordinary, i.e. commonsense and/or realistic way of thinking in relation to the world". The difference, however, between Misra and Nayak is : while the former (as Bagchi thinks) maintains that Śaṅkara's philosophy is only linguistic analysis, for the latter Śaṅkara has some metaphysical axis to grind in addition to linguistic analysis or *vākyārtha vicāraṇa* and that directs specifically to a vision. In this connection, Bagchi's own view is that Advaita Vedānta "is neither merely conceptual analysis nor merely a vision but a phenomenology of one's experience of Brahman". In order to clarify his view-point, Bagchi takes Prof. K.C. Bhattacharya's observation (made in a different context) that philosophy for Śaṅkara is "self-evident elaboration of self-evident". He admits that for this philosophical programme, conceptual exercise is necessary, "but such exercise actually amounts to a spelling out of concept as the experience of Brahman". Thus, Bagchi thinks that "it is not linguistic clarification or analysis of concepts but stratification or elaboration or spelling out the consciousness of Brahman that Śaṅkara has in mind as a philosopher".

I think, Bagchi's own point of view on Śaṅkara Advaita, while departing from both Misra and Nayak's standpoints, is quite significant and it definitely is worthy of critical appraisal.

In a sense, Prof. Panneerselvam's (University of Madras) essay "Śaṅkara and Vākyārthavicāraṇa : A Study of Prof. G.C. Nayak's Understanding of Advaita" is a continued discussion on the issue initiated by Bagchi, since he too deals with Nayak's understanding of Śaṅkara along with brief reference to Misra's point of view. He has noted Nayak's rendering of *Brahmānubhava* in terms of analysis. It is also important for Nayak according to Panneerselvam, to stress the point that analytical understanding is not of any utterance but only of the Vedantic *mahāvākyas* like "That thou art" which can provide enlightenment. Panneerselvam concedes this point of Nayak as against Misra's view which (according to him and also Nayak) suffered from fallacy of reductionism by holding that Śaṅkara's stand only is confined to linguistic analysis. He further differs from Misra's view (along with Nayak) that *śabda/śruti* in Śaṅkara's Advaitic framework does not stand for authority at all.

According to Panneerselvam "the true purport of *śruti* is to show that Brahman as the eternal subject is never an object". In that way, the ordinary expressions which deal with the knowledge of the object cannot be of any relevance so far as *Brahma jñāna* is concerned. That is how, there is special importance of *mahāvākya* in Śaṅkara Advaita. But, it is to be marked that, to Śaṅkara, Brahman is indescribable. So, strictly speaking, it transcends both objectivity and subjectivity. So the analytical understanding of *mahāvākya* is to lead, from Śaṅkara's point of view, pure indescribable non-dual or advaita. Further, it is notable that Śaṅkara, for his philosophical programme, takes the meaning of ordinary sentence like "fire is hot" for analysis. And, it is also worth noting that the Vedāntic *mahāvākya* is not exclusively analysed by Śaṅkara; it is taken up also by other interpreters of Vedānta. In fact, the different Vedāntins, while discussing and interpreting Vedic utterances, are clearly found to be choosy and selective. They read the utterance through their respective philosophical standpoints. This activity is not at all arbitrary in the sense that something foreign is grafted or superimposed from outside. Rather, on the contrary, the different philosophical views are original and bear distinctive mark of their own.

Saṅkara Advaita is interpreted by Nayak as revealing "absolutistic ontology". Panneerselvam, though readily approves ontology being operative at the conceptual plane, holds that it looses its significance at the higher level. According to him, Saṅkara Advaita "is not only transempirical but also transontological". Brahman "transcends everything and there is no place for any ontology". It is evident that Panneersevam's concluding remark is novel and it requires further analytical study.

Prof. S.S. Rama Rao Pappu (Miami University, Ohio, Oxford) starts his discussion by pointing to shifting of emphasis, made by some Western philosophers, from legalistic to virtue ethics. So far as the classical Indian point of view is considered, he attempts to explore the primacy of virture-ethic in contrast to legalistic or duty-ethic. Advancing number of references from the *Rāmāyaṇa,* the *Bhagavad Gītā* and the *Dharmaśāstras*, he comes to the conclusion that dharma can reasonably be regarded as virtue and not as duty. In this context, he has touched upon the Indian concept of *puruṣārtha* and he rightly holds, I think, that "dharma is the most important *puruṣārhta*". To him, all "other *puruṣārthas* have been subsumed under dharma".

Dharma has (like many other concepts) varied meanings, but, according to him, the central meaning of the concept is law. In this context, he maintains that as law, dharma is both moral and natural, prescriptive and descriptive. Dharma as cosmic law means *Ṛta*. It is viewed as natural law, meaning thereby, what happens "necessarily happens" and even "ought to happen". Dharma, Pappu continues, also means social norm, duty or obligation. But, even then he holds that "dharma cannot be identified with a normative ethic".

Then he elaborately discusses dharma as virtue. Quoting passages from the *Rāmāyaṇa* and the *Gītā* with citing views of Manu, Praśasthapāda and Patanjali he tries to substantiate his stand that dharma is understood in terms of virtue. However, he concedes that dharma is also used in the sense of duty, but dharma is, according to him, "primarliy a virtue ethic". He then has raised the case of virtuous person in the Indian context. He has discussed the role of a paradigmatic individual who is obviously a sincere follower of dharma (virtue) but not necessarily an ascetic or *sannyāsin*, who is rather treated as an escapist. Virtuous person, on the other hand, is regarded to be an exampler so far as his conduct is concerned. He is considered as not innovator of standard but as "standard bearer". In this context, Pappu has touched upon the *Gītā* concept of *puruṣottama* and, in modern times, Gandhi as *mahātmā.*

His essay is well composed and carries definitely an air of freshness.

The next essay on *Svarāja* or self-rule is by Prof. Rajendra Prasad, a noted philosopher of recent India. The essay deals with rethinking of the two faces of *svarāja* : pre-independence and post-independence. Prasad, first of all, brings out the reason as to why there is the need of rethinking *svarāja* that is there in India today. In what sense, the existing form of *svarāja* has gone astray from the original form. That means, he admits that *svarāja*, found in post-independent stage, is not on the same track on which it was in the pre-independent stage and definitely there is some derailment. He suggests, by way of revaluation, some measures by means of which it can be brought back on the right rail.

Basing on the Gandhian concept of *svarāja*, Prasad finds certain conditions which are to be satisfied if India can be regarded as having *svarāja*. It must imply that there is political independence; but that is not enough. It is necessary, Prasad points out, that Indians must be free from any unreasonable, dogmatic cultural foundation of their own, however deep-rooted it may be. There should not be any sort of domination of any culture, either foreign or native. The individual must have free choice to operate, within the parameters of good reason of course. In the Gandhian scheme, the *svarāja* of the country depends upon the *svarāja* of each individual. He must have the living with self-respect and self-dignity and that cannot be accomplished unless there is the involvement of moral element. Prasad rightly holds that morality is a social phenomenon. It contributes to social cohesion. The moral consideration is to override the political, economic and even religious factor. Dharma in the Indian context, is to be understood in terms of morality.

Prasad thinks that the primacy of the moral and respect for the intrinsic dignity of the individual are the two basic components of *svarāja*. To him, the Gandhian model of *svarāja* is neither utopian nor idealistic. It, of course, needs reevaluation and reconstruction and for that the role of intellectuals cannot be set aside. However, by intellectual he does not mean those who are just formally well educated, but are opaque to any moral sensibility. His presentation has analytical clarity. It is an insightful study of the concept of *svaāja*.

So far as the issue of equality in the social sector is concerned, there are quite a good number of essays (included in the volume) which have touched the point and have dealt with the issue from different angles. Srivastava has appealed for a philosophical reflection at the practical set-up. Pappu, through the discussion of dharma, has raised the point of moral justice at the social as well as individual level. Prasad has referred to the class-discrimination in the Indian social set-up and has dealt with this point at the background of the Gandhian concept of *svarāja*. Prof. Arun Mookherjee (from Jadavpur, Kolkata) too is interested with the problem of equality in the social phenomena which, to him, is a common concern for a sociologist as well as social philosopher.

He points out as to how far "equality" turns out to be a mere slogan, while "inequality" is a socio-political fact based upon the feeling of inequality. Mookherjee argues that "only a felt inequality moves individuals and groups to socio-political action for equality". In this context, he has cited illustrations both from Western and Indian sources as to how the slave or the śudra "was made to believe that servility was his element and has given nature". In course of his critical discussion, he has also dealt with various ways in which equality is understood in different situations. In modern democratic set-up, equality is said to have been understood in terms of civil rights. Mookherjee holds that equality has acquired different meanings, one for the liberal world, and quite another for the socialist world. At certain sphere, equality is also accepted as "tolerable inequality". In this connection, individual liberty is regarded as of prime concern in certain dominant Western circle. Such sense of individual liberty can be ensured in a socio-political set-up, often identified as "minimal state". In such a situation, Mookherjee thinks, the issue of equality and inequality is not that important. He refers, in this regard, Bernard William's view-point who is found to be somewhat close to the sense of tolerance and fraternity. Finally he comes to the conclusion that equality as a round full concept is a myth.

Mookherjee's essay, though concise, evinces in-depth reflection.

The essay on Commonism is exclusively on the philosophical position which Prof. Nayak has advocated and that, in his own language, is philosophy of commonism. By this expression, he means that the commonistic elements in religion can be supported by commonistic philosophy and that is, what he hopes, to play a vital role in future. His point of view has raised interesting debate and discussion in certain philosophical circle. The essay of mine is a modest critical review of his philosophical position. Nayak finds commonistic element most significantly in Hindu dharma and, according to him, if that is properly comprehended and is well implemented in the practical plane, then it can effectively counter the challenge of the present religious crisis.

I have discussed his stand in detail and I have seen his attempt of reviewing religious framework at the background of human and secular perspective to be in the right direction. Dharmic consciousness, it is true, is meant primarily for the man of flesh and blood in the empiric, mundane plane and the idea of transmundane or sacred or divine cannot reasonably play a superior role in this set-up. Religious crisis can be overcome if religion is viewed essentially as of human concern than of any trans-human and transmundane source. The sense of divinity and spirituality in religious framework has to be accommodated only in so far as it possesses dharmic sense of morality and is both conceivable and workable by men here and now. Otherwise, the religious protagonist's appeal for divine or spiritual excellence turns out to be mythical and thus it never becomes convincing to the ordinary common man, having regard for a minimum sense of moral reasoning. The sense of commonism is, according to me, of great significance by having the undertonal basis of humanism.

Bijayananda Kar

1

Śaṅkara on Human Embodiment

John M. Koller

It would seem that Śaṅkara cannot be expected to have a philosophy of the body, for his view, as expressed in the *Upadeśasāhasrī,* for example, is that the pure consciousness *(cidātman)* alone is ultimately real; everything else, including the body, is only an illusion. The Self (*Ātman)* that I truly am, he says, is "ever free, pure, transcendentally changeless, invariable, immortal, imperishable, and thus always bodiless".[1] Further, being bodiless means that the true self neither experiences nor acts. In Śaṅkara's words, "The false belief that *Ātman* is doer is due to the belief that the body is *Ātman*".[2] Thus, when a student approached his teacher, a knower of Brahman, and asked how he could obtain release from the suffering of *saṁsāra,* the teacher advised him that he must overcome the ignorance through which he mistakenly thinks that he is an agent, an experiencer and a transmigrator, when in fact he is none of these, but the highest *Ātman.*[3]

After all, from Śaṅkara's perspective, though I frequently identify with the body, this identification *(adhyāsa)* is a mistake, the result of ignorance, for the truth is that I am pure consciousness, *Ātman,* eternal and unchanging, having nothing to do with the body. But how is this mistake to be explained? What is this ignorance wherein I identify with the body and regard myself as an actor and experiencer? For the sake of showing that this identification is a mistake, that it results from ignorance, Śaṅkara needs to develop a philosophy of human existence that explains what the body-mind is and how it comes to be falsely imposed on *Ātman*. Even more importantly, he needs a philosophy of the embodied self as the basis for liberation from karmic bondage.

The crucial question here is, what is the relation of the Self *(Ātman)* qua pure consciousness *(caitanya)* to the body? The first thing to note is that for Śaṅkara, as for all of the Indian systems, body includes mind. That is, the ontological line is drawn not as in modern Western philosophy between the mind and the body, where mind is identified with soul or self and body with unconscious matter, but between the body which has both physical and mental dimensions on the one hand, and the Self on the other, where Self transcends both the physical and the mental.

Although the theoretical issues involving the relation of Self to body-mind are notoriously difficult, and while it is true that for most of the systems it is the pure Self that has paramount ontological status, the lived body-mind is of the greatest practical, soteriological importance because the path to liberation is followed by the embodied Self. It is the embodied Self that is to be liberated; the bonds to be loosened are those created by the body-mind and only the lived, experiencing, acting body-mind can loosen them. Thus, in *Upadeśasāhasrī* (II. 1.11), in response to the student's question about getting out of the ocean of *saṁsāra,* the teacher says, "When you are dead your body will be eaten by birds or will turn into earth right here. How then do you wish to get out of the ocean of *saṁsāra?* Because if you turn into ashes on this bank of the river you cannot get across to the other side of the river". The point is that only the embodied Self can achieve the purity of action and knowledge needed to dissolve the bonds of karma.

So overpowering is the conviction that consciousness is inoperative without the body-mind organism that in Nyāya the Self *(Ātman)* in disembodied condition is held to be without consciousness or knowledge.

Indeed, neither the sorrow nor the happiness resulting from karma could be experienced except in the context of mind, senses, and body. Any existence of the Self outside that context is unintelligible in karmic terms; it appears incompatible with the function of the karmic mechanism.[4] It is only the embodied Self that is bound by karma and only the embodied Self that can be released from karma. That is, both karma and *mokṣa* are relevant only to embodied existence. This is why Śaṅkara views the subtle body *(sūkṣma śarīra)* as the agent of the Self, carrying it from one gross body *(sthūla śarīra)* to another. The linkages between gross and subtle bodies are well established, with each shaping and being shaped by the other. It is through the subtle body that the *karmasāya*, the effects of karma, are impregnated into the gross body, while, in turn, the gross body encapsules its effects into the subtle body, much like a plant encapsuling itself in its seeds, which then reproduce it.

But neither *sthūla* nor *sūkṣma śarīra,* which are to be viewed as sets of integrated process constituted by a variety of instrumentalities and functions, are to be confused with *Ātman,* of which they are only the agents. For Śaṅkara, the *jīva,* the living person, refers to the *Ātman* in relation to the body. But this is not the relationship of parts making up a whole. It is, rather, the relationship of a guiding light to a traveller in the night, or a supervisor to the persons supervised. As Śaṅkara says in *Brahamasūtra bhāṣya* 1.1.6, "The word '*jīva*' indicates the conscious principle exercising supervision over the body and sustaining the vital airs".[5]

Just as supervisor is different from what is supervised and light different from what is illuminated, so is *Ātman* different from the body. Thus, in *Upadeśasāhasrī*, Śaṅkara says that if the student seeking the sacred knowledgse which brings release from *saṁsāra* says, "I am eternal and different from the body. The bodies come and go like a person's garment," the teacher should say, "you are right," and then should explain how the body is different from the Self.[6]

There follows a remarkable passage in which Śaṅkara explains what the body is and how it comes into existence. Positing an unmanifest name-and-form *(avyākṛte nāmarūpe)*, Śaṅkara declares that this unmanifest evolved into the world of name-and-form as we know it through an evolutionary process according to which it first became manifest as ether, air, fire, water, and earth, in that order. Having characterized the *paramātman* as "different from *nāmarūpa* and bodiless",[7] Śaṅkara says, "This [*paramātman*] is the Evolver of the unevolved name-and-form merely by being existent since It is possessed of inconceivable power. The unevolved name-and-form is different in essence from this [*Ātman*] and is the seed of the world, abiding in It, indescribable as this or something else, and known to It".[8]

He then goes on to say, "[originally] unevolved, this name-and-form took the name-and-form of 'ether' in the course of its evolution from this very *Ātman.* And in this manner this element named 'ether' arose from the highest *Ātman* as dirty foam from clear water. Foam is neither [identical with] water nor absolutely different from water since it is not seen without water. But water is clear and different from foam which is of the nature of dirt. Likewise, the highest *Ātman* is different from name-and-form which corresponds to foam; *Ātman* is pure, clear and different in essence from it. This name-and-form, [originally] unevolved, took the name-and-form of 'ether,' which corresponds to foam, in the course of its evolution".[9]

Śaṅkara then describes an evolutionary process by

which the five basic elements, ether, air, fire, water and earth, appeared. As each of these elements became impregnated with the previous elements, finally earth appeared, as a combination of all five elements. He goes on to say, "And from earth, rice, barley, and other plants consisting of the five elements are produced. From them, when they are eaten, blood and sperm are produced, related respectively to the bodies of women and men. Both blood and sperm, produced by churning with the churning stick of sexual passion driven by ignorance *(avidyā)* and sanctified with sacred formulas, are poured into the womb at the proper time. Through the penetration of fluid from the womb, they become an embryo and it is delivered in the ninth or tenth month".[10] He then explains how this body is named at birth, how it gets its student name, its householder name, and also the name of the forest dweller and *saṅnyāsin.* Repeating that "the body is different from you *(Ātman),*" Śaṅkara says that the teacher should remind the student that the mind and the sense organs consist only of name-and-form, and quotes passages from the *Chāndogya Upaniṣad* (VI. 5,4; 6,5; and 7,6) which declare that the mind consists of food.[11] The point the student must understand is that mind is a function of the body and should not be mistaken for consciousness itself.

Explaining how the Self is bodiless, free from caste, family and purifying ceremonies, the teacher says, "The Evolver [*paramātman*] of name-and-form, by nature different in essence from name-and-form, created this body in the course of evolving name-and-form. And [the Evolver] entered the name-and-form [of the body], Itself being free from the duties of purifying ceremonies. Itself unseen by other, [the Evolver] is seeing; unheard, It is hearing; unthought, It is thinking; unknown, It is knowing".[12]

Rather like the *prakṛtic* self of Sāṅkhya, this self of name-and-form is said to be unconscious ("like food"), but nonetheless constituted by an awareness enabling it to experience, act, and identify itself (mistakenly) as a transmigrating, experiencing, acting self. Unlike *prakṛti,* however, name-and-form, whether manifested or as *avyākṛte,* is not regarded as ultimately real, thus avoiding the Sāṅkhya problem of interaction between the two totally different realities of *prakṛti* and *puruṣa.*

Except for his denial of the ultimate reality of name-and-form and its relation to *Ātman,* Śaṅkara's view of embodied existence is quite similar to the Sāṅkhya-Yoga view. According to Śaṅkara a person consists of *Ātman,* the foundation, and name-and-form, which consists of (1) the body, both gross *(sthūla)* and subtle *(sūkṣma);* (2) core vital energy (*mukhyaprāṇa*); (3) five organs of action (*karmendriya*); (4) five sense (*buddhīndriya*); and (5) the internal organ *(antaḥkaraṇa).*[13]

The subtle body is constituted by the subtle parts of the elements, their "seeds". The *sūkṣma śarīra* is the seed of the *sthūla śarīra,* and when the *sthūla śarīra* perishes at death the *sūkṣma* carries the encoded energy structures of the elements forward into the next life. But upon achieving *mokṣa* the *Ātman* is liberated from the *sūkṣma sárīra.*[14] It is the core vital energy, the *mukhyaprāṇa* that is responsible for breathing, digestion, and the release *(udāna)* of *Ātman* from the body at death.[15] The *mukhyaprāṇa* belongs to life at a deeper than conscious level, whereas the *karmendriya* and *buddhīndriya* belong to embodied consciousness.

The distinction between physical and subtle bodies *(sthūla śarīra* and *sūkṣma śarīra)* is very important, for it recognizes a distinction between mere physicality and humanly embodied physicality. It is a way of insisting on the bodily character of what we think of as mental functions, for the *sūkṣma śarīra,* constituted by the five vital airs, the *buddhi* and *manas* through which the *antaḥkaraṇa* functions, as well as the ten organs (five cognitive-sensory; five conative-motor), is not only itself viewed as a body, *sūksma śarīra,* but is itself further embodied in the *sthūla śarīra.* The senses and agencies of action are seen as instruments of the mind, linking mind with the outside world, just as mind links senses with reflective consciousness, and reflective consciousness links up with Self. But senses, vital force, mind and reflective consciousness can function only when embodied; ultimately the inner organ (*antaḥkaraṇa*) cannot function except through the bodily self; through its *indriya* or instruments.

The problem with all this, however, is that in the end Śaṅkara insists that the true self, *Ātman,* is not really embodied; that body is not self. Further in trying to maintain a strictly non-dualist position, he is forced to deny the reality of bodily existence. To avoid the problems of dualism, Śaṅkara denies that name-and-form is ultimately real or that it really embodies the Self. For him this account functions to explain only the *appearance* of bodily existence and experience, the reality of which is never admitted. This view is deeply problematic, however, as Śaṅkara himself recognized, when he said not only that *avyākṛte nāmarūpa* evolved from *Ātman,* but also that it is different in essence from *Ātman.* How can it be both essentially different from, and evolved from, *Ātman* in a philosophy committed to *satkāryavāda? Satkāryavāda,* as a causal principle, insists that what is produced, the effect, cannot be a different kind of reality than its cause. Thus, *Ātman* could produce only *Ātman,* never *nāmarūpa,* which is non-*Ātman.*

The analogy Śaṅkara introduces to explain this evolution of *nāmarūpa* from *Ātman* reveals the problem, for he says,

> In this manner this element named 'ether' arose from the highest *Ātman* as dirty foam from clear water. Foam is neither water nor absolutely different from water, since it is not seen without water. But water is clear and different from foam, which is of the nature of dirt. Likewise, the highest *Ātman* is different from

nāmarūpa, which corresponds to foam; *Ātman* is pure, clear, and different in essence from it.[16]

Here bodily existence, *nāmarūpa,* is said to correspond to foam, different in essence from *Ātman,* which corresponds to clear water. It would seem then that *avyākṛte nāmarūpe* would correspond to the dirt, of which foam is the manifestation. But clearly this analogy breaks down, for dirty foam arises not simply from clear water, nor simply from dirt, but from the combining of clear water and dirt. Unless both dirt and water were real, and different from each other, how could they combine? Since Śaṅkara cannot admit such a duality, he denies the reality of *nāmarūpa,* relegating it to the level of *māya* or illusion, as superimposition on *Ātman* through ignorance. Thus, Advaita confronts a dilemma: though body-mind must be assumed to account for experience, action and transmigration, in order to preserve the non-dualism that allows nothing other than *Ātman* to be real, its reality must be denied.

It is hard to see how positing *avyākṛte nāmarūpe* resolves this dilemma. If *avyākṛte nāmarūpe* is different from *Ātman,* but equally real, non-dualism is abandoned, bringing the system perilously close to Sāṅkhya-Yoga. If *avyākṛte nāmarūpe* is real but not different from *Ātman,* then either *Ātman* must be bodily existence or else *Ātman* and *avyākṛte nāmarūpe* must be distinct though not different, a view that appears indistinguishable from the *Bhedābhedavāda* that Śaṅkara finds unacceptable. On the other hand, if *avyākṛte nāmarūpe* is unreal, and is only falsely imposed on Brahman through *avidyā,* then bodily existence is also unreal, merely an illusion. To accept this latter alternative, *avidyā* must be explained. If *avidyā* is real, how is it related to Brahman? If *avidyā* is unreal, how can it cause anything to appear?

Śaṅkara regards *avidyā* as *adhyāsa,* superimposition. But if *avidyā* is *adhyāsa,* and *adhyāsa* is the imposition of *avyākṛte nāmarūpe* on *Ātman,* then unless *avyākṛte nāmarūpe* has real ontological status, there is nothing to be imposed on *Ātman.* But if *avyākṛte nāmarūpe* has real ontological status, then the non-duality of *Ātman* is abandoned.[17] This is probably why Śaṅkara sometimes regards *avidyā* as a kind of psychic affliction, a *kleśa,* like *kāma, rāga* and *doṣa.*[18] But of what is it a *kleśa* or affliction? If an affliction of the body-mind, then unless the body-mind is given ontological status, there is no locus for *avidyā.*[19]

This is the basic problem of Advaita, the problem of the unreality of everything other than *Ātman.* If everything other than *Ātman* is unreal, merely a false construction, then to what can *avidyā* belong other than *Ātman?* What Śaṅkara says in the *Upadeśasāhasrī* is that there is no ignorance in *Ātman.*[20] In *Brahamasūtra bhāṣya* he says that for the ignorant, *avidyā* belongs to them in their ignorance, while for the enlightened there is no *avidyā.*[21] This is a way of dismissing the question of locus *(āśraya)* typical of Śaṅkara.

In *Upadeśasāhasrī* (II.2.64), the teacher also evades the question of locus. The student asks, "Is the mutual superimposition of the body and *Ātman* made by the composite of the body and so on or by *Ātman?*" The teacher replies, "What would happen to you if made by the composite of the body and so on or if made by *Ātman?*" The student answers: "If I am merely the composite of the body and so on, then I am non-conscious, so I exist for another's sake; consequently, the mutual superimposition of body and *Ātman* is not effected by me. If I am the highest *Ātman* different from the bodily composite, then I am conscious, so I exist for my own sake; consequently, the superimposition (of body), which is the seed of every calamity, is effected upon *Ātman* by me who am conscious". Here we might expect the teacher to protest that the *Ātman,* free of ignorance would not superimpose anything on *Ātman,* but instead the teacher evades the metaphysical issue, and makes a soteriological point instead. He says, "If you know that the false superimposition is the seed of calamity, then do not make it!"

It appears as though Śaṅkara is more interested in the question of liberating this bodily existence than in metaphysical consistency and completeness. This, of course, is in keeping with his emphasis on revelation *(śruti)* as the ultimate source of truth and on *parisaṁkhyāna* meditation as the final means of release from the accumulated *karmas.*[22] Reason serves a useful role in understanding and interpreting experience and revelation, but it is not their final arbiter.

Notes and References

1. *Upadeśasāhasrī,* I. 13.3. As translated by Sengaku Mayeda in *A Thousand Teachings: The Upadeśasāhasrī of Śaṅkara,* Tokyo: Tokyo University Press, 1979, p. 132.
2. *Ibid.,* I. 12.16, p. 130.
3. *Ibid.,* II. 2. 50, p. 235.
4. Padmanabh S. Jaini, in "Karma and the Problem of Rebirth in Jainism", pp. 217-38, in O'Flaherty, ed., *Karma and Rebirth in Classical Indian Traditions,* p. 210.
5. *Brahamasūtra bhāṣya,* I.i.6: *Jīvo hi nāma śarīrādhyakṣaḥ prāṇānām dhārayita.*
6. *Upadeśasāhasrī* II. 1.12,13, p. 215.
7. *Ibid.,* II. 1.18.
8. *Ibid.*
9. *Ibid.,* II. 1.19.
10. *Ibid.,* II. 1. 20, pp. 216-217.
11. *Ibid.,* II.1.21, p. 217.
12. *Ibid.,* II. 1.23.
13. See Sengaku Mayeda, *A Thousand Teaching: The Upadeśasāhasrī of Saṅkara,* pp. 28ff.
14. *Upadeśasāhasrī* I.15.10.
15. See *Brahamasūtra bhāṣya* II. 4.12.

16. *Ibid.*, II.1.19, p. 216.
17. Sengaku Mayeda, *A Thousand Teaching: The Upadeśasāhasrī of Saṅkara,* 82: If *avidyā* is mutual imposition of *Ātman* and *non-ātman,* neither can be said to exist, for as the pupil points out in *Upadeśasāhasrī* II. 2.55, what is superimposed on another does not exist in the other. Mutual superimposition is nihilism.
18. See *Yoga Sūtra,* II.3.
19. See Sengaku Mayeda, *A Thousand Teaching: The Upadeśasāhasrī of Saṅkara,* 78.
20. *Upadeśasāhasrī,* I, 16,37.
21. *Brahamasūtra bhāṣya,* IV, 1,3.
22. *Upadeśasāhasrī,* II.

2

The Spirituality of Līlā

K.R. Sundararajan

I plan to explore here the Vaiṣṇava doctrine of play (*līlā*) and hope to explicate what could be described as the spirituality of play. The term "spirituality" is rather ambiguous, used in a variety of ways especially in the context of Christianity. Therefore, there is a need to give a working definition of spirituality before engaging in the task of exploring the spirituality of *līlā*. Here the term is used in a general way on the lines indicated by Dr. Ewert Cousins, who, introducing a series of volumes on *The World Spirituality*, writes:

> The series focuses on that inner dimension of the person called by certain traditions "the spirit". The spiritual core is the deepest center of the person. It is here that the person is open to transcendent dimension; it is here that the person experiences the ultimate reality.

Thus, the topic of the spirituality of *līlā* would require a careful exposition as to how the notion of divine play enables one to gain access to transcendence. Towards the end of the paper, I hope to compare the spirituality of *līlā* with the spirituality of *māyā* as elaborated in the Advaita tradition, since both of them define a certain attitude towards the world, and through which one could gain access to the experience of *Brahman*. While for a non-dualist, the access to the transcendent dimension is gained through the realization of the ultimate illusoriness of the world of plurality and multiplicity, *(māyā),* for a Vaiṣṇava, the access to the transcendence is made possible by the realization that the world is created out of divine playfulness and for the divine sport, (*līlā*). I hope to show through my analysis of *līlā*, that the attitude towards the world becomes more positive when looked at from this perspective, than from the perspective of Advaita which looks at the world as ultimately illusory *(māyā)* or even from the perspective of selfless action (*niṣkāma karma*) of the *Bhagavad Gītā.*

Līlā in the Vaiṣṇava Tradition

The concept of *līlā* has a central place in the Vaiṣṇava tradition. It provides an explanation as to the way God creates, and thus a proper perspective to understand the world and also the purpose of human life. I would like to hold that the very purpose of human life, from as Vaiṣṇava perspective, is "regain" a *līlā* perspective of the world, a vision which was lost under the conditions of *saṁsāra.* I would draw my resources for the exposition of the concept of *līlā* mainly from the writings of Rāmānuja, the chief exponent of Viśiṣṭādvaita Vedānta.

In order to understand the concept of *līlā* properly, it may be useful to situate it first in the context of Viśiṣṭādvaita notion of three eternal principles (*tattvas*), God (*Brahman/Viṣṇu*), individual self (*ātman*) and matter (*prakṛti*) in a relationship which Rāmānuja states a "Qualified Oneness" with Brahman as the Supreme Principle upon which *ātman* and *prakṛti* are *totally dependent.* The individual self and matter exist for the sake of Brahman, outside which they do not have independent, substantial existence. Rāmānuja calls the relationship of these three principles as body-soul (*śarīra-śarīri*), body constituted of *ātman* and *prakṛti*, and the soul (*śarīri*) by Brahman. In the above situation it is clear that the body (*śarīra*) cannot function without the sustaining power of the soul (*śarīri*) which is the Supreme Self. Brahman is described as the supporter of the individual self, and it is in this role that the Vaiṣṇava tradition comes with the notion of the inner presence of the divine (*antaryāmi*) which I shall elaborate later. Brahman is the ground of all existence since God is both the efficient as well as the material cause (*upādāna kāraṇa*), like a spider and its web, or clay and clay pots. Whereas the dependent relationship of the individual Self (*ātman*) to the Supreme Self (*Brahman/ Viṣṇu*) is expressed in terms of devotion *(bhakti)*, the dependent relationship of matter (*prakṛti)* to the Supreme is expressed in terms of *līlā* or play.

Līlā, understood as divine sport, explains the process of creation, its origin, maintenance and destruction. Here Rāmānuja's dedicatory verses to Viṣṇu in the very beginning of *Śrī Bhāṣya*, Rāmānuja's commentary on Bādarāyaṇa's *Vedānta Sūtra,* is worth noticing.

> May my understanding attain the nature of devotion to the Supreme, the abode of Śrī [Laksmī], the Brahman who is luminously revealed in the crown of scripture [the *Upaniṣads*], whose sport [*līlā*] consists in such acts as origination, maintenance and destruction of the worlds, who has dedicated Himself entirely [*eka-dikṣā*] in protecting and saving [*rakṣā*] hosts of various kinds of creatures who bow before Him.[1]

Līlā in the context of creation underlines divine freedom and spontaneity in the act of creation. The nature of God is such that He is not compelled to create, but creation issues forth spontaneously. This freedom and spontaneity on the part of the Supreme is highlighted by Rāmānuja in his description of Brahman as one who is free from all imperfections and defiling qualities, whose actions are not regulated by the law of karma as in the case of human beings.

> The motive which prompts Brahman—all whose wishes are fulfilled and who is perfect in himself—to the creation of world

comprising of all kinds: sentient and non-sentient beings dependent on his volition, is nothing else but sport, play. We see in ordinary life how some great king, ruling this earth with its seven *dvīpas*, and possessing perfect strength, valour and so on, has a game at balls, or the like, from no other motive than to amuse himself; hence there is objection to the view that sport only is the motive prompting Brahman to creation, sustentation and destruction of this world which is easily fashioned by his mere will.[2]

Being a sportive action, creation is therefore not purposive, and it could be stated appropriately as "purposeless purpose". According to S.R. Bhatt:

Thus the world is *līlā*, a purposeless purpose, which implies disinterestedness, joyousness, free will and super abundance of energy on the part of Brahman, and it must be distinguished from conscious volitional effort. The creation follows the mere will, or free choice, of Brahman. It is to preserve the supreme perfection of Brahman that the Sūtrakāra has given *līlā* as the motive for creation.[3]

Rāmānuja is anxious to maintain the theme of "purposeless creation" in order to avoid charges that Brahman is partial, "in so far as the world contains beings of high, middle and low station gods, men, animals and immovable beings...". Rāmānuja maintains that though the act of creation itself was without hierarchy, due to the association with karma the created world has become hierarchical in the above fashion. This association with karma is the result of human choice and not a design in creation itself. Rāmānuja writes:

The heart of the whole *śāstra* is this: The individual selves are essentially of the nature of pure knowledge, devoid of restriction and limitation. They get covered by nescience in the shape of karma. The consequence is that the scope and breadth of their knowledge is curtailed in accordance with their karma.... The first truth to be taught by the *śāstra* is that the individual selves are not intrinsically divided into several kinds like gods, men, etc., and they are fundamentally alike and are equal in having knowledge as their essential nature.[4]

Śruti and *Smṛti* alike declare that the connexion of the individual souls with bodies of different kinds—divine, human, animal, and so on—depends on the karman of those souls... what causes the difference in nature and status between gods, men, and so on, is the power of the former deeds of the souls about to enter into a new creation....[5]

Playful creation is in fact an invitation to the *jīva* to participate in the delight of the *līlā* world. Such a delight is experienced when the *jīva* undertakes a life dedicated to the service of the Lord. Hence the concept of *kaiṅkarya*. service to the Lord, assumes a central place in the post-Rāmānuja Srī Vaiṣṇavism of southern India. *Kaiṅkarya* becomes the proper way to respond to God and also to participate actively in the *līlā* world. Service to the Lord is the eternal birthright of the *jīva* according to Vedānta Deśika, a post-Rāmānuja Vaiṣṇava theologian.

The *Jīva* is thus entitled, by his essential nature, to the service of his Master as his birth right....But sunk in the sleep of beginningless Māyā, he has fallen into wilderness of matter (*prakṛti*), has had repeated births in quick succession, has lost the primary aim of existence, has found no comfort or consolation, has lost the splendour of his real nature....[6]

Now the world which has been created out of the sportive action of God, has become an ever binding *saṁsāric* world for those who did not participate in the *līlā* world. Each one of us have created our own worlds thus becoming responsible to them directly and in that very process we have been caught in the cycle of karma. It is the freedom exercised by the *jīva* to move away from the "original purpose" of participation in the creative play of God, that has added a new dimension to creation. Now the creation instead of being "purposeless" has become "purposive". To the karmic world, God is not playful, but God is "gracious", "a merciful protector" entrusted with the task of "saving" those trapped in *saṁsāra.* God now comes to possess the following auspicious qualities: *kāruṇya* (compassion), *sauśilya* (gracious condescension), *vātsalya* (forgiving and protecting love), and *audarya*, (generosity). By these auspicious qualities, God takes the role of a moral governor maintaining the natural and social order, and also providing opportunities for the *jīvas* to gain freedom from the entanglement of *saṁsāra.*

It should be noted that from a strict Vaiṣṇava theological point of view, even for the act of drifting away from joyful participation in the *līlā* world, the *jīva* requires "assent" from God's side. The relationship of total dependency on God, though is forgotten by the *jīva* in the *saṁsāric* state, still holds as a matter of fact. In the Vaiṣṇava tradition, free will and free choice, which perhaps determines the extent of one's individuality, are those granted by God and actively supported by God, for without God's support the *jīva* cannot be engaged in any action whatsoever. It is in this context that the manifestation of God in every *jīva* as its inner presence, *antaryāmi.* becomes important. It is this inner presence of God that enables one to engage in action. It is indeed the power source without which no action would be possible for the individual. Therefore, it may be true to say that,

> It is by the will of the Supreme Person that an individual soul is either in the state of bondage or release. He hides the true essentially blessed nature of the soul who has committed sins in his beginningless chain of *karman*— It is He, who as the inner soul, brings about even the spiritual relationship (by means of which an individual soul can attain release). Thus B (Brahman) is not only the object to be attained by worship, but is also the means of performing worship itself.
>
> But this immanence of B. in the souls is not to be construed as to leave no room for freedom of action on their part. The souls resting in B. and furnished by it with bodies and sense-organs as well as with powers to use them, apply themselves of their

own accord and in accordance with their own wishes, to works either good or evil. No action is indeed possible without the assent (*anumati*) of the Inner Soul; but in all actions there is the volitional effort (*prayatana*) made by the individual soul; and the Supreme Soul, by giving assent to it, carries out the action.[7]

It is the same *antaryāmi* presence that permits us to create our karmic world, that is also willing to save us from the same karmic world, once we decide to abandon it and surrender ourselves at the feet of God. In the Vaiṣṇava tradition, both *bhakti* and *prapatti* express a state of abandonment of the karmic world. It is through devotion (*bhakti*) and self-surrender (*prapatti*) that one recaptures the consciousness of one's total dependency on God thus becoming God's willing instrument to participate joyfully in the *līlā* world. Though in Rāmānuja's theology there is no concept of *jīvanmukta,* I believe that if we work out the implications of the *lila* theory on the above lines, we could speak meaningfully of a person, who is "freed", but still active in the world, whose actions are not any more "binding". Here bondage or freedom is not based on whether we accept the worthiness of the world or its unworthiness but on the attitude with which we engage ourselves in "worldly actions". If we are engaged in action in the spirit of joyful participation in a world created out of divine play, our actions are free and not binding. Being engaged in actions with notions of "mine" "yours" and "ours", we continue to extend our life in bondage.

In terms of the worldview that emerges in the context of the *līlā*, it may be necessary to see its implications for "purposeless creation" as well as for "purposeful creation" where the world has changed from a *līlā* world into a karmic world. For Vaiṣṇavism, in the purposeful world the upholding of dharma as defining one's code of moral behaviour, is important. It is only by following the principles of dharma one could maintain some quality of life in this karmic world. The *Bhagavad Gītā* is a standing testimony to the affirmation that our dharma, whatever it be, is fulfilled. However, *līlā*, as purposeless creation, may encourage one to transcend the dharmic order, as the dharmic order has only a provisional meaning and significance. But the metaphor of play suggests that we should continue to play and not abandon the play itself. This means that we should continue to fulfil our assigned role, but without any personal attachment. The spirit of *līlā,* is shown in our *attitude* towards the external world. Instead of looking at it from a karmic perspective, we see it now from the angle of *divine sport*. Therefore, the one who has achieved a "sportive vision" captures divine spontaneity and joy and participates in the created world in the same spirit. He/she is not opposed to dharma but is free from karmic consequence of his/her actions. Commenting on a verse from the *Gītā* where Kṛṣṇa suggests renunciation of all dharma in an act of total surrender to God (*Gītā* xviii.66), Rāmānuja is cautious to suggest renunciation of the fruits of dharmic actions, instead of renunciation of dharma itself.

Renouncing all *dharmas*... consist of... complete renunciation of the sense of agency, possessiveness in works, fruits and such other things, in the manner taught: (having done so) continuously think of Me as the agent, the object of worship, the goal of attainment and the means.[8]

Commenting on Ramanuja's interpretation of the above verse S.S. Raghavachar writes:

The renunciation enjoined is not giving up the practice of Dharma but the spiritual dissociation from the three-fold egoism; of sense of authorship of the deeds, the attachment to deeds as one's own and of hankering after the fruits for oneself.[9]

On this interpretation the renunciation of Dharma does not mean giving up everything. It just signifies that the aspirant is fully convinced of the impossibility of realizing the ideal of liberation through Dharma....The impossibility is realized owing to the aspirants' lack of requisite knowledge, incapacity for fruitful practice, impatience to await full maturation of Bhakti and the non-fulfillment of other accessory conditions laid down in the *Śāstras.* When the seeker is fully and firmly established in this extremity of hopelessness the pathway of *Prapatti* is enjoined. He has to surrender himself to God wholly and place the burden of effectuating salvation in the hands of God entirely.[10]

Concluding Remarks

While the *līlā* attitude towards involvement in the world shares in common with the *Gītā* notion of selfless action (*niṣkāma karma*), the spirit of renunciation of the fruits of action, instead of action itself, by stressing on the theme of playful creation, the former encourages more an attitude of joyous and positive involvement with the world in contrast to the latter. Again unlike the *jīvanmukta* in the Advaita tradition, a Vaiṣṇava who has succeeded in gaining the *līlā* perspective of the world could interact with the world in the spirit of joy. The attitude of the *jīvanmukta* is generally of one who is *in the world* but not *of the world.* The *jīvanmukta* realizes the oneness of the self (*Ātman-Brahman*) and having realized this refuses to have a positive and appreciative relationship with the *māyā* world. Saṅkara describes the life of a *jīvanmukta* in his commentary on the *Vedānta Sūtra* thus:

> Quietly devoted to his duty, let the wise man pass through life unknown; let him step on the earth as if he were blind, unconscious, dead.[11]

The Vaiṣṇava theology of *līlā* provides a more adequate basis for joyful participation in the world than the theological framework of Advaita, which has been characterized by a quest for the underlying substratum rather than appreciation of its manifestations. However, it should be noted that modern Hindu thinkers such as Swami Vivekananda and S. Radhakrishnan, affirming the relevance of Advaita to the modern world, see the role of a *jīvanmukta* differently, more positively. Commenting on the same passage of Śaṅkara cited above, S. Radhakrishnan describes the life of a *jīvanmukta* as a "life in the spirit full of meekness and peace, holiness and joy, and not sinking into the state of contemplative inertia. For Swami Vivekananda, it is the experience of non-duality that "provided the motive power behind his activities of service...".

Having perceived his own identity with the Absolute, he had that same knowledge with respect to others: thus, seeing God in man, he worshipped God in man. The perception also formed the basis for his preaching activities later on. As he then declared: "I am bringing Vedānta from the forest place to the market place...".[12]

Notes and References

1. *Śrī Bhāṣya.* 1.1.1, *Thibaut Vedānta Sūtra* with Rāmānuja's Commentary, reprint, Delhi: Motilal Banarsidass, 1977, p. 2.
2. *Śrī Bhasya.* II.I.33, *Thibaut,* p. 477.
3. S.R. Bhatt, *Studies in Rāmānuja Vedānta*, New Delhi: Heritage Publishers, 1975, p. 99.
4. *Vedārtha-saṅgraha of Śrī Rāmānujācārya,* S.S. Raghavachar, trans., 1978, Mysore: Sri Ramakrishna Ashrama, pp. 79-80.
5. *Śrī Bhāṣya.* II.I.33, *Thibaut,* p. 477.
6. *Vedānta Desika, Śrīmad Rahasyatrayasāra,* trans. M.R. Rajagopala Ayyangar, Kumbakonam, 1956, p. 13.
7. V.A. Suktankar, "Teachings of Vedānta According to Rāmānuja", *Vienna Oriental Journal,* Vol. XXII-3, 1909, p. 302.
8. *Gītābhāṣya of Rāmānuja,* trans. M.R. Sampatkumaran, Bombay: Ananthacharya Indological Research Institute, 1985, pp. 474-475.

9. S.S. Raghavachar, *Śrī Rāmānuja on the Gītā,* Second Print, Mangalore: Sri Ramakrishna Ashrama, 1979, pp. 206-207.
10. *Ibid.,* p. 209.
11. III.IV.50, See Radhakrishnan, *Brahma Sūtra: The Philosophy of Spiritual Life,* New York: Greenwood Press, 1968.
12. Claude A. Stark, *God of All Sri Ramakrishna's Approach to Religious Plurality,* Cape Cod: Claude Stark, Inc., 1974, p. 129.

3

Early Mīmāṃsā on Language

John Brockington

As a scholar who is primarily a linguist, I approach with some diffidence the task of contributing to this volume honouring such a noted philosopher as Prof. G.C. Nayak, welcome as it is to honour him in this way at the invitation of our mutual friend, Prof. Bijayananda Kar.

This essay presents some thoughts on the Mīmāṃsā system on meaning and language and the term 'essay' is used deliberately to indicate both its discursive character and the fact that it does not incorporate any primary research. It was tempting in fact to entitle this piece 'Mīmāṃsā and meaning' or even 'Śabara on *śabda'* as a way of indicating by the play on words its relative slightness.[1] However, although it concentrates on Jaimini and Śabara, there are occasional remarks on later figures.

While Jaimini has quite rightly defined the subject matter of the Mīmāṃsā as *dharma* in the opening words of his *Mīmāṃsāsūtra (athāto dharmajijñāsā,* MS 1.1.1) and *dharma* itself as complete obedience to the Vedic commands *(codanālakṣaṇo artho dharmaḥ,* MS 1.1.2), the system is also with good reason known as the *vākyaśāstra,* 'the science of sentences', since it was within this *darśana* that detailed study of sentences and elaborate canons of interpretation were first developed, though more by Śabara and his successors than by Jaimini, in whose *Mīmāṃsāsūtra* only the first *adhyāya* explores such issues. These views on the nature of language are of continuing interest, forming a significant contribution to the study of language (which otherwise became the exclusive preserve of the grammatical schools) and attesting a firm belief in the power of language in shaping reality (though in a very different fashion from Bhartṛhari's *Śabdabrahman).* Let us not forget either that the Mīmāṃsā view of language has been influential elsewhere. Śaṅkara, for example, rejects the concept of *sphoṭa* in favour of the Mīmāṃsā view that *varṇas* constitute a word, quoting from Upavarṣa in this connection (*Brahmasūtrabhāṣya* 1.3.28), and also upholds the Mīmāṃsā view of the eternality and authorlessness of the Veda. Indeed, Parpola has suggested that the Pūrva and Uttara Mīmāṃsās were effectively one system at least until the time of Śabara.[2]

Jaimini's main thesis is that *dharma* can only be known from the Vedic injunction *(codanā)* and so the sacrifice is to be performed because it is enjoined in the Veda through language, which is from the beginning part of experience and inherently related to purpose, *artha.* Therefore, in order to establish the infallibility of the Vedic injunctions, the Mīmāṃsā system seeks to prove that words, their meanings, and the relationship of word and meaning are all eternal, while the meaning of the sentence is derived solely from the component words. Sentences which may appear to be incoherent are to be treated in context: all Vedic sentences have to be taken as related to, and collectively bearing on, some action which is enjoined to be done. In the process Mīmāṃsā also distinguishes two methods of interpretation of words, by etymology and by actual usage, affirming that the latter is always to be preferred. Above all, however, Mīmāṃsā is concerned with distinguishing the commands from the explanations, for the rules are intrinsically valid but the auxiliary material does not affect the command and must not be construed as the reason for the act.

The basic standpoint of Mīmāṃsā, then, is that the

Veda, being eternal and uncreated, possesses absolute authority (further developed in Kumārila's emphasis of the theory of *svataḥprāmāṇya)* and that the Vedic commands *(vidhi)* constitute man's entire duty *(dharma),* and its method of exegesis is designed to demonstrate the consistency and non-ambiguity of the Vedic revelation. The textual material is arranged in such a way that conflicts and ambiguities can always be eliminated: an *arthavāda* cannot contradict a *vidhi,* and the testimony of *śruti* is by definition stronger than that of *smṛti.* In this way it deduces logical principles for the consistent application of the apparently unsystematic Vedic texts.[3] Although certain sentences in the Veda appear incoherent or meaningless, this is not really so; it is incorrect to take any Vedic utterance out of context and treat it in isolation. For the Mīmāṃsā, in fact, Brāhmaṇa is that part of *śruti* which lays down direct ritual action: it is everything which is not *mantra* or *arthavāda (śeṣe brāhmaṇaśabdaḥ,* MS 2.1.33). The Brāhmaṇa part of *śruti* is always and unconditionally valid in itself, since it contains the commands (cf. Śabara's comment *vidhilakṣaṇa* on this *sūtra).* Accordingly, as Kumārila subsequently points out, frequent imperative endings are found in Brāhmaṇa material and consequently many commands, while non-imperative endings are rare (*TV* 2.417.9).

The Mīmāṃsā system thus began not as a school leading to *mokṣa* (as the other orthodox *darśanas* claim to be) but as a direct successor to the ritual *sūtra* literature, whose aim was to ensure the correct interpretation of the Vedas. Accordingly, it systematises the interpretation of Vedic sentences and evolves canons of interpretation, formulating general rules of a meta-linguistic nature. Such meta-rules, often called *nyāya,* are further used and developed in *dharmaśāstra;* the term *nyāya* was later commonly used to denote logic and the system of logic. While the Mīmāṃsā is indeed based on the ritual *sūtra* tradition (and was willing to borrow ideas from individual Vedic schools), it is nonetheless important to realize that it took a broader view of the sacrificial ritual than those belonging to particular Vedic schools. It does, though, follow through the Brāhmaṇa position on the centrality of action, at least in Jaimini's work (where the affirmation of the Brāhmaṇa path of action may perhaps be seen as an implicit response to criticisms from early Buddhism as much as from the *Upaniṣadic* thinkers), although the introduction of *apūrva* as something transcendent in Śabara, who reads it into MS 2.1.1-5, may be the beginning of a shift of attitudes.

Since the Veda is the sole source of authority, the authority of *smṛti* is derived from it on the assumption that there is a corresponding Vedic text to back up the assertion of a *smṛti* text or it was once, for the Mīmāṃsā, with the realism that it often shows, accepts the possibility that Vedic texts may have been lost: the theory of the lost or scattered Veda. If all *smṛti* injunctions are based on Vedic commands, then those *smṛtis* for which we cannot find a Vedic basis in the extant Veda must be based on texts that are either lost or unavailable, as Kumārila acknowledges when, in his comments on MS 1.3.1, he advances the theory of the scattered Veda, according to which it is difficult to know all the Vedic texts because the Vedic *śākhās* within which they are preserved are scattered around India.

The Mīmāṃsā is thus not a theology either, in the sense that it attempts to justify belief in a deity or deities, any more than it is a philosophy on the model of other *darśanas,* but rather its apologetic function relates a textual corpus which is presented ontologically as existing eternally. Nor does it attempt to claim any kind of Vedic status for itself, despite its close links with the Veda, and Śabara and his successors do not try to derive their teachings on epistemology or on the philosophy of language from the Veda. But, although the Mīmāṃsā is often represented as being simply a school of Vedic exegesis (and the remarks made above may seem to reinforce such a view), this underrates its philosophical implications, which are clearly visible in both Jaimini and Śabara, long before the arrival of its two overt philosophers, Kumārila and Prabhākara. These arise, in fact, from one of its central beliefs and arguments, that of *apauruṣeyatva,* which is much more than, indeed is not really in any significant sense concerned with, the claim that there is no name of any historical person found in the Veda (cf. the elaborate arguments at *Śabarabhāṣya* 1.1.27-31, concluding *paraṃ tu śrutisāmānyamātram iti).* For Śabara a *codanā* is valid because it cannot be falsified and so *śabda* makes itself known in all its purity as the supreme *pramāṇa;* he emphasizes that there is no human interference with a Vedic statement and *śabda* is the only *pramāṇa* (cf. *ŚBh.* 1.1.1), 'because of the impersonality of the relationship between word and meaning' *(apaurṣeyatvāt saṃbandhasya siddham iti,* 1.1.5).

The authorlessness of the Veda means that its meaning must be sought within itself and does not depend in any way on external factors – essentially it is the view that the unity of the Vedic language is found in the injunctive force that underlies all Vedic utterance. It is this that prompts Jaimini's view of a sentence as a self-sufficient unit directed to a single purpose (e.g. MS 2.1.46) and his assertion that praise, *stuti,* should be understood as auxiliary to injunctive sentences, *vidhi (*MS 1.2.7-18). This view of the Vedic language as injunctive was extended to include the principle that its meaning does not differ from that of ordinary language, since otherwise religious commands would be incomprehensible and so useless *(*MS 1.3.30 and Śabara's commentary). Hence Jaimini's assertion that the relationship between a word and its meaning or denotation is innate, *autpattika (autpattikas* *tu śabdasyārthena saṃbandhah,* MS 1.1.5), and specific (cf. *nityas tu syāt* at MS *1.1.18,* where *nitya* has rather its original meaning of 'proper, specific' than its more usual sense 'eternal', cf. also Śabara's gloss on 1.1.5: *autpattika iti nityaṃ brūmaḥ).*

Śabda is consequently the chief *pramāṇa* for the Mīmāṃsa system, since it is the sole means for knowing injunctions and prohibitions (*dharma).* In order to establish the inerrancy and utter reliability of the Vedic command, the Mīmāṃsā seeks to prove that words, their denotations and the relationship between word and denotation are all eternal, that the meaning of the sentence is understood by understanding the meanings of the component words and the sentence has no meaning by itself. Sentences which may appear to be incoherent are to be treated in context. All Vedic sentences have to be taken as related to, and collectively bearing on, some action which is enjoined to be done. The word, its meaning or denotation, and the relationship between them are all considered to be inborn, eternal and therefore not subject to creation by anyone. When words come from human sources, there are many reasons why the validity or truth of the words may well be doubtful (the reliability of the speaker, his source of information, and so on). But if a word does not come from a human source, it is not open to such defects and there can be no doubt about its impersonal truth. So the Veda is held to be impersonal, eternal and infallible concerning everything beyond the reach of the senses.

Since the Mīmāṃsā system was committed, by its view of the authority of the Veda, to the doctrine that *śabda* ('sound', perhaps better 'word') is unproduced and hence eternal, Śabara develops an effective answer to the problems of its particular, localised realization — how, for example, can the word be eternally unchanging when it is not always present in one's consciousness, and when it requires human effort for its production? Śabara borrows both from the theories of the grammarians and from the Vaiśeṣika theory of sound, responding to such criticisms by saying that what is brought about by human effort is only the making present of the pre-existent word. He declares that during speech, breath mounts from the abdomen, strikes the speech organs, and is modified by their opening and shutting *(saṃskṛta).* The air thus modified is called sound *(dhvani* or *nāda)* and moves from the speaker's mouth through the surrounding air until it reaches the ear of the hearer. It is not itself heard but affects the ear and enables it temporarily to perceive the eternal word *(śabda)* which otherwise it would not be able to hear; when it is no longer heard, this is not because the word, has vanished, only the perception of it. The same partless *(niravayava) śabda* is manifested in spite of any variation in volume, which characterizes only the *nāda;* the phonetic structure of the word is nonetheless explicitly recognized *(ŚBh.* 1.1.5) and serves to distinguish the proper form *(sādhuśabda),* which alone is beginningless, from any corruptions *(apabhraṃsa,* 1.3.26). This theory had the great advantage of allowing the origin and propagation of sound *(dhvani, nāda)* in air and not in ether (as the Vaiśeṣika system propounded, hence also Śabara's emphasis on the *aikarūpya* and the *niravayava* nature of *śabda* at 1.1.13-17 in implicit rejection of the Vaiśeṣika standpoint), thus explaining a number of problems such as the attenuation of sound by intervening barriers or simply by distance. Thus, despite its obvious cumbersomeness, the theory is not without its merits and indeed approaches a distinction between the semantic and phonetic aspects of language.

Śabara offers five proofs for the eternality of *śabda.* The most important is that *śabda* cannot perish since its purpose is to reveal, not so much itself, as its meaning; the implication is that continuity is necessary for meaning to be grasped. His second argument is that when the word 'cow' is uttered, the *ākṛti* (species, genus, perhaps more generally typical form) cow is denoted and, since there is an innate relationship between word and *ākṛti, śabda* like *ākṛti* must be eternal. From the fact that normally we speak about a word being repeated so many times rather than so many words being uttered, this recognition of it as the same word demonstrates its eternality. Whereas objects, such as mountains, whose production no one has witnessed, are known to consist of perishable materials and so to be perishable themselves, 'in the case of *śabda* we do not observe any such cause, at the disintegration of which *śabda* would also perish'. Śabara's final 'proof' is a citation of the scriptural phrase *vācā virūpantyayā* as implying the eternality of *śabda.*

Kumārila and the Bhāṭṭa school, unlike Prabhākara, do not restrict *śabdapramāṇa* to Vedic commands but divide it into the two classes of *pauruṣeya* and *apauruṣeya.* Under *pauruṣeya* are included all words uttered by trustworthy people (basically the Nyāya view) and under *apauruṣeya* come the words of the Veda; both are valid. The reason given for this view is that the only ground for the invalidity of a word lies in its emanating from an unreliable source, and this is no more the case with the words of trustworthy people than with the words of the Veda. The reason why Śabara defined *śabda* in terms of *śāstra* is, according to Kumārila, not that he confined valid verbal cognition to scripture alone but that it is this alone which is relevant to the subject studied, *dharma,* since this is known from the Vedic injunctions *(codanā).* The ideal sentence is still for Kumārila a command and he investigates it in detail. At its heart he finds an efficient force, called *bhāvanā,* which is responsible for the connection, co-ordination and mutual qualification of the word-meanings. The sentence-meaning is thus shown to arise from the word-meanings but at the same time it is proved that it cannot be reduced to the sum of the word-meanings because of this *bhāvanā.*

In relation to the sentence, the Mīmāṃsā was indeed the first to put forward the three factors of *ākāṅkṣā* (expectancy), *yogyatā* (consistency) and *samnidhi* (contiguity) among the word meanings in a sentence as the basis for the unity of the sentence; it also stressed the importance of *tātparya* or the general context. Jaimini himself lays out the principles for determining the proper division of sentences at *Mīmāṃsāsūtra* 2.1.46-49: firstly the principle of syntactic connection (if there is *ākāṅkṣā* between certain words so that after some are spoken more are still awaited in order to complete the sense, then they all belong to the same sentence - *arthaikatvād ekaṃ vākyaṃ sākāṅkṣam ced vibhāge syāt,* 46), secondly the principle of syntactic split (if the groups of words can be understood separately, they should be taken as separate sentences -*sameṣu vākyabhedaḥ syāt,* 47) and thirdly the principle of elliptical extension (where a statement seems incomplete, the words needed to complete it should be supplied from a parallel complete context, provided nothing else intervenes - *anuṣaṅgo vākyasamāptiḥ sarveṣu tulyayogitvāt,* 48).

Jaimini also asserts emphatically that the sense conveyed by the words of the Vedas is not in any way different from that found when they are used in everyday speech (MS 1.3.30): this is shown by the fact that the texts lay down injunctions about the performance of certain acts and, if these are to be obeyed, they must first be understood and so must be couched in language that is intelligible to all; Śabara's commentary on this *sūtra* states simply that there is no difference between words in the Veda and in ordinary life, since we do not notice any difference, while the opening sentences of his commentary affirm that the words of the *sūtras* are to be understood in the same senses as in ordinary speech. This fits well with Mīmāṃsā efforts to establish how *śabda* escapes the limitations of the other *pramāṇas,* such as perception, in terms of the fallibility of the individual. It enabled the Mīmāṃsā to assert the superiority of *śruti* over all other *pramāṇas* (thus neatly reversing the Nyāya listing which had placed *śabda* last).

On the issue of the relationship of word and meaning, the Mīmāṃsā view is that *śabda* is *pratyāyaka* and *artha* is *pratyāyya* and so the *paratyāyapratyāyyabhāva* should exist between them. But in that case we would expect a word to convey its meaning even on its first hearing. However, our experience is that a word heard for the first time is not *pratyāyaka.* Already the *vṛttikāra* counters the argument that this refutes the assumed relationship by affirming that we do not say that the eye is not the seer because it cannot see where there is no light, which is its *sahakāri kāraṇa,* and in the same way repeated hearing is the *sahakāri kāraṇa* for *śabda.* According to the Mīmāṃsā, the primary meaning of a word is the universal *(ākṛti)* which is the quality common to all the particular instances of a class. Both Jaimini and Śabara use the term *ākṛti* to refer to the universal, the typical form, while later Kumārila declares explicitly that the term is used in the sense of *jāti* or universal *(jātim evākṛtiṃ prāhur vyaktir ākriyate yayā, Ślokavārttika,* '*Ākṛti,* 3-4).

More importantly still Mīmāṃsā distinguishes two methods of interpretation of words—*yoga,* the meaning based on analysis and etymological derivation, and *rūḍhi,* the meaning established by convention—and lays down the firm principle that *rudhi* is stronger than *yoga.* In other words, we must define the meaning of a word as used in actual texts or speech and, if possible, must interpret the word always in that way, without regard to its derivation (real or apparent), since this involves the minimum intervention of reasoning: the presumption is that words mean the same in the Veda as in ordinary speech. This well-known principle, termed the *rathakāranyāya* from its stock example, is a prime example of the Mīmāṃsā realism; after all, etymologically the term *rathakāra* simply means a maker of chariots and could theoretically be used of any individual, and it is only by usage that it denotes a member of a particular low caste, thus rendering problematic the Vedic injunction that 'a *rathakāra* shall lay the sacred fires in the rainy season'. Nevertheless, Jaimini does accept that sometimes context dictates that a word should be understood in a secondary sense and lists six types *(tatsiddhi, jāti, sārūpya, praśaṃsā, bhūma* and *liṅgasamavāya,* MS 1.4.23), for which Śabara then provides examples. Similarly, in deciding between two different interpretations of a Vedic statement, Śabara regularly prefers the 'nearest meaning' *(saṃnikṛṣṭa artha)* to the 'more remote meaning' *(viprakṛṣṭa artha)* and has an extended discussion of such factors in his commentary on MS 3.3.14, taking a common-sense position on what is the most direct meaning.

However, this attitude goes much further still. In their commentary on MS 1.3.10, both Śabara and Kumārila include an important discussion on the interpretation of foreign loanwords in Vedic lexts, in which they come close to subverting the standard Mīmāṃsā arguments for the eternality of the Veda at the same time as they display a keener awareness of linguistic problems than they are usually credited with. The point at issue is whether certain words in the Veda that are not in use among the people of 'Āryāvartta should be given the meanings attested among *mlecchas.*[4] The *pūrvapakṣa* presented is that, since orthodox Vedic brāhmans even halt their recitation of the Veda on seeing a *mleccha,* how can *mleccha* usage possibly be accepted as authoritative in explanation of a Sanskrit word? The *siddhānta* is that, if a Vedic word is no longer used in the language of Āryāvartta but precisely the same term is used by *mlecchas,* the sense given by them must be accepted and Śabara even counters the argument that *mlecchas* are not authoritative and elite by declaring that they are authoritative and learned in their own particular ways and must be accepted as being so. The linguistic realism shown here is quite remarkable.

In conclusion, let me bring together some of the points made. It is important to remember about the Mīmāṃsā views of language that, starting from a body of Vedic *mantras* and Brāhmaṇa passages connected with them, they evolved a much more general theory of sentence interpretation, and that they adopted certain views mainly because they dealt not with a total grammar but with specific sentence types, for, while the Pāṇinian grammarians were concerned with the totality of the language (though concentrating on morphology), the Mīmāṃsā system was concerned only with *śruti*. This explains, for example, why in his treatment of the verb Śabara ignores the past tenses and why the law of contradiction is discarded, since use of the negative particle with the imperative or the optative does not function in the same exclusive fashion as with the indicative. Overall, the Mīmāṃsā system is concerned to adopt positions which demand the minimum intervention of fallible human understanding, since the purity of the Veda is threatened by mental activity, whether in its composition or in its interpretation. To this end it is prepared to assert the absolute primacy of *śabda*. The eternality and authorlessness of the Veda are the buttresses to its absolute validity *(svataḥprāmāṇya)* and lend authority to its commands. Ultimately, all that the Mīmāṃsā has to say on language, on words and their meanings, on semantics and phonetics is subordinate to *dharma*, as Jaimini asserts in his opening *sūtra*.

Notes and References

1. Accordingly, I shall not overburden it with an extensive array of footnotes but I must here acknowledge my indebtedness to much earlier research on Mīmāṃsā, from Ganganath Jha's *Pūrva-Mīmāṃsā in its sources* first published in 1942 to more recent studies such as the fine collection of papers in *Studies in Mīmāṃsā: Dr. Mandan Mishra Felicitation Volume,* ed. R.C. Dwivedi (Delhi, 1994), and also Francis X. Clooney, *Thinking Ritually: Rediscovering the Pūrva Mīmāṃsā of Jaimini* (Vienna, 1990), Othmar Gächter, *Hermeneuties and Language in Pūrva Mīmāṃsā: A Study in Śābara Bhāṣya* (Delhi, 1983) and Lars Göhler, *Wort und Text bei Kumārila Bhaṭṭa* (Frankfurt am Main, 1995).
2. Asko Parpola, 'On the formation of the Mīmāṃsā and the problems concerning Jaimini', *Wiener Zeitschrift für die Kunde Südasiens* 25, 1981, pp. 145-77 and 38, 1994, pp. 293-308.
3. Although the Mīmāṃsā sought for complete consistency, it accepted that when injunctions contradict each other there is an option, *vikalpa,* to follow one or the other. The regular example of a *vikalpa* concerns the kinds of grain used in a ritual; some texts enjoin rice and others barley (cf. Śabara on MS = Mīmāṃsā sūtra (already made clear by the writer [vide p. 23]) 12.3.15) and so Mīmāṃsā allowed the use of either rice or barley. However, it developed the theory of the eight faults of an option and avoided option whenever possible.
4. There is an interesting discussion of this by Madhav Deshpande in his *Sociolinguistic Attitudes in India: An Historical Reconstruction* (Karoma Publishers, Ann Arbor, 1979), on which my comments are based.

4

Plotinus and the Contemplative Life

Rabindra Raj Singh

Porphyry's account informs us that Plotinus' thought showed itself in his way of life. It was a life devoted to the contemplation of the Real, the One, *to agathon,* the Father of all Being. Porphyry was a witness to the realizations of this thinker, for whom philosophy was neither a study of abstractions, nor a building of systems. "To this godlike man who often raised himself in thought, according to the ways Plato teaches in the *Banquet,* to the first and transcendent god that god appeared who has neither shape nor intelligible form",[1] Porphyry paints the picture of a man who lived his philosophy. According to him Plotinus "never relaxed his self-turned attention except in sleep; even sleep he reduced by taking very little food. . .and by his continuous turning in contemplation to his *nous*".[2]

Plotinus' philosophy is aptly considered as a pioneering work of neo-platonism, for he clearly builds upon the foundations laid by Plato's metaphysics. The notions of the Good (*to agathon*), *nous* and soul are all exposed systematically at first in Plato's writings. However, Plotinus shows remarkable originality in his orderly description of reality based on the intertwining roles of these three hypostases. But perhaps, such sparks of originality are spontaneous rather than deliberately pursued for as Pierre Hadot remarks, among the writers of late antiquity, not originality but fidelity to a tradition was considered the foremost duty.[3] In its aim to construct an outline of Plotinus' thought on the theme of contemplative life, this paper will attempt to illustrate Plotinus' fidelity to Plato's thought with respect to the all-important human activity called contemplation. I will particularly explore how exactly Plotinus exposes and supplements the insight contained in Plato's *Phaedo* concerning the connection between death and contemplation. For the practice of death has been called the essence of contemplative life in the *Phaedo*.

Contemplation is viewed as a turning away from the "matters bodily" or thoughtless and excessive worldliness by Plato, who is second to none in his downgrading of the visible and the mundane for the sake of a vision of the real and the ideal. In keeping this ideal of contemplation alive in his life and works, Plotinus too shows a longing for the absolute based upon a "turning away" from excessive worldliness. The Platonic themes of man's bond with the absolute, the pursuit of death-contemplation on the part of the philosopher and contemplative and virtuous living, receive Plotinus' creative attention in the *Enneads*.

Heidegger in his essay "Plato's Doctrine of Truth"[4] attempts to correct to overly ethical interpretation of *to agathon* implicit in its usual translation as "the Good". According to him, *to agathon* is Plato's concept of Being and must be treated as an ontological notion. It is remarkable that Plotinus understands the One as not only beyond any ethical characterization and beyond the intelligible realm of *nous* but also beyond Being. He calls it "not Being but the generator of Being".[5] He conceives man's bond with this attributeless ultimate as the most vital and most fulfilling of all relations and involvements.

To know the One does not mean being able to describe it. But it is more like thought's constant quest to appropriate something real but elusive. Plotinus remarks in the fifth *Ennead* that "we ought not to apply any terms to It; but we should so to speak run round and outside of it trying to interpret our own feelings about it, sometimes drawing near and sometimes falling away in our perplexities about It".[6] This seems to be an accurate description of the contemplative attitude in which the object of one's meditation is elusive, yet the onward swell of one's devotion brings one to the brink of an experience of a momentary but momentous union only to lapse into an inevitable but renewed return to the familiar mundaneness. According to Plotinus, man has an instinctual bond with the absolute, but remains for the most part forgetful of it. "Men have forgotten that which from the beginning, now still, they want and long for. For everything reaches out to that and longs for It by necessity of nature, as if divining by instinct that it cannot exist without It".[7]

This contemplative realization has been recognized as the best attainment of human life by Plotinus. Human being is hardly human without this experience. It is described as a challenge and a "contest" by Plotinus; a contest in the double sense. It is a contest as a striving for something most valuable as well as a hard won and rare communion between man's longing and divine grace: "Here the greatest, the ultimate contest is set before our souls; all our toil and trouble is for this, not to be left without a share in the best of visions. The man who attains this is blessed in seeing that blessed sight, and he who fails to attain it has failed utterly".[8] In outlining the conditions requisite for such a contemplative practice, Plotinus seems to rely upon the exposition of contemplation given in Plato's writings. A brief consideration of what Socrates is supposed to have said concerning the philosophical life on his death-day as reported in the *Phaedo* will prepare us for Plotinus' rejoinders to Plato's classical account of contemplation.

Plato's *Phaedo* is a pioneering work of the contemplative tradition of western philosophy. The connection between death, contemplation and contemplative living is elucidated in such an insightful and definitive way in this seminal text that generations of western thinkers will be inspired by it. The "idea of philosophy as a rehearsal of death" is the central message of *Phaedo's* dramatic account of Socrates' death day. Among the thinkers who do subscribe to the Platonic contemplative tradition, the following convictions concerning the nature and task of philosophy are quite visible: (a) philosophy is a contemplative activity, (b) death-contemplation is the soul of all contemplation, that is, death-contemplation is "the" task of philosophy not just one of its possibilities, (c) contemplation must lead to a contemplative living. Among this class of contemplative thinkers we may include Plotinus, St. Augustine, Schopenhauer, Kierkegaard and Heidegger. All these philosophers adopt and build upon the insight contained in the *Phaedo* that reflecting on death is a pre-requisite to genuine philosophizing as well as an authentic philosophical life.

It is easy, however, for an innocent reader of the *Phaedo* to be bogged down by the various reported arguments of Socrates concerning the immortality of the soul and miss what the drama indicates on the whole concerning the connection between death and contemplation. Most analytical interpretations of the dialogue continue to be literal applications which sidetrack the issue of death and philosophy. Many comparative studies of Plotinus and Plato, and several translators' notes tracing the roots of Plotinus' allusions to Plato's dialogues also concentrate, especially in case of the *Phaedo* on the various proofs of the soul's immortality or refer to those parts where mythological accounts are given of the soul's destiny after death and its journey towards

Hades. The chief insight of the dialogue concerning the reason why death-contemplation must be cultivated by a genuine philosopher is only mentioned in passing by such analytical readers of the dialogue. Thus, Socrates' influence on Plotinus is not to be traced merely in Plotinus' literal references to Plato in the *Enneads* but also in his general attitude towards contemplation as such and in what Porphyry tells us about Plotinus' philosophical life and solitary death.

The dialogue in the *Phaedo* shows us that a clear choice was made by Socrates to remain engaged in philosophizing with his friends in his very last hours. Socrates is reported to have said that his readiness and willingness to die was not anything strange, given his life as a philosopher. "The true votary of philosophy is...of his own accord...always engaged in the pursuit of dying and death".[9] This "dying and death" is not meant as an actual rejection of the corporeal body but an ongoing attempt to secure freedom from an indulgent service of the body that is, a freedom from the vulgar and thoughtless materialistic pursuits. What is crucial for the realization of a higher contemplative life, is a continuing attempt to free one's soul from "matters bodily" and making it ready for pure thought:

> Thought is best when the soul is gathered into itself...when it takes leave of the body, and has as little as possible to do with it, when it has no bodily sense or desire, but is aspiring after true Being.[10]

It is described in the *Phaedo* that true Being can only be intuited by the soul's dwelling in thought, "dwelling in its own place alone, as in another life, so also in this, as far as it can".[11] According to Socrates, as the philosopher's life becomes a continual rehearsal of such a death, i.e. death of the subservience to the body, the soul experiences the here and the hereafter in this very life. The dwelling in the "other life" is particularly useful for the philosopher for it enables him or her to acquire a critical distance from things he or she is supposed to philosophize about. Thus death-contemplation is bound to deliver, not only a holistic and existential perspective but also the capacity for a detached outlook. The contemplative life also enables one to be free of the fear of actual death, as Socrates demonstrated, for such a philosopher has already realized that not-being (for the sake of the world) is no evil, but contemplation is human life's highest and most blissful potential.

Plotinus seems to have imbibed this contemplative culture very well in his own life and seems to have taught by example to his disciples, according to Porphyry's reports. To the Socratean call to the true philosopher to dwell, "as far as possible" away from the body, "as if in another life", Plotinus adds: "shut your eyes and change to and wake another way of seeing, which everyone has but few use".[12] If we take the *Enneads* literally, Plotinus has a lot to say about the desirability and rewards of contemplation and about the necessity to downplay the matters bodily. At the same time, when we take into account his life and work on the whole, he appears to be an excellent practitioner and expositor of the kind of death-contemplation outlined by Socrates.

Plotinus' treatise that is believed to be his last, happens to be a meditation on death and in the Socratean fashion or in the Phaedoian fashion, offers a summary of its author's entire philosophy. This is why Porphyry placed it in the first ennead. St. Ambrose translates and quotes it in his sermon *De bono mortis*:[13]

> If life and the soul exist after death, then death is good, all the more so in that the soul is better able to carry out her proper activities without the body.... In general... there is no evil for the soul who has maintained her purity; and if she has not maintained it then it is not death that is an evil for her but rather life. It could perhaps be said that, in and of itself, life within

the body is an evil but that thanks to virtue, the soul can come to be within the Good, not by living the life of the composite (of soul and the body) but by separating herself from it already in this life.[14]

That the contemplative life is neither to be a ruthless suppression of the body, nor an embracing of pre-mature death is obviously maintained in Plotinus' standpoint. The above mentioned statement seems to endorse what Socrates is reported to have said to his friends just before his death. The death that the contemplative life undergoes is a death of excessive bodily involvements, a practice of virtue whereby the soul attempts to achieve a separation, as far as possible from the body in this very life. Plotinus seems to allude to the Socratean notion of the desirability of a rehearsal for death in the fourth treatise of the ennead I:

> The common life of body and soul cannot possibly be the life of well being. Plato was right in maintaining that the man who intends to be wise and happy...must look to that Good and be made like it and live by it....
>
> He must give to this bodily life as much as it needs and he can, but he is himself other than it and free to abandon it, and he will abandon it in nature's good time, and always plans for it with independent authority.[15]

According to Plotinus the world of sense itself is not to be disparaged or dismissed. It mirrors the absolute and represents its mystery:

> Will anyone be so sluggish in mind and so immovable that when he sees all the beauties of the world of sense all its proportion and mighty excellence of its order, and its splendour of form which the stars for all their remoteness make manifest, he will not be seized with reverence and think "what wonders and from what a source?" If he does not, he neither understands the world of sense nor sees that higher world.[16]

The world of sense and the higher world are not mutually exclusive and the outright dismissal of the visible reality is not desired. Plotinus' thought is imbued with love and blissful enjoyment of all that is in Being. At the same time, he seems to understand the reasons for Plato's body-soul dualism. Plotinus is fascinated by the Platonic dismissal of the body but realizes that the body stands not for the human physique as such but for "matters bodily" or human being's thoughtless and matter-of-course involvements in mundane projects. The rewards of contemplation do not end with the ending of the meditative moment of union with the One but the contemplator returns to the worldly life with a new resoluteness and renewed inclination towards the contemplative life:

> When a man falls from the vision, he wakes again the virtue in himself in all his order and beauty, and is lightened and rises through virtue to *nous* and through wisdom to the divine. This is the life of gods and divine and blessed men, deliverance from the things of this world, a life which takes no delight in the things of this world, escapes in solitude to the solitary.[17]

The contemplative life is based on a "turning away" from the things of this world or the common worldly concerns which flood the mind and impede its progress through wisdom to the divine. Such a turning away in thought is not an outright dismissal or denial of the visible world but a life of beauty, virtue and moderation. It is an invitation to death to abide in the midst of and alongside life. In outlining his concept of contemplation, Plotinus certainly responds to the insight concerning the practice of death spelled out in the *Phaedo*. He seems to demonstrate and supplement the Platonic notion of death-contemplation in an original way in his life and work.

Notes and References

1. Porphyry's "Life of Plotinus" in A.H. Armstrong, ed. and trans., *Plotinus,* New York: Collier Books, 1962, p. 48. [Subsequently abbreviated as *Plotinus*].
2. *Ibid.,* p. 46.
3. Pierre Hadot, *Plotinus or the Simplicity of Vision,* trans. Michael Chase, Chicago: University of Chicago Press, 1993, p. 17.
4. Martin Heidegger, "Plato's Doctrine of Truth", trans. John Barlow in W. Barrett and H.D. Aiken, ed., *Philosophy in the Twentieth Century,* New York: Random House, 1962, Vol. III, pp. 251-270.
5. *Plotinus,* V. 2. 1, p. 51.
6. *Ibid.,* VI. 9. 3, p. 55.
7. *Ibid.,* V. 5. 12, p. 62.
8. *Ibid.,* I. 6. 7, p. 126.
9. Plato, *Phaedo.* trans. Benjamin Jowett in *The Dialogues of Plato* (Chicago, Encylopaedia Britannica, 1952, 64 a.
10. *Phaedo.* 65c.
11. *Ibid.,* 67c.
12. *Plotinus.* I. 6. 7-8, p. 127.
13. Hadot, *Plotinus or the Simplicity of Vision,* p. 107.
14. *Ibid.,* I. 7. 3, p. 108; quoted by Hadot.
15. *Plotinus.* I. 4. 16, pp. 132-133.
16. *Ibid.,* II. 9. 16, p. 134.
17. *Ibid.,* VI. 9. 11, p. 148.

5

Humanism in Swami Vivekananda's Philosophy : Some Critical Observations

S.B.P. Sinha

I propose to study here the humanistic elements in Swami Vivekananda's thought. Before coming to this point, it would be desirable to observe that in India philosophy is vitally connected with life. So, here one may be regarded as a philosopher even if one is not technically trained in the discipline of philosophy. In fact, philosophy in India is not confined to intellectualism and logicism. Here, philosophy is regarded not only as the foundation of all knowledge (*Sarva-vidyā-pratiṣthā*) but it is also considered to be highest purpose or goal of human life as Max Müller visualizes it. So naturally, of late, I have been trying to study some such non-technical philosophers in my various essays. It has been seen that such non-technical philosophers like Ramakrishna Paramhansa, Swami Vivekananda, Maharsi Ramana, Mahatma Gandhi and others have made important contributions in contemporary Indian thought. It would not be fair to denigrate their importance simply because they are not trained in analytical and formal methods of philosophy. I have tried to show the limitations of linguistic and formalistic trends of recent philosophy which has really divorced philosophy from life. This may be regarded as one of the causes of the present human predicament concerning crisis of values and other maladies rampant at the global level. Therefore, it is quite justifiable to study Swami Vivekananda's humanistic approach in this brief essay.

Before coming to his humanism, it would be proper to point out here some important elements of humanism. Here, we may quote William Benton:

> Humanism, an attitude of mind attaching prime importance to man and human values, is regarded as the central theme of Renaissance civilization. Renaissance humanist is traceable to the 14th century Italian humanist Patriarch.... Philosophically humanism made man the measure of all things.[1]

Again, Dr. S. Radhakrishnan makes more or less similar observations thus, "Humanism is a protest against naturalism on the one hand, and religion on the other. The soul of man is not a thing of nature, nor is it a child of God".[2]

Instead of referring to others views, it may be observed here that humanism is the doctrine which attaches pivotal position to man. Naturally, we find that the history of humanism can be traced back to quite ancient period and continues up to the present era. It would not be out of place to mention name of Protagoras whose famous maxim 'Man is the measure of all things' is well known. Then instead of making detailed historical study, we may just refer to names of Comte, Schiller and Sartre who also championed the cause of humanism in their respective writings.

Now, so far as humanism in Indian philosophy is concerned, here it really stands on somewhat different footing. Protagoras' approach smacks of scepticism and solipsism, likewise we find predominance of positivistic elements in Comte and existentialism paves the way for humanism in Sartre. But our Indian thinkers, barring some materialists, both in ancient and contemporary period are more and less inclined towards spiritualism in their humanistic approach. This is quite natural because our thinkers were more interested in self-observation, *Ātmānam Viddhi* 'know thyself' has been the keynote of their philosophical method. This introspective attitude has been conducive to the growth of idealistic philosophy. But this does not mean that the story of Indian philosophy is the story of idealism alone. As a matter of fact, Indian philosophy is characterized by its multisided trends. So there are various types of philosophies here, e.g. materialism, realism, dualism. Even trends of analysis also find place here. But it cannot be denied that idealism finds its pivotal place. Here humanism goes beyond materialism, naturalism, positivism and existentialism. It is not expected to deal with all such thinkers, that is why, we shall try to study briefly and critically Swami Vivekananda's approach only. In fact, he was a great intellectual and spiritual giant which India has produced. His eastern and western disciples have rightly realized the difficulty in assessing him.

> It is impossible to give an adequate picture of his sublime character, so potent, so complex, so all comprehending, with infinite facets, each facet representing a variation of the light within. His was a harmonious development of all sides of nature, intellectual, emotional and spiritual, to perfection which is seldom found in man, and which drew men to his feet in love and adoration.[3]

He is really the dynamic counterpart of the one of the greatest persons of the present time, namely, Ramakrishna Paramhansa who started his career as an extraordinary devotee of the Divine Mother and is said to have vision of the Mother. It is further seen that he experimented with different religious sects and demonstrated their essential identity. He is also known for his synthetic approach to Vedānta and held that formless Brahman and Divine Mother (*Kāli*) are one and the same. Swami Vivekananda was attached to him and naturally became devoted to him. Subsequently, he really presented master's ideas and ideals clearly and systematically before the world as Plato did for Socrates.

Swami Vivekananda also developed the philosophy of practical Vedānta so far as ontological constructions are concerned and propagated the ideals of synthetic and universalistic approach in the domain of religion also. It is interesting to see that he added practical dimension to the philosophy of non-dualistic Vedānta. Of course, we may not agree fully with following observations of Brodov who tries to see Swami Vivekananda from his materialistic standpoint, "Vivekanada was an adherent of the objective idealist Vedānta Philosophy, but he also raised Vedantism to a new and higher level, making some concessions to materialism".[4]

Here, Brodov does not fully realize the fact that Vivekananda essentially championed the cause of non-dualistic Vedānta where the sole reality of Brahman alone is emphasized. So, the question of accepting or rejecting materialism does not arise. From that point of view, matter is also Brahman in this scheme of things. So the question of its independent status does not arise. But at the same time it would be interesting to note that Vivekananda does not dismiss the reality of this World as phantasmagoric production of nescience. In fact, he sees Brahman or God everywhere. He holds:

> From the highest to the lowest and most wicked man, in the greatest of human beings and the lowest and most wicked man in the greatest of human beings and the lowest of crawling worms under our feet, is the soul, pure and perfect, infinite and ever blessed. In the worm that soul is manifesting only an infinitesimal part of its power and burette and in the greatest man it is manifesting most of it the difference consists in the degree of manifestation, but not in the essence. Through all beings exist the same pure and perfect soul.[5]

So it is obvious that Swami Vivekananda saw Brahman or God in every being. In fact, one can easily see his humanistic approach in above lines as well because he really identifies "*Jīva*" with "*Śiva*". To make this point more clear, we may quote following observations of J.C. Banerjee.

> The humanism of Swami Vivekananda is this focal vision of the transcendence as immanental. God as man and not God in man, *Jīva* as Shiva. It is from this view point of realization that service to humanity is a service of God. God, self, Brahman (Absolute) are names of the same being. On this concept of identity of God and self one can claim to understand the synthesis of *Jñāna* and Karma, the reality of man and the appearance of man. This is the keynote of Vivekananda's humanism, a synthesis of the transcendent and the immanent.[6]

Here, one can further observe that the famous poet of Bengal, Chandidas also advocated humanistic ideals in his own way and this tradition is said to have been further propagated by Shahajiā cult of Bengal. This cult stands for common sense realistic approach to view, where the superior reality of man is affirmed.

Now instead of further dwelling on this aspect, it would be befitting to mention here that Swami Vivekananda, though does not allow any concession to materialism, has definitely obliterated the distinction between self and non-self or between man and God. In fact, as indicated earlier, man is divine being essentially. There is the hidden and innate divinity in him. So, naturally according to him religion is realizing this innate divinity through different yogas namely *Jñāna Yoga*, *Karma Yoga*, *Bhakti Yoga* and *Rāja Yoga*.

Instead of discussing the yogas in details, it would suffice to point out that Swami Vivekananda takes religion in more realistic, rationalistic and universalistic sense So, for him ritualism and such other practices do not form part of the real religion. One has to simply realize one's true nature, i.e. divinity in him or in her through yogas. One is free to choose the particular yoga according to one's temperament and capacity.

It would be further interesting to see in this context that here one can easily come across his humanistic approach, so far *Karma Yoga* is concerned. We may quote R.K. Dutta Gupta's following lines,

"Seekest thou God?" says Sri Ramakrishna," then seek him in man. Divinity is more manifest in man that in other objects"..... The many sided works of service rendered by the Ramakrishna Mission in India and abroad according to local needs derive their inspiration from this aphoristic saying of Sri Ramakrishna:"*Jīva* is *Shiva*".[7]

Here it may be observed that he sometimes clearly holds that religious and spiritual practices cannot be expected from persons who are ill-fed. In other words, he preferred serving the suffering human beings in comparison to religious ritualism etc. His concern for poor and suffering countrymen shows his patriotism as well as his sublime humanistic philosophy. His humanism transcends the ideal of personal salvation. Like Buddha, he postpones his personal salvation for the cause of suffering humanity. Swami Ranganathananda also says,

Vivekananda's lectures from Colombo in Srilanka in the far south to Almora in the Himalayas in the far north, created a great national awakening. For, his main theme was the awakening of the Indian humanity and strengthening it to meet the modern challenges and utilise the vast opportunities of the modern age to evolve a truly humanist social order....[8]

Here, one should not try to see parochial and nationalistic approach in this great humanist. He means the entire human race. This is also confirmed by his various writings and addresses including the historical address at Parliament of Religion at Chicago. By way of further clarification, we may again quote Swami

Ranganathananda who has categorically remarked:

> The humanism expounded by Vivekananda is intensely human and universal.... A humanism that is strengthened and sustained by the ignition of the divine spark in man is far different from the current humanism of the west, including its scientific humanism.[9]

Swami Vivekananda stands for superior or divine type of humanism. As such, it must be differentiated from positivistic, pragmatic and existentialistic humanism. It may be relevantly remarked here that these humanistic philosophers have not taken into account, all the dimensions of man whereas one can clearly see that Swami Vivekananda's treatment of man does not touch only periphery. To make this point more clear, it may be observed here that Swami Vivekananda also takes into account the spiritual and divine dimensions of man. For him, man is not only psycho-physical being but essentially spiritual and divine. Swami Rangnathananda has rightly appreciated this point:

> It was this philosophy of man in depth, adhyātma-vidyā as Vedānta calls it, this science of human possibilities to use a fine phrase that biologist and humanist, the late Sir Julian Huxley coined to express what he wanted modern western physical science to develop into, that Vivekananda made the core of his humanism. It is a science of man that India investigated and developed over three thousand years ago in her immortal literature, the Upanishads.[10]

Perhaps this type of approach cannot be found either in Comte or in Schiller or in Sartre or even in M.N. Roy. Perhaps it is difficult to find such a humanistic approach where the dignity of man has been so much exalted. So, it would not be unjustified to name it as 'super humanism'. In fact, this approach has got not only its theoretical importance, but it is of far reaching practical implications. This is because at present we are subject to consumeristic culture and have meagre regards for our fellow beings. We have become self-centred and more concerned with our own interests. It may be noted, not unfairly, that various discoveries and inventions of science have made us more self-seekers in the sense of our cravings for various luxuries. Of course, science has provided modern men with tremendous amenities of life but it has also generated grisly greed for various luxuries. That may not be very bad, but to be less concerned for our fellow beings is certainly unfortunate. Here this sublime humanism of Swami Vivekananda comes to our rescue. We can be enlightened and inspired by his gospel of service and sacrifice for our fellow beings, for everything and being of this globe. This will inspire us to serve the suffering man and as well as everything and being of the universe. Various social, political, ecological and other imbalances and problems can be remedied to a great extent if we try to acquaint ourselves with his ideas and ideals of humanism. Then, we can develop a sense of respect and love for our fellow beings, and, for entire universe. Then problems of violence not only to man or to nation but also to nature can be solved at least to some extent. Swami Vivekananda's gospel of humanism which is the practical counterpart of his philosophy of practical Vedānta needs to be studied and practised more zealously and ardently for saving the modern man from various maladies. It is really the need of the hour to pay heed to this clarion call Swami Vivekananda:

> Arise, awake, and stop not till the goal is reached.... Teach yourselves, teach every one his real nature.... Power will come, glory will come, goodness will come, purity will come and everything that is excellent will come, when this sleeping soul is roused to self-conscious activity.[11]

So, we, the "children of immorality" have to arise and awake and realize our real nature. This would inspire us to tread on the path of Dharma which would lead us to both *Nihshreyasa* and *Abhudaya*. Indeed, his humanism is thus needed both for worldly and spiritual welfare. So. its importance and relevance at present can be hardly overemphasized.

Notes and References

1. William Benton, *The New Encyclopedia Britannica*, inc. Vol. V, London: Helen Hemingway Benton, Publishers, 1973-74, p. 199.
2. Dr. S. Radhakrishnan, *An Idealist View of Life*, London: George Alien & Unwin Ltd., 1967, p. 48.
3. *Vivekananda: The Man and His Message* by his eastern and western disciples, Advaita Ashrama (Publication Department), 5 Dehi Entally Road, Calcutta-700014, p. 175.
4. V. Brodov, *Indian Philosophy in Modern Times*, Moscow: Progressive Publishers, p. 290.
5. *The Complete Works of Swami Vivekananda*, Mayavati Memorial Edition, Volume VI, Advaita Ashrama, 5 Dehi Entally Road, Calcutta-700014, pp. 24-25.
6. J.C. Banerjee, *Humanism of Swami Vivekananda, Parliament of Religions*, Swami Vivekananda Centenary, 163, Acharya Jagadish Bose Road, Calcutta-700014, p. 104.
7. R.K. Datta Gupta, *Swami Vivekananda's Gospel of Divine Humanism: Parliament of Religions*, Swami Vivekananda Centenary, 163, Acharya Jagadish Bose Road, Calcutta-700014, pp. 210-2.
8. Swami Ranganathananda, *Swami Vivekananda: His Humanism*, Moscow University Lecture, Advaita Ashrama (Publication Department) 5 Dehi Entally Road Calcutta-700014, p. 41.
9. *Ibid.*, pp. 46-47.
10. *Ibid.*
11. *Op. cit., Complete Works*, Vol. III, 1960 edition, pp. 192-93.

6

The Buddhist Theory of Two-Faceted Knowledge

S.R. Bhatt

Knowing something virtually implies knowing that one knows. In every case of knowing besides an awareness of an object, there is also an implicit awareness with regard to that awareness. Implicit in this meta-awareness there is an awareness of the truth of that awareness. Thus in every knowledge there is not only cognitivity-claim but also a truth-claim. So to say that 'this is a pen' necessarily involves (a) an awareness of the presence of a pen but it also involves (b) an awareness of that awareness together with (c) an awareness of the truth of that awareness. In other words, my knowledge that 'this is a pen' necessarily implies (a) "I know that I know that : this is a pen" and (b) "I know that my knowledge that 'this is a pen' is *true*".

Now the question is, how are we aware of (a) and (b)? Dignāga, advocating the theory of self-intimating and self-evidencing character of knowledge, insists that every knowledge cognizes itself and also evidences itself for its truth. To substantiate this view he puts forth the theory of two-faceted knowledge (*dvairūpya jñāna*).[1] According to him every knowledge is produced with a two-fold form, viz., that of itself as a subject (*svākāra= svābhāsa*) and that of the object (*viṣayākāra= viṣayābhāsa= arthākāra= arthābhāsa*).[2] In other words, every knowledge has an epistemic form and an ontic form. Rejecting the succession-model of the Nyāya system, according to which we first have (a) as, proto-reflection (*vyavasāya*) and (b) and (c) as post-reflections (*anuvyavasāya*), Dignāga puts forth a simultaneity-model, according to which all the three occur together under the same set of conditions.

II

In its epistemic form (*svābhāsa*) a knowledge cognizes itself and also distinguishes itself from other knowledge This is the doctrine of self-intimating character of knowledge known as *svayamvedyatā* or *svaprakāśatā*.[3] This doctrine has been a fundamental tenet of Dignāga's epistemology put forth in the background of the theory of momentariness. If a knowledge is just a momentary psychic state ceasing to exist the next moment then either we have a cognition of that knowledge in the very moment of its origin or we shall have to deny the very possibility of the cognition of that knowledge, because the next moment that knowledge will no longer be there to be cognized by the subsequent cognition. (Without accepting momentariness also this doctrine can be upheld as is done by Prabhākara in the Pūrva Mīmāṃsā system). Since the cognition of a knowledge is a fact given in experience, it can only be understood in the context of the doctrine of self-intimating character of knowledge which means that at the very moment of cognizing an object it also cognizes itself.

III

The ontic form of knowledge (*viṣayābhāsa*) establishes the truth of knowledge because of its being determined by the object. The object is the very ground upon which a knowledge is based. In fact, the object not only serves to give rise to knowledge but it also differentiates it from other cognitions. This determination of cognition by the object is metaphorically called the cognition having the form of the object. When a cognition possesses the form of the object it is a sufficient condition for its being true. Thus Dignāga writes, "The evidence for the truth of a cognition is simply its having the form of the object".[4]

A true cognition cognizes an object but the question is, does it cognize any object whatsoever or a particular object because of the cognition of which alone it becomes true. Dignāga contends that since a true cognition is due to a particular object, only it has to be in the form of that object. In other words, there is a specific object corresponding to every cognition and it is that object which determines the content of the cognition and this determination alone is the evidence for the truth of that cognition. Thus when we have a distinct cognition of something blue, this cognition is recognized as being determined by the cognition of something blue and not something yellow and this determination is made by the appearance (*ābhāsa=akāra*) of something blue in the cognition itself.[5] Then only the cognition can be said to be a true presentation of the object. If the cognition is at variance with the object (*visamvāda*) it will not then be determined by the object and this will amount to its falsity. In order that a cognition should be true it has to represent its object in its proper form. This is possible only when the cognition is arising in the form of the object. The truth of a cognition therefore consists in this sameness of form with the object, Dignāga illustrates this by saying, "Whatever form of the thing appears in the cognition as, e.g., something white or non-white, it is an object in that form which is cognised".[6] When Dignāga talks of similarity of form it should not be taken literally because the cognition can never be similar to the object.[7] Cognition and object belong to two different categories.[8] One is epistemic whereas the other is ontic. Therefore it will be meaningless to talk of their similarity. All that it means is that every cognition necessarily refers to an object and every true cognition has to refer to its object as it is. To refer to the object as it is has been figuratively expressed as the cognition having the form of the object. This point is made clear by Prajñākara[9] with the example of a new-born child, who showing similarity to his father, is said to have taken the form of his father, although in fact he has no such function as taking his father's form. It is just a metaphorical way of saying things.

The theory of two-faceted knowledge is based on a more basic theory of *Sākārajñāna* according to which knowledge is never devoid of a form of its own. This is opposed to the Nyāya view that knowledge simply represents the form of the object but does not itself possess any form.[10] However it must be made clear that the advocacy of two facets of knowledge in no way implies that these are two different epistemic entities. These two are to be distinguished only for the sake of conceptual analysis.

Dignāga has mainly been adherent of the *yogācāra* school and there is sufficient theoretical basis for the theory of two-faceted knowledge in that view. According to the *Yogācāra* school consciousness itself appears as subject and object.[11] In reality there is neither subject nor object. These are thought-constructions (*parikalpita* or *utprekṣita)*. By attaining detachment from the subject-object dualism (*pariniṣpanna daśā* or *grāhaka-grāhya rahita daśā*) a man comes to realize the state of pure consciousness (*vijñaptimātratā*).

Notes and References

1. *Dvairūpya sādhanenāpi prāyaḥ siddham svavedanam. Pramāṇa Vārtika II. 425.*
2. (i) The word 'cognition' is used in this paper as a generic term. The word 'knowledge' stands for true cognition.

(ii) The present paper aims at presenting the theory of two-faceted knowledge on the basis of which Dignāga and his followers constructed a very interesting system of epistemology. It is attempted here to present this theory in as clear form as possible keeping off from the two below given different interpretations of it from the Sautrāntika and the Yogācāra points of view, both of which Dignāga himself has referred to in the *Pramāṇa Samuccaya* and its *Vṛtti*. In writing this paper I am greatly benefitted by M. Hattori's 'Dignāga on perception'.

(a) *Sautrāntika Interpretation*:

Yadātu bāhyevārthaḥ prameyaḥ tadā 'viṣayākarataivāsya pramāṇam'. Tadā hi jñānāni svasamvedyāmapi svarūpamanape-kṣyārthābhāsataivāsya pramāṇam. P.S.V.I.g. Cf Sautrāntika pramāṇam sārūpyam bāhyórthaḥ prameyo' dhigatiḥ phalam vyavasthāpyādhunā vijñaptau pramāṇaphala vyavasthām nirdidikṣuḥ. Pramāṇavārtika vṛtti of Vibhūticandra, p. 215 (R. Sankrtyayana edition) also, *ye'pi Sautrāntika pakṣam evam vyācakṣate - bāhyo'rthaḥ prameyam vijñānasya viṣayākāratā pramāṇam svasamvitti phalamiti. Ślokavārtika Vyākhyā* of *Bhaṭṭa Umbeka*, p.139. (Madras University Sanskrit Series).

The Sautrāhtika position can be represented in the form of a diagram taking help of Nyāya phraseology also as follows:

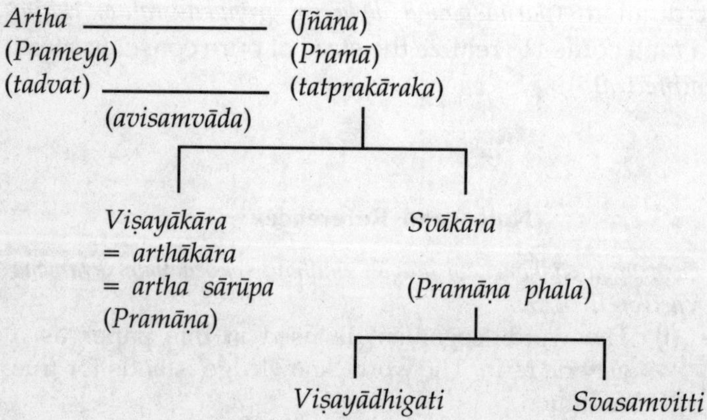

Here *artha* is *tadvat* and *jñāna* is *tatprakāraka* and therefore there is *avisamvādakatva* or *sārūpya* which is a *pramāṇa*. In other words, in every knowledge the epistemic content must have an ontic correlate supplied by the object. Thus knowledge has an ontic form and an epistemic form, the latter resulting from the former. The Sautrāntika admits the existence of an external object. Thus the similarity of form (*sārūpya*) represented in a cognition to that of the object is held to be the *pramāṇa* of the resulting *viṣayādhigati* and *svasamvitti*.

(b) *Yogācāra interpretation:*

(a) *Dvayābhāsam hi jñānamutpadyate svābhāsam viṣayābhāsam ca. Tasyobhayabhāsasya vijñānasya yatsvasamvedanam tatphalam. P.S.V.I.9.*

(b) *Tasmād dvirūpam astyekam yadevamanubhūyate. smaryate Cobhayasya samvedanam phalam. P.V.III. 337.*

The Yogācāra position can be represented in the form of a diagram as follows:

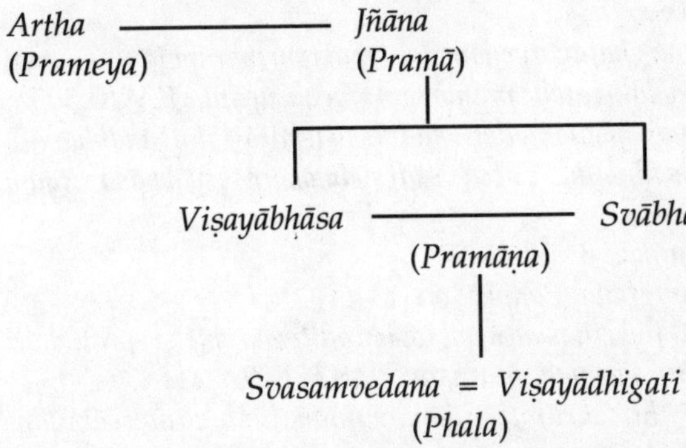

Every cognition is produced with a two-fold appearance, namely, that of itself and that of the object. Self-cognition is the result of these two appearances. This is the Yogācāra view that the cognition itself appears as subject and object. As Dignāga puts it,

Yadābhāsam prameyam tat pramāṇa phalate punaḥ grāhakākāra samvitti trayam nātaḥ pṛthak kṛtam. P.S.I. 10.

In the Slokavārtika Vyākhyā (p. 139) a slightly different account is available which is as below:
Yogācāra pakṣe' pi... bāhyo' arthonāsti, vijñānasya viṣayākāratā premeya, svākāratā pramāṇam. svasamvittiḥ phalamiti.

In a diagram form it can be put as follows:

Jñāna

Artha = *visayākāratā* (*prameya*)

Svākāratā (*pramāṇa*)

Svasamvittiḥ (*phala*)

3. *Svarūpa vedanayānyad vedakam na vyapekṣate. Na cāviditam astīdam ityartho' yam svasamvidaḥ. Tattva Samgraha 2012.*
4. (i) *Viṣayākārataivāsya pramāṇam. P.S.I. 9.*
   (ii) *Sārūpyamasya pramāṇam. Nyāya Bindu I.19.*
   (iii) *Tasmāt prameyadhigateḥ sādhanam meya rūpatā. P.V. III. 306.*
   (iv) *Arthena ghaṭayatyenam nahi muktvārtharūpatām, Tasmāt prameyādhigateḥ pramāṇam meyarūpatā. P.V.III.305.*
5. *Yasmādviṣayaj jñānamudeti tadviṣayasadṛs' am tadbhavati. Yathā nīla sadṛsam. Tacca sādṛsyamākāra ityābhāsa ityapi vyapadiśyate.*
   Nyayā Binduṭīkā, p. 18.
   Cf. Tattvasamgraha Panjikā on 1346.
6. *Yathā yathā hyarthasyākāraḥ śubhrāditvena jñāne pratibhāti tattatrūpaḥ sa viṣayaḥ pratīyate. P.S.V.I. 9.*
7. *Sarvātmanā hi sārūpye jñānamajñānatām vrajetsāmyam kenacidamśena sarvam syāt sarvavedakam. T.S. 1357.*
8. *Grāhyasādhāraṇākāram yasmājjātyantaratvatah, Rasa rūpādivaj-jñānam naiva cedupapadyate. T.S. 1355.*
9. *P.V.B.P. 344.*
10. *Ārthenaiva viśeṣo hi nirākāratayā dhīyam. Nyāyakusumāñjali, IV. 4.*
11. *P.S.I. 10.*

7

A Note on Contemporary Indian Philosophy

R.P. Srivastava

Let us first analyse what is meant by the expression 'Contemporary Indian Philosophy'. The word contemporary means[1] (i) happening, existing, living, or coming into being during the same period of time; (ii) simultaneous, (iii) marked by characteristics of present period: Modern. If we have a look at the various books bearing the title 'Contemporary Indian Philosophy', we find that generally post-Vedāntic philosophy of India is considered as Contemporary Indian Philosophy. These authors have not taken the term 'Contemporary' in its first sense because a period of over two hundred years cannot be contemporary for any individual. It is possible, then, that the word has been being used in its third sense, that is, in the sense of being a philosophy marked by the characteristics of the present period. But it will not be an easy task to identify the characteristics available commonly in the philosophy originating from the time of Raja Ram Mohun Roy towards the close of the 18th century up to the present age. If we take the word in its true connotation, we should use it now for post-independence period.

The word 'Indian' also deserves attention. The word means pertaining or belonging to India. It has a geographical connotation. An Indian tree means a tree of Indian origin, found within the geographical boundaries of India. Similarly Indian within the geographical boundaries of India. Similarly Indian Philosophy means a philosophy with an Indian origin. Classical systems of India are in this very sense Indian. Although thoughts and ideas are not bound by geographical limits and it is always possible to have same thoughts propagated by different thinkers on different soils, e.g. Spinoza and Vidyāpati, Kabir and Eckhart, etc., some systems of thought are unique to bear some particular heritage of a country. Classical systems of India are in this very sense truly Indian. But the question is, can we say this about our present day philosophizing also? I am afraid it will not be proper to call all philosophizing of our time Indian. It is Indian only in the sense that we are discussing it in India with Indians. Otherwise it is more proper to call it 'Contemporary Trends in Philosophy in India'.

Now coming down to contemporary trends, we find a vertical division among the persons claiming to be engaged in philosophizing. On the one side these are those who are engaged in philosophical pursuit in its academic sense and on the other side are those who claim to be practical philosophers and who have a band of followers engaged in some sort of socio-religious activities. Karl H. Potter[2] makes a division of Indian Philosophy into Progress Philosophy and Leap Philosophy. I am tempted to accept his division particularly in the context of contemporary philosophizing. The former group of philosophers may be treated as progress philosophers and the latter as leap philosophers. The leap philosophers of our time preach not only unconditional submission to God but they declare they are themselves God. So there is a difference between the leap philosopher like Ramakrishna Paramhansa and those of our time. While the former's preaching is Bhaktized Advaita[3] (to use Potter's term once again), the latter's is something like sermons on the Mount. I do not intend to examine it as I am inclined to take it as pseudo-philosophy.

I would like to quote here Nirad C. Choudhury who says, "the idea that the Hindus had great love and reverence for philosophy and respect for philosopher is a figment of the European mind. What we respect are the Sadhus, possessors of occult power not philosophers who professed to possess only knowledge and that is useless in our eyes".[4] This statement only confirms that there is a sharp division between pure philosophers and pseudo-philosophers and the common man is more enchanted towards the latter than towards the former.

Let us now consider the pure philosophical activities of our time. Discussions on this issue have been made exhaustively at many places. The general editor of the *Muirhead Library of Philosophy* says in the foreword of *Contemporary Indian Philosophy* that, "it was in the conviction that in present day philosophy there is more than a trade and that, owing partly to the inherent genius of the race, partly to the fructifying contact with western thought, the tree of knowledge has recently put forth fresh flower and fruit that the idea of publishing the book was mooted." There are people inside and outside the world of academics who believe that contemporary Indian philosophers have nothing of their own to add to the ancient Indian wisdom and their so-called philosophies "are either various interpretations of ancient Indian thought or intellectual positions relevant to local problems in Great Britain, France or America".[5] The editors of *Current Trends in Indian Philosophy* mention five main types of philosophical activities of our time. It includes exposition of classical Indian systems, comparison of Indian systems with western ones, looking for solutions of Indian problems in western ways, exposition of western thoughts and attempt of constructing a world-view incorporating and reconciling different philosophical positions. I do not think it necessary to go into the details of the merits and demerits of these different types of activities. However I do feel that those who are engaged in the work of exposition of ancient Indian texts or current western thoughts are doing it for acquainting our generation with those thoughts and this acquaintance may help in determining one's priority for a particular kind of philosophy for life. So even these expository works have their philosophical value.

The merit of any constructive philosophy is to be judged by its insight of perceiving the contemporary problems which a man is confronted with and its readiness to put forward possible ways out. There may be people who think that classical Indian systems are still relevant in modern context. For example, Karl H. Potter feels that domination of western thought over Indian mind today may prove "a real danger" and "the relevance of classical Indian thought to recurrent problem of philosophy may be lost sight of and the whole tradition lapse from want of attention".[6] Without making any critical comment on such an opinion as the above, it may be pointed out that things have been changing very rapidly particularly during the last few decades. Monstrous growth of industrialization has given serious jolts to our traditional concepts of values and howsoever hard we may strive for re-establishing those old values, we may not succeed as the whole weltanschauung has changed. Human values and human endeavour have forced their entry into the forefront and it is in appreciation of these things that we find discussions regarding different sorts of humanism today. When Sri Aurobindo called his philosophy 'Realistic Advaita' as contrasted with 'Illusionistic Advaita' of Śaṅkara he was but responding to the intellectual climate coming up gradually with the critical comments of Albert Schweitzer and others about the nature of Indian philosophizing.

Today we have reached a stage when philosophy has got to re-establish its identity. For our philosophy to be Indian it is essential to identify the problems of man of today and their possible solutions suitable to our own historical and geographical conditions. Potter[7] has taken pains to identify ten current problems, purely, philosophical, for an Indian philosopher. No doubt these points deserve serious considerations. What I wish to add is that in contemporary situation philosophy stands in need of coming closer to the sciences concerned with social dynamics. A man of today is confronted with three predicaments, apart from the normal predicament of social injustice, unequal distribution of human resources and unavailability of equal opportunity of progress:

(a) Alienation
(b) Futility of human endeavour
(c) Pangs of mediocrity

Marx speaks of three kinds of alienation — (i) alienation of the worker from his product, (ii) self-alienation of the workers, i.e. the alienation of the worker in the process of production and (iii) the alienation of man from one another in social relations. Mahatma Gandhi adds three other kinds — (a) alienation of man from nature, (b) alienation from his inner self and (c) alienation of consumption from production. But the problem of alienation has taken a different dimension on our subcontinent and that is the alienation of people of one caste, creed, region and religion from those of another threatening the very existence of the country.

The futility of human endeavour is particularly manifest in our country which has been made to be so by ruling elite encouraging the devils of corruption, frustrating the honest means of progress, individual or social and promoting an atmosphere of total valuelessness. As a natural corollary mediocrity has been made to rule and every intellectual effort has to bear its pangs resulting in suicide. Every Indian today is conditioned to this situation. Now is it not for a philosopher to find a way out of it? This is not to suggest that Advaita Vedānta or Navya Nyāya, etc., have lost their relevance today. They undoubtedly reflect the outcome of some of the subtlest minds of the world but when the very human existence is threatened, what is needed primarily is to find out ways and means to safeguard it. Intellectual brilliance will naturally follow. It may sound like suggesting that India today needs social or political philosophers who can guide the course of social change in the desirable direction in order to re-establish the dignity of human existence, to secure a place for man as man and to provide an atmosphere in which a man can actualize his potentialities in reaching his ultimate destiny. Contemporary Indian philosophizing is yet to come up to this.

Notes and References

1. Webster's *Third New International Dictionary.*
2. See his book *Presuppositions of India's Philosophies,* New Delhi: Prentice-Hall of India, 1965.
3. *Ibid.*, p. 253.
4. Nirad C. Chaudhury, *The Continent of Circle,* London: 1966, p. 149.
5. Mulk Raj Anand, Quoted in the Preface of *Current Trends in Indian Philosophy,* edited by K. Satchidanand Murty and K. Ramkrishna Rao, Asia Publising House, 1972.
6. Karl H. Potter, *Prosuppositions of India's Philosophies,* p. 257.
7. *Ibid.,* pp. 257-59.

8

On the Very Idea of Metaphysics

R.C. Pradhan

The theme which I would like to develop in this article is concerning the very idea of metaphysics as a serious philosophical inquiry. The idea of metaphysics has undergone radical changes across the centuries both in India and the West. However, there has been an underlying continuity amid all these changes which keeps metaphysics at the centre stage of philosophical inquiry. The metaphysical inquiry can be summed up in the question: Why is there something rather than nothing?[1] This question which is the most fundamental and according to some, the deepest question ever raised by philosophy constitutes the core of metaphysical investigation. However, no two metaphysical systems have agreed on what that something is which is sometimes called the 'reality' or the 'absolute' or sometimes the 'essents'.[2] No one who goes through the history of metaphysics can miss the divergent ways of describing the reality or the 'something' which is the ungrounded bedrock of all metaphysical inquiry.

My aim here is to argue that metaphysics ensures a vision of reality and that it is bound to lead us beyond language and scientific thought. Metaphysics is a higher order activity than science and therefore it is necessary to overcome both descriptive and revisionary metaphysics to arrive at a true vision of the transcendent reality.

What Metaphysics is Not

The first step in understanding metaphysics lies in defining what metaphysics is not or cannot be. Metaphysics cannot be a mere survey of the reality around us nor can it be a classification of the furniture of the universe. It is not in that sense a trivial account of what there is. The contemporary metaphysics, in contrast to its classical counterpart, has become a trivial study of what is there in the world in view of the fact that it has been content to describe the existing conceptual structure. Much of what is known as descriptive metaphysics[3] leads to the trivialization of metaphysics in the sense that it abdicates the responsibility of inquiring into why there are things at all. As Strawson writes:

> Descriptive metaphysics is content to describe the actual structure of our thought about the world, revisionary metaphysics is concerned to produce a better structure.[4]

Thus descriptive metaphysics is limited in its approach as it decides to be content with bringing out the actual conceptual structure of the human beings. It refuses to consider whether there is a better structure available at all. That is the very bane of descriptive metaphysics.

Strawson further argues that "there is a massive central core of human thinking which has no history- or none recorded in histories of thought".[5] Thus he suggests that descriptive metaphysics presupposes a permanent conceptual structure that underlies our thought and language. If there is an essential structure[6] of our thinking about the world as Strawson claims there is, then metaphysics cannot be a mere description of that structure. It must inquire why such a structure exists at all, that is, it must find out if there is no better structure available. If it is inevitable that we must have only that structure, then it becomes all the more imperative to know why it is so. This itself opens up the possibility of a more fundamental metaphysics that Strawson calls revisionary metaphysics. The revisionary metaphysics has been bracketed with speculative metaphysics just because it has raised a fundamental why–question.

Descriptive metaphysics is not possible for the simple reason that we can never reach the final world-view which we can describe. Alternative world-views are possible. We may be in illusion that we have got the ultimate conceptual structure at our disposal, but what we have is only the concepts which are in practice at the moment. Thus descriptive metaphysics has to give way to revisionary metaphysics if it has to sustain its interest in the nature of reality. In that case descriptive metaphysics will be at the service of revisionary metaphysics and not the other way round. Revisionary metaphysics itself makes room for further revision in its quest for the ultimate nature of reality. Thus metaphysics goes on revising itself till it grasps the reality as it is.

Davidson has aptly proposed that the very idea of a conceptual scheme[7] has something wrong with it because we are misled into believing that through a conceptual reorganization we could comprehend the reality. But the fact remains that we cannot understand reality through the conceptual network alone. We may have to overcome the conceptual scheme for reaching reality. As Davidson rightly claims, truth and reality are not relative to any conceptual scheme and therefore they are not subject to any further revision.[8] That is to say that we must admit the absolute truth that metaphysics seeks as the culminating point of its inquiry. But that is not a thing to be described but only to be encountered as the final destination of the philosophical journey.

Thus metaphysics in the fundamental sense is neither revisionary nor descriptive but visionary in the sense that it encounters the reality as it is in its ultimate character. It is not that the ultimate reality is readily available as it is; it requires bold intellectual effort to understand reality. It defies all conceptual organization and so has to be posited beyond the conflicting conceptual systems. Reality remains beyond our conceptual system. The task of metaphysics is to understand the reality in its ultimate character. Metaphysics is in this sense an intellectual inquiry into the ultimate truth about reality. In A.E. Taylor's words,

> Metaphysics sets itself, more systematically and universally than any other science, to ask what, after all, is meant by being *real,* and to what degree our various scientific and non-scientific theories about the world are in harmony with the universal characteristics of real existence.[9]

This is a reiteration of the Aristotelian view that metaphysics is the science of being *qua* being. Metaphysics, for Aristotle, is the first philosophy[10] that inquires into the fundamental principles of reality. Aristotle writes:

> There is a science which investigates being as being and the attributes which belong to this in virtue of its own nature. Now this is not the same as any of the so-called special sciences; for none of these others treats universally of being as being.[11]

This science is obviously what he calls the first philosophy which seeks the ultimate principles concerning being.

The First Philosophy: Beyond Realism and Antirealism

The idea of first philosophy has been subjected to attack in recent times especially by Quine[12] in his search for a relativistic account of ontology. According to this account, all ontology is relative to a theory or conceptual scheme; that is to say, what exists in the world is a matter of what we posit as existing in the theory. This conforms to his canonical dictum: "To be is to be the value of a variable".[13] That is, existence is, broadly speaking, a matter of our conceptual structure and so it is impossible to have a first philosophy at all. Metaphysics as the first philosophy is itself the product of our language and science. Hence, according to Quine there is a continuum between science and philosophy. He observes:

> The philosopher's task differs from the others', then, in detail; but in no such drastic way as those who imagine for the philosopher a vantage point outside the conceptual scheme that he takes in charge. There is no cosmic exile. He cannot study and revise the fundamental conceptual scheme of science and common sense without having some conceptual scheme, whether same or another no less need of philosophical scrutiny, in which to work.[14]

Quine's concept of philosophy as continuous with science rules out metaphysics as a first philosophy and replaces it by a general system of science that keeps on changing its conceptual structure in response to the external world. This idea of revision of conceptual structure makes science itself a fallible instrument of conceptual organization of experience. That is why Quine looks for a holistic method to make science weave together the bits of human knowledge into a system. Nevertheless, he feels the necessity of the fundamental principles of science at the centre of his system so as to give it the semblance of stability and conceptual coherence. This in a way is a reminder of the fact that there is a distant hope of a first philosophy even in Quine's system.

We need a first philosophy for the sake of science itself because there are fundamental principles which all sciences presuppose. These principles concern the very nature of human knowledge, the structure of human thought and the structure of reality which we think about and know. These fundamental principles cannot be studied by any particular science and therefore metaphysics must come forward to study and examine them. This is the source of the idea of a first philosophy which Aristotle felt to be necessary. First philosophy raises fundamental questions about the ultimate principles regarding reality. The most fundamental question as already mentioned is: "Why are there essents rather than nothing?" which Heidegger characterizes as follows:

> We do not inquire into this or that, or into each essent in turn, but from the very outset into the essent as a whole, or, as we say for reasons to be discussed below: into the essent as such in its entirety[15].

This why-question "penetrates to the 'underlying' ...realms and indeed to the very last of them, to the limit: turning away from the surface, from all shallowness, it strives towards the depths; this broadest of all questions is also the deepest".[16] Thus we are led to the depth of reality and to the very limits of all existence by the metaphysical questions. This only proves that first philosophy is *a sine qua non* for all intellectual inquiry.

Metaphysics has, however, remained bogged down in the realism-antirealism controversy just for the reason that we have not been able to decide whether we can understand reality within our conceptual structure or independently of it. The realist has pressed for the argument that reality is independent of our conceptual schemes and that we have direct access to it independently of how we think. This is the standpoint of what Putnam calls the metaphysical realist[17] who puts forward the view that there is a reality beyond our cognitive capacities. On the contrary, the antirealist or what Putnam calls internal realist believes that it is the conceptual structure within which alone the reality is understood. Thus for the internal realist our thinking makes a difference to the reality.

Both the arguments, however, seem to have missed the fundamental question which we have mentioned earlier. That question does not demand a clear-cut choice as to whether the reality is dependent on us or is independent of us. Reality or the being is inquired into with the presupposition that only the human intellect can penetrate it and therefore there is a metaphysical route to reality. So it cannot be denied that we have to understand the reality through our categories. But this does not mean that the reality is nothing but how we project it. There is a limit to our conceptual innovations. Therefore nothing regarding the nature of reality follows from the fact that there are limited conceptual choices we can make. If the reality is dependent on us, then it is no more the reality that metaphysics is all about. In that case reality is still a matter of our thought and not the ultimate reality which is the object of metaphysical inquiry. The best way therefore to go about it is to dissolve the idea that metaphysics either discovers reality or constructs it. It can do neither. It simply puts forward the way the reality reveals itself to us. That is, it makes us aware of the fact that the ultimate reality is beyond language and our descriptive apparatus. Nevertheless, it is the ground of all existence including language. If metaphysics puts forward the reality as it is or the being that underlies all beings, then it is imperative that we go beyond realism and antirealism. Neither realism nor antirealism can solve the problem of metaphysics; it is because each point of view excludes the other point of view and thereby fails to understand the reality. Reality or Being is neither man-made nor not man-made because the whole idea of man making reality or not making it does not arise in view of the fact that reality stands as it is. There is no reason to believe that our categories make a difference to the reality or being. If they make a difference, then they are not categories of reality. Therefore Putnam's idea that the world is projected through our categories and so must be internal[18] to the categorical scheme of ours is half true. Putnam says:

The perspective I shall defend has no unambiguous name. It is a late arrival in the history of philosophy, and even today it keeps being confused with other points of view of quite different sort. I shall refer to it as the *internalist* perspective, because it is characteristic of this view to hold that *what objects does the world consists of ?* is a question that it makes sense to ask only *within* a theory or description (p.49)[19] (italics original).

The internalist perspective thus presented makes the very talk of the world and its objects dependent on a theory or conceptual framework. Putnam seems to regard this perspective very conducive as a metaphysical world-view as it is supposedly replaces what he calls the externalist perspective which demands a God's eye point of view.[20]

However, the idea of reality being internal to a conceptual scheme could be questioned. If reality is internal to our concepts, then it is not reality at all; if it is not internal, then reality can never be known or understood. Thus to say that reality is internal or not internal is meaningless. Reality is not a category that can be placed among other categories.

It is important to note that metaphysics is not a science which can encapsulate reality at all in this or that category. Metaphysics leaves everything as it is and transcends the limits of all description. It does not use any language like science; it holds language itself as a matter to be understood. Language represents the reality that metaphysics treats as belonging to the lower-order because what language describes belongs to the arena of science. That is why metaphysics is not a science of any kind. It investigates the very foundations of science. By that it removes itself from all modes of scientific talk. The more we are concerned with the fundamental reality the less talk we can have about reality.

Metaphysics and the Limits of Language

Language is constrained in not capturing the essence of reality which metaphysics seeks to unravel. Language remains unsuccessful in its search for the essence of reality. There are two modes of language which have remained glued to world, namely, the descriptive mode or the mode of representation, and the mode of language being an active agent in shaping the reality. Both modes have a scientific bias, since both are connected with the world. This has resulted in the idea that metaphysics must be linked with language either in the form of a description of reality or of an instrument of making reality. This is how contemporary metaphysics remains tied down to the reality of our ordinary experience. We have not reached the level of reality that stands beyond the categories of language. We have remained confined within the language that we use and the conceptual scheme that we have found entrenched in language. The philosophers have been the prisoners of language and have lost their way in the labyrinth of language. Metaphysics liberates us from language and its categories.

Language has limits as emphasized by Wittgenstein.[21] It cannot encapsulate the reality as it is, that is, it cannot put in words what the reality ultimately is. It cannot tell us why there is any reality at all. Besides, in our search for reality we go on moving from one category to another. We move within language and therefore fail to reach reality. Ultimately we get imprisoned in our own language-games. This spells doom for metaphysics. We cease to wonder about language itself and about the very reality we are searching for. This state of affairs occurs because of our species-habit to take language for granted. Language holds us captive[22] as Wittgenstein tells us. There is a deep reason why we fall a prey to language. Language presents an illusion of truth rather than the truth itself. Though language is the only means of expressing truth, it does not constitute truth itself. Truth stands independent of language and so we have to cross the limits of language to arrive at truth.

It is not the case that there is nothing beyond language as many linguistic thinkers believe. According to some, there is nothing beyond the limits of language. But this is wrong. Beyond language there is reality–the absolute reality. The linguistic representations are only the landmarks on the way to truth. Truth is the peak and the linguistic and mental representations are only the way through which we have to go to reach the peak. Therefore all sciences which take language as their sole ground are only half-way houses on the way to truth. Truth is not a material entity to be captured, nor is it a substance to be located. It is the end of all inquiry and the highest mark of our intellectual quest.

The idea of the limits of language arises because we have the tendency to limit everything to language. The transcendent realm of existence is either denied or reduced to the ordinary existence. This makes the task of metaphysics totally superfluous. The reason why metaphysics finds no favour with some is that they do not recognize the transcendent realm at all. But if we admit that there is a greater reality than what we experience in ordinary life, then admitting the possibility of metaphysics becomes inevitable. From time immemorial, metaphysicians have admitted the vast domain of reality that remains beyond the ken of ordinary knowledge. Therefore it is necessary that metaphysics is admitted as an inquiry into the higher-order realm of existence.

The Metaphysics of the Transcendent

We can admit that the physical and empirical realm is not the only realm of reality. It is only a fragment of a vast realm of reality that no language can decipher. It is the total reality or being that includes language and mind themselves. Our little understandings and cogitations are a part of the network of language which we must overcome with a view to reaching reality. Overcoming language does not mean having no language at all. It only means that we shall never demand that everything should be expressed in language. That is, we can leave room for the fact that there is a residual reality that needs no language at all. For example, we cannot express in language that there is reality or being at all instead of nothing. This fact is beyond language because the existence of language itself suggests that there is reality already. Language carries its own ontology and so there is already the ontic affirmations following from the reality of language. Thus besides language there is already the reality which language carries with itself. Thus some ontology is already there to begin with. Now the question is whether metaphysics would accept this ontology as final or go beyond it. If metaphysics accepts the given ontology, then it becomes localized and loses its global appeal. Besides, it loses its global vision and gets reduced into a partial and localized ontology.

There are two disadvantages with the local ontology. First of all, it is limited to the entities that have only a local significance, e.g. material bodies, persons, etc. Secondly, it has only a regional appeal in the sense that the entities it introduces are products of some conceptual bias. If the materialists argue that the material bodies alone make up the universe, then they have a very narrow view of the universe and so their ontology suffers from a local bias. If there is an attempt, on the contrary, to deny the material bodies altogether, that also takes us nowhere because common sense says that there are material bodies besides minds and persons. Thus we are limited to the narrow views about reality offering only narrow or local ontologies. Therefore there is a need to overcome these ontologies in search for a global view of the universe. This leads us to what Heidegger calls the fundamental ontology[23] which investigates into the nature of being in the fundamental sense.

The transcendent realm that beckons us in our search for being is the realm of the extraordinary, the infinite and the ungrounded reality. What that reality is nobody knows, but it is there as the source and the limit of all existence. It is not a nothingness either because it is the source of all beings. The source of all beings must be a being, that is, being of a higher order. The higher-order being is not a material body nor is it a spirit of any kind. The higher-order being is the being *simpliciter*. It has no colour, no shape, no size and it is neither born nor does it die. It is beyond all categories as no category is rich enough to describe it. It makes no difference by what description we characterize it because it is in a sense beyond all descriptions.

In Western thought, the realm of the transcendent lost its significance because of the positivist attack on the language in which the transcendent reality was described. The language of the transcendent was declared meaningless because it did not fit the framework of the physical sciences. The standard of cognitive significance accorded to physical sciences obviously did not match the language of metaphysics. This led to the conclusion that metaphysics consists of meaningless statements.[24] This made philosophers shy of the realm of the transcendent. Many thought this realm is a figment of wild imagination or at best the product of a speculative mind. Thus the concept of transcendent fell into disrepute and the subsequent neglect. Husserl, Heidegger and Wittgenstein have realized the futility of the positivist attack on metaphysics and have given in their own restrained way the hints of the possibility of a metaphysics of the transcendent.

Indian metaphysics is fully rooted in the idea of the transcendent because of which there has been a continuous talk of the transcendent realm from the *Upaniṣadic* times to the present. Sri Aurobindo in his *Life Divine*[25] has brought into focus the nature of the transcendent reality which lies concealed in the *Upaniṣadic* literature. His glorification of the transcendent as the essence of all metaphysical quest is built into the Indian response to the metaphysical questions raised in the West. For Sri Aurobindo, the Divine Reality is beyond all our mental plane and belongs to the realm of the supramental.

The Metaphysics of the Immanent

The realm of the immanent has been in the focus in the West after the retreat of the metaphysics of the transcendent. The former has held sway for the reason that the realm of the immanent is easily accessible to the methods of science and experience. The metaphysics of the immanent therefore has been acceptable to the majority of philosophers. This metaphysics admits a variety of word-views on the nature of reality. From Aristotle to Strawson there is effort to pin down the reality to what is already known through science and common sense. Here metaphysics does nothing but put forward a view of reality that suits the language and logic we are already familiar with. The categories we have employed in describing the reality have come from either ordinary language or from the language of the logical systems. Thus there is no effort here to go beyond language or the logic already available. That is why there is need to keep reality within the framework of logic we have adopted for the purpose of understanding reality. Immanent metaphysics is thus based on logic as in Aristotle, Kant, Strawson and so on. Thus we have the metaphysics of the substances, attributes and modes and so on all derived from a particular logical system we have followed. We have varieties of metaphysical concepts such as space, time, events, processes, meteorological sums, numbers and so on for understanding reality.

The major difficulty with this metaphysics is that it does not take us very far. We are provided with conflicting pictures of reality. No two pictures of reality agree on what the reality is. Whereas one tells us that the world consists of things, another says that it consists of events and processes. Thus we are led from one metaphysics to another without being enlightened about what the reality is. This may lead to antinomies as Kant[26] has pointed out. These metaphysical systems most of the time are engaged in an unending battle about the nature and the structure of the universe. The result is: we are nowhere near the reality. We are puzzled about the multiplicity of the world-views and their conflicting claims.

Kant suggests that we must get rid of these systems of antinomous[27] metaphysics. We have to go beyond the categories that are employed in metaphysics. According to Kant, these categories like substance, causality and number have application only to sensible objects and so have no significance beyond the realm of the sensible. This has led him to denounce the metaphysics of the super sensible for the obvious reason that such a metaphysics does not give any cognitive access to reality. The super sensible which is recognized by Kant as real, however, is not accessible through the categories but is nonetheless presupposed by all our intellectual endeavour including our moral and religious life. Thus in Kant's philosophy we are not deprived of the reality of the super sensible but only of our knowledge of a such a reality.

However, the question arises, why should we not be allowed to have a metaphysical access to reality? If the reality is a noumenon as Kant says it is, it is not the case that we are in total ignorance about it. We have constant interaction with it even if we have no scientific knowledge of it. Scientific knowledge is not the whole of knowledge we have; there are other ways of encountering reality. For example, philosophy provides an access to reality through its metaphysical vision. The greatest contribution of philosophy in this task is that it tells us to transcend the limited sphere of the knowledge of science. We cancel the scientific knowledge with the assurance that we have a broader and better vision of reality. Scientific knowledge is only a fragment of the totality of human knowledge. Therefore metaphysics goes beyond science in revealing us the reality which has a transcendent face.

Modern science is dwarfed by its own limiting categories; it cannot go beyond a certain level of thought. As Heidegger says:

> Modern science today in all its branches is a technical, practical business of gaining and transmitting information. An awakening of the spirit cannot take its departure from such science. It is itself in need of an awakening.[28]

This indicates the fact that science has been irresponsive to the higher demands of the human spirit and so it remains indifferent to the demands of metaphysics. There is every reason to believe that metaphysics is a higher-order activity than science and so we must take a more positive view of metaphysics.

The immanent metaphysics which sometimes goes in the name of scientific or logical metaphysics is in need of a revision. It cannot fulfil all the demands of reason and so falls short of making any effort to reach the transcendent. That the transcendent is a logical and metaphysical possibility cannot be denied by science. Science remains wedded to an immanent metaphysics at best. What, however, we need is a transcendent metaphysics. That alone can show us the real nature of being.

Concluding Remarks

The idea of metaphysics has come from man's quest for truth. It is therefore a higher-order activity. It takes us back to the ultimate nature of things. That makes the task of metaphysics all the more important because we have the responsibility of conceptually locating the transcendent in the overall framework of human knowledge. Metaphysics ensures the possibility of a vision of reality.

Notes and References

1. See Martin Heidegger, *An Introduction to Metaphysics,* trans. Ralph Manheim, New Haven: Yale University Press, 1959, pp. 1-51.
2. *Ibid.*
3. P.F. Strawson, *Individuals: An Essay in Descriptive Metaphysics,* Methuen, London: 1959.
4. *Ibid.,* p. 9.
5. *Ibid.,* p. 10.
6. *Ibid.*
7. See Davidson, "On the Very Idea of a Conceptual Scheme" in *Inquiries into Truth and Interpretation,* Oxford: Clarendon Press, 1984.
8. *Ibid.*
9. A.E. Taylor, *Elements of Metaphysics,* Methuen, London and Barnes and Noble, New York: 1903; University Paperback, 1961, pp. 4-5.
10. Aristotle, *Metaphysics.*
11. *Ibid.,* Book IV.
12. W.V. Quine, *Word and Object* (MIT Press, Cambridge and Massacheusetts: 1960).
13. *Ibid.*
14. *Ibid.,* pp. 275-76.
15. Heidegger, *op. cit.,* p. 2.
16. *Ibid.,* p. 3.
17. Hilary Putnam, *Reason, Truth and History,* Cambridge: Cambridge University Press, 1981.

18. *Ibid.*
19. *Ibid.*
20. *Ibid.*
21. Wittgenstein, *Tractatus Logico-Philosophicus,* trans. D.F. Pears and B.F. McGuinness, Routledge and Kegan Paul, London: 1961, 5.6-5.61
22. Wittgenstein, *Philosophical Investigations,* trans. G.E.M. Anscombe (Blackwell, Oxford: 1953), sects. 109-15.
23. Heidegger, *op. cit.*
24. See A.J. Ayer, *Language, Truth and Logic,* Penguin Books, 1971.
25. Sri Aurobindo, *Life Divine,* 2 vols., Pondicherry: Aurobindo Ashram, 1972.
26. Kant, *Critique of Pure Reason,* trans. N.K. Smith, Macmillan, 1929.
27. *Ibid.*
28. Heidegger, *op. cit.*

9

Wittgenstein and Kant

S. Shyamkishore Singh

In recent years, we have witnessed a revival of interest in Kantian ideas and modes of thought, and interesting general suggestions concerning the interpretation of Kant and his relevance to the contemporary scene have been brought to the sharp focus. We have also noticed the reverence shown by the present-day analytical thinkers to Wittgenstein and the way in which they study the works of Wittgenstein with near religious fervour. Every student of philosophy knows that Kant and Wittgenstein are prominent landmarks in the history of philosophy. Kant has heralded a "Copernican revolution" in philosophical thinking towards the later part of the eighteenth century and his works opened new vistas to latter European thought. Wittgenstein's philosophy is equally revolutionary and original. In fact, Wittgenstein has directed twentieth century philosophy towards entirely new channels. But although Kant and Wittgenstein developed two original and independent philosophies, it will be found on closer study of their works that these two intellectual giants shared parallel and almost similar views on certain fundamental issues of philosophical inquiry.

In both *Tractatus Logico-Philosophicus* and *Philosophical Investigations,* Wittgenstein was concerned with determining the limits of sense, and demarcating the boundary between what can intelligibly be said and what cannot be said.

Wittgenstein was convinced that these tasks can be carried out through a careful study of language. He maintained that "All philosophy is a critique of language".[1] There are however, differences between the *Tractatus* and the *Investigations,* in drawing the boundary between what can be said and what cannot be said, and in the detailed description of the boundary. As George Pitcher says, "still to draw some boundary is one of Wittgenstein's major aim in both. In pursuing this task, he was carrying on, in his own way, the work started in modern philosophy by Locke, Hume and Kant".[2] In the *Tractatus,* Wittgenstein stated the functions of philosophy as follows:

> Philosophy aims at the logical clarification of thoughts.
>
> * * *
>
> A philosophical work consists essentially of elucidations.
>
> * * *
>
> Without philosophy thoughts are, as it were, cloudy and in—distinct: its task is to make them clear and to give them sharp boundaries.[3]

Thus, according to Wittgenstein, the proper task of philosophy is the clarification of confusing and indistinct thoughts through subtle logical analysis and also to draw limits to thought.

This line of thinking in which a boundary is drawn between the experienciable and the inexperienciable, the thinkable and the unthinkable, thereby, the sayable and the unsayable was pursued by Kant. In the *Critique of Pure Reason,* Kant maintains that any enquiry into the objects of cognition leads to the conditions of knowing, which in turn leads to the inquiry into the limits of cognition itself. Kant holds that cognition is permitted within the bounds of experience only, because the formal *a priori* conditions of knowledge can be applied solely within the limits of experience. Thus the enquiry into the objects of cognition leads us to the description of conceptual boundary. Now since cognition (hence, thought) and language are intimately related, prescribing limit to cognition is tantamount to assigning similar limit to language, if at all our language should be intelligible. Thus, a 'critique of thought' is in essence a 'critique of language'. Yet, Kantian thought is not merely confined to drawing such a boundary line of thought, for Kant puts a great stress upon the role of reason which has unsatiable tendency for diving into the unfathomable depths of the transcendental supersensible. Reason roams about the garden of metaphysics tasting the forbidden fruits, i.e. the transcendental ideas. But the intrusion meets with its inevitable punishment. Reason ends in contradictions, 'antinomies' and 'paralogisms'. Thus Kantian thought shows that what began as a warning, ends in a precarious situation.

We find almost similar line of thought in the philosophy of Wittgenstein. In the *Tractatus,* Wittgenstein worked out the internal grammar of the sensible, and demarcated the spheres of the sensible and non-sensible, in simple and straightforward way. Wittgenstein defines the aim of the *Tractatus* in his preface thus: ' to set a limit to thought or rather not to thought, but to the expression of thoughts" Concerning the method, he expressed it in the following illuminating lines:

> The correct method of philosophy would really be the following : to say nothing except what can be said, i.e. propositions of natural science i.e. something that has nothing to do with philosophy and then, whenever someone else wanted to say something metaphysical, to demonstrate to him that he has failed to give meaning to certain signs in his propositions. Although it would not be satisfying to the other person—he would not have the feeling that we were teaching him philosophy—this method would be the only strictly correct one.[4]

The *Tractatus* concludes with a frank admission, along with a warning:

> My propositions serve as elucidations in the following way: anyone who understands me eventually recognizes them as nonsensical when he has used them as steps to climb up beyond them. (He must, so to speak, throw away the ladder after he has climbed up it). He must transcend these propositions; and then he will see the world aright. What we cannot speak about we must pass over in silence.[5]

Wittgenstein maintains that what we cannot speak about falls within the subject-matter of ethics, religion and aesthetics. Wittgenstein has passed certain remarks on these disciplines in the closing pages of the *Tractatus* as well as in the *Notebooks.*

Just as Kant pursued the flight of reason in the spheres of ethics, religion and aesthetics in his *Critique of Practical Reason* and *Critique of Judgement,* Wittgenstein in his *Philosophical Investigations* makes an assessment of the philosopher's predicament in breaking the "Silence" he had enjoyed in the *Tractatus.* Philosophy, the latter Wittgenstein maintains, begins with perplexing riddles and generally ends with bewilderment. Being a philosopher, therefore, is being in an unhappy, puzzling situation. To know a philosophical problem entails being thus bewildered. This happens so because the philosopher by employing his reasoning processes tries to tackle the philosophical problems but is led to consequences which turn out to be absurd. As Wittgenstein says: "A philosophical problem has the form: I don't know my way about".[6]

The philosopher proceeds with high hopes that he will be able to find his way out, only to be baffled in the end. The philosophical puzzles have certain characteristic features. Most of them are like paradoxes in which both the assertion and negation of the same statement seem to have equal weight in an argument. Regarding the puzzles George Pitcher writes:

One does not have to look far for examples of these Wittgenstein Puzzles: Zeno's paradoxes of motion and multiplicity, and Kant's four antinomies are known to all students of philosophy. Book I of F.H. Bradley's *Appearance and Reality* consists almost entirely of the exposition of such puzzles.[7]

There are hordes of examples of the philosopher's puzzlements. It may be said in a sense that philosophy starts from puzzles. Malcolm in his Memoirs mentions a remark passed by Wittgenstein:

A person caught in a philosophical confusion is like a man in a room who wants to get out but doesn't know how. He tries the chimney but it is too narrow.[8]

What is the root cause of philosophical perplexity? Wittgenstein says that the most important source of philosophical puzzlement is the philosopher's misconceptions about language. "Philosophy" he says, "is a battle against the bewitchment of our intelligence by means of language".[9] He thinks that a thinker who is bewitched by language is like a person suffering from an illness, in this case confusion. After diagnosing the philosopher's illness, Wittgenstein proceeds to cure the disease. In his later writings Wittgenstein upheld a therapeautic conception of philosophy. He thinks that the philosopher's illness needs treatment, and, definitely the cure can be found out. If the philosopher's puzzle is compared with the situation in which a person is entrapped in a room without any accessible outlet, then the cure for this puzzlement lies in the escape from the room. "What is your aim in philosophy ?" Wittgenstein asks himself, and pat came the reply, "To shew the fly the way out of the fly bottle".[10] The philosopher is the fly in the fly bottle, and his escape route from the bottle of puzzlement consists in understanding the proper function of language and the correct use of words and sentences in their appropriate moorings. The philosopher has to play his role in the "language game" (*Sprachspiele).*

In Kant's *Introduction to Logic* (tr. T.K. Abott, N.Y., Philosophical Library, 1963) Kant conceived of Dialectic in the therapeautic sense. Kant wrote:

...We should therefore have two parts of logic; the Analytic, which should treat of the formal criteria of truth and the Dialectic, which should contain the marks and rules by which we should be able to know that something does not agree with the formal criteria of truth, although it seems to agree with them. Dialectic in this respect would have its use as a *Cathartic* of the Understanding.[11]

Again, in the *Critique of the Pure Reason* in the part entitled 'Transcendental Dialectic', Kant was concerned with certain kind of philosophical "puzzlements" or "bewilderments" which he called "the Transcendental Illusions". Kant was aware of the aberrations of Reason when it employs the "Ideas of Pure Reason". Reason fails to define the nature of such metaphysical entities as God, the immortal soul, and the world conceived as a totality, because the forms of *Sensibility and Understanding* cannot be applied beyond experience. If the forms are valid in experience only because they are necessary conditions of experience, there is no way of judging their applicability to objects transcending experience. Hence when Reason tried to have theoretical (demonstrative) knowledge of the transcendental objects, it meets with the "antinomies" and the "paralogisms". The more Reason tries to delve into the transcendental Ideas, the more it is surrounded by some quite natural and inevitable illusions. "Which can no more be prevented than we can prevent the sea from appearing higher at the horizon than at the shore".[12] According to Kant, "Transcendental illusion...does not cease even after it has been detected and its invalidity clearly revealed by transcendental criticism".[13] The transcendental dialectic exposes "the illusion of transcendent judgements, and at the same time taking precaution that we be not deceived by it".[14] Thus we find that Wittgenstein's "puzzles" are similar to Kant's "illusions". Kant sums up his philosophical standpoint as follows:

> All our knowledge starts with the senses, proceeds from thence to understanding, and end with reason, beyond which there is no higher faculty to be found in us for elaborating the matter of intuition and bring it under the highest unity of thought. Now that I have to give an explanation of this highest faculty of knowledge, I find myself in some difficulty.[15]

Both Kant and Wittgenstein recognize reason's cravings for the highest unity and completeness.

> What makes it difficult for us to make this line of investigation is our craving for generality—completeness.... This tendency is the real source of metaphysics, and leads the philosopher into complete darkness.[16]

Both the philosophers, however, admit that reason's great expectations in the realm of the Indefinite are expressive of some very deep human needs. It was Kant's purpose in his critical philosophy to search if some misunderstanding lies at the root of the conflicts and contradictions, and felt that the resolution of these conflicts will provide the way for a "lasting and peaceful reign of reason over understanding and the senses".[17] Similarly, Wittgenstein was looking for "the real discovery". "The real discovery is the one that makes me capable of stopping doing philosophy when I want to—The one that gives philosophy peace, so that it is no longer tormented by questions which bring itself in question".[18] It must, however, be admitted that although the two thinkers agree with their goals of "peace" in philosophy, there are differences in the mode of striving to achieve the goal. Kant allows Reason to pursue its flight and employ its Idea, as the regulative principles of morality in Ethics; He also explains man's yearning for the supersensible in religion through the idea of Infinity. Again by means of the idea of infinity he accounts for aesthetic experiences. Wittgenstein's solution of philosophical problem, on the other hand, lies in the proper use and analysis of language. In effect, the two approaches do not conflict with each other, in so far as the proper use of language covers all the things that Kant strives to achieve.

We have to bring out some other features of Wittgenstein's thought for comparison with that of Kant. Regarding the nature of logic, Wittgenstein wrote in the *Tractatus* that "Logic is transcendental".[19] This remark is significant in view of its deep philosophical significance. It revives a theme of Kant's *Critique of Pure Reason*. However, this statement can be interpreted in more than one sense. It may mean, literarily, that logic in so far as it is a pure formal science transcends actual and possible experience. But this is not the only sense which Wittgenstein meant. By "logic" he meant "the logic of language" which shows "logic of the world". Wittgenstein thought that logic has philosophical and ontological implications. Logic is the basis of ontology and logical studies lead to certain ontological implications. He finds that there is intimate connection between logic and world order. He thinks that there is an order in the world and that the ideal of logic is to determine *a priori* the form of the world. In the *Notebooks* Wittgenstein wrote, "The great problem round which everything that I write turns is : Is there an order in the world *a priori* and, if so, what does it consist in".[20] This order according to him, must be precise, it must be free from accidental connections. Now what Kant's transcendental deductions are intended to perform, Wittgenstein's logical analysis of language purports to perform. Just as Kant declared "Understanding is the law-giver to nature," the analysis of language yields the *a priori* determination of the nature of the world. Wittgenstein even believed that understanding the nature of a proposition leads us to the knowledge of the world. It was also the purpose of Kant to yield *a priori* knowledge of the world of experience by means of the transcendental method. In case of Kant it was the analysis of experience which leads us to the *a priori* conditions of experience.

Wittgenstein even raised such Kantian questions as "How is pure mathematics possible ?" in his writings on the nature of pure logic and the foundation of mathematics. On this issue Max Black writes,

Kant in the *Kritik* held undoubted knowledge of 'Universal necessary connections' in logic and mathematics to be incomprehensible either from the standpoint of Hume's empiricism or from that of Leibniz's rationalism. Wittgenstein would have agreed that if experience is the source of all knowledge, mathematical conclusions ought to be tentative and approximate; while if reason supplies only analytical truth it remains mysterious how mathematics escapes triviality. Pure mathematics cannot be 'about' the world in the way that Physics is; yet if grounded in thought alone, how can it *apply* to the world? Wittgenstein was absorbed by this ancient puzzle of the connection between thought and reality. The great question was: "Is there an order in the world *a priori,* and if so, what does it consist in?" That there must be "an order in the world" was a conviction he never abandoned while composing the *Tractatus;* though he came to see that *a priori* proposition 'say nothing', he still maintained that in them the 'logical form of reality' manifests itself.[21]

A.M. Quinton, in a paper, explains Wittgenstein's view on the above issue thus:

...broadly speaking, the *Tractatus* sets out a general theory of language in relation to the world. It gives an answer to the Kantian looking question: how is language, and so thinking possible? Wittgenstein was not, as Russell supposed in his introduction to the book, projecting an ideal language in conformity with the most stringent standards of logical perfection. He was attempting, rather, to reveal the essential structure that must be possessed by any language capable of being significantly used and which must, therefore, be hidden behind the familiar surface of our actual language.[22]

In view of Wittgenstein's contribution to the critique of language (and hence, of thought) some commentators have suggested that *Tractatus Logico-Philosophicus* can be given the title: The *Critique of Pure Language.*[23]

Alexander Maslow also interpreted Wittgenstein's thought in similar lines when he wrote, "in my interpretation of the *Tractatus* the basic philosophy underlying it has become a kind of Kantian phenomenalism, with the forms of language playing a role similar to Kant's transcendental apparatus. Language in this interpretation is not only an instrument of thought and communication but also an all pervading factor in organising our cognitive experience".[24] Both Kant and Wittgenstein have emphasized the intimate relation between thought and the expression of thought (in language).

Further, the attitudes of Kant and Wittgenstein towards philosophy show obvious similarity. Wittgenstein considered philosophy as an activity rather than a subject, ("Philosophy is not a body of doctrine, but an activity".) This activity view of philosophy reminds us of Kant's illuminating statement : "Philosophy can never be learned, ...we can at most learn to philosophize".[25] As a teacher of Philosophy in Königsberg, Kant's guiding principle was to teach his students not so much philosophical doctrines as how to "Philosophise".[26] The philosophical activity may consist either in prescribing limit to thought or to language or even in salvaging thought from the lulling and confusing effect of language in the service of uncritical metaphysics (Kantian view in the *Prolegomena to Any Future Metaphysics,* p. 132; L.W. Beck's translation) or as "a battle against the Bewitchment of our intelligence by means of language" (Wittgenstein's standpoint in the *Philosophical Investigations,* 109). We must take up philosophy as an activity. Wittgenstein has carried the activity-view of philosophy to the further extent of saying (in a remark to his friends) that "philosophy is an art-form".

There are many other issues of philosophical activity in which Wittgenstein's thinking goes parallel to that of Kant. In recent years, some thinkers have taken keen interest in the comparative study of Wittgenstein and Kant.[27] However, further research into their philosophical works will reveal many more valuable materials for the comparative study of Wittgenstein and Kant. It can be rightly said that many new insights on understanding Kantian thought will come out when we study Kant in the light of Wittgensteinian philosophy. It may also be proper to say that the right approach to Wittgenstein will be the one from the Kantian standpoint.

Notes and References

1. *Tractatus Logico-philosophicus,* 4.0031 (translated by D.F. Pears and B.F. Mc Guinness, N.Y.: Humanities Press, 1961).
2. G. Pitcher, *The Philosophy of Wittgenstein,* Prentice-Hall, 1964, p. 326.
3. *Tractatus,* 4.112.
4. *Ibid.,* 6.53.
5. *Ibid.,* 6.54; 7.
6. *Philosophical Investigations;* p. 123 (translated by G.E.M. Anscombe, Oxford, 1953).
7. G. Pitcher, *The Philosophy of Wittgenstein,* p. 190.
8. N. Malcolm, *Memoir,* p. 51
9. *Philosophical Investigations,* p. 109.
10. *Ibid.,* p. 309.
11. Kant, *Introduction to Logic,* p. 7. (translated by T.K. Abott, N.Y.: Philosophical Library, 1963).
12. *Critique of Pure Reason,* A297=B254 (*A* refers to the First Edition (1781); *B* refers to the Second Edition (1787).

13. *Ibid.*, A 297=B 353.
14. *Ibid.*, A 298=B 355.
15. *Ibid.*, A 299=B 355.
16. Wittgenstein, *Blue and Brown Book,* pp. 17-19.
17. *Critique of Pure Reason,* A 465=493.
18. *Philosophical Investigations,* p. 133.
19. *Tractatus Logico-Philosophicus,* 6.13.
20. *Notebooks,* 53 (II).
21. Max Black, *A Companion to Wittgenstein's Tractatus,* Cambridge, 1964, pp. 5-6.
22. A Quinton's paper is included in G. Pitcher (ed.), Wittgenstein, *The Philosophical Investigations,* p. 3.
23. Eric Stenius, *Wittgenstein's Tractatus : A Critical Exposition of its Main Lines of Thought,* p. 220.
24. A Maslow, *A Study in Wittgenstein's Tractatus,* California University Press, 1961, pp. XIII-XII.
25. *Critique of pure Reason,* A 837=B 865.
26. S. Körner, *Kant,* Penguin Paperback, 1955, p. 220.
27. S.M. Engell "Wittgenstein and Kant", *Philosophy and Phenomonological Research,* 1969-70, pp. 483-513.

10

Reason and Revelation in Śaṅkara

R.L. Singh

Reasoning in Indian Logic is of several kinds. Here we may mention two in the main (i) syllogistic (ii) Non-syllogistic (especially *sāmānyatodṛṣṭa anumāna*). Example of syllogistic reasoning : smoke implies the existence of fire. Here there is smoke, here there is fire. Of the other type is the analogical reasoning. Here the inference is, on the basis of resemblance. In Advaita Vedānta of Śaṅkara, analogical reasoning has been used. The pots imply the potter, the world implies a cause. But potter considered as a concept, is an empirical concept. There are different types of concept. Non-empirical concepts are *a priori*.

Brahman, according to Advaita Vedānta of Śaṅkara, is the unconditioned. It, as a concept, is thoroughly *a priori* and transcendent. It means, it cannot be an object of knowledge in the manner in which the potter is. I can verify the truth of the statement that an intelligent being is the cause of '*ghat*' but I cannot verify the same in case of the cause of the world. So it can conclusively be said that analogical inference cannot establish the existence of Brahman or give us the knowledge of Brahman. Then, is analogical reasoning entirely useless? No, not altogether useless. It can be made to yield a highly probable conclusion, provided that this kind of *anumāna* is yoked to another *pramāṇa* as *Tarka* or *Yukti* clarifying and developing what has been given by that *Pramāṇa*. What is that *Pramāṇa* which gives us the awareness of this cause of the '*bhutāni*'. *Śruti* or revelation, e.g. the *śrutivākya, yato vā imānibhūtani jāyante* or *yukti* or *tarka* may be helpful in justifying to us a supramental seeing of the Brahman, a vision expressed in the *śrutivākyas* like *sarvam khalu idam Brahma, so ayamātmā Brahma, Tattvamasi*, etc. The basic proposition is Brahman alone is real. The question is how could we account for the world and the individual souls? In other words, how could we correlate these diverse propositions: (i) Brahman is real (ii) the world is *mithyā* (iii) The *jīva* is identical with Brahman. We can correlate these diverse propositions through the hypothesis of *Māyā*, which is the logical paradigm of Advaita Vedānta of Śaṅkara for explaining manyness along with oneness. Here again we take recourse to analogical reasoning. Just as the snake is the effect of the rope, so the world is effect of Brahman. Just as the one moon appears as two to a man of defective vision, so does the Brahman appear as *jīvas.* Analogical reasoning has been used both for indicating that the world has a cause as also for indicating that the effect is merely an illusory transformation of cause (*Vivartamātra)*. But unless one has a disposition, temperament or awareness, an acquaintance with the cause in question and/or the kind of relation that exists between the ground and consequent, the inferential procedure even if it is stated, it would not lead to any ascertainably tangible conclusion.

Now the question is, can reasoning give us the knowledge of reality according to Advaita Vedānta of Śaṅkara? A reasoning which is not the unfolding of a seeing, a vision or a clear and distinct perception is no reasoning at all. It may be a useless dialectical argument, which may have a lot to do with words and random ideas, but which does not give us knowledge. Reasoning is the unfolding of a vision in the medium of intellectual understanding; but itself it cannot lead to the vision. The only sin to which our intellect is all too prone finds expression in the belief that intellect or reasoning can give us the knowledge of truth or reality. In our opinion every piece of a reasoning which is not merely a pretension or self-deception is the intellectual unfolding of a seeing, perceiving or vision. We make a distinction between false seeing and true seeing, part and fragmentary seeing and whole seeing. So reasoning is logic but there is not one logic. There will be as many logics as there are perceptions or seeing. If I see things in a fragmentary manner, each divided from each, resting on negation, supporting affirmation, my logic will be the logic of finite. But if my seeing is seeing square and whole, my logic will be the logic of absolute affirmation, the logic of the infinite. From logic there is no passage to the seeing or the vision though from the vision there is a passage to logic or reasoning.

Is there antagoism between revelation and reason? We have first to know what is revelation. Revelation has been sometimes identified with scriptural statement or dogma. This is mistaken. Revelation is seeing or the direct perception of reality. Scripture simply bears testimony to this seeing. Once you have seen, you can argue and translate this seeing into reasoning. So there is no antagonism between revelation and reasoning. But there is also a situation in which the relation between them might be misconceived. Reasoning does not lead to seeing or revelation; without seeing there can be no argued ontological knowledge. Sometimes after having mastered the stock of arguments of various philosophical systems, we profess to be Kantians or Śaṅkarites. We do not therefore, have the knowledge of Brahman by mastering the dialectical subtleties of the *Khaṇḍana-khaṇḍakhādya* or *Tattvapradīpikā*. Reasoning itself does not lead us anywhere. It leads to ignorance, to vanity and self-deception. What is needed is knowledge or seeing. Unless the intellect is divested of its pride and false self-confidence it will continue to be distempered. A distempered intellect can only enter into *logomachy*. It cannot be a means to knowing. So reasoning is not useless. It can unfold to the intellect the contours and forms of a vision, if we have it but it is useless if cut off from such a vision.

The thing or *vastu* to be known is the Brahman, The question is how can it be known? Brahman being not an ordinary *vastu* like those cognized by ordinary means of knowledge requires an extraordinary means of knowledge. This extra-ordinary means of knowledge is intuition. The knowledge of Brahman is not a cognition in the ordinary sense. It is a vision, in which the knower, known and knowledge stand in an indistinguishable unity. This knowledge can be described as integral experience through and through *aparokṣa* in nature, without a trace of mediation in it. This knowledge is neither descriptive in nature nor it is conceptual in nature. It is the vision of the unity of all existence. This vision of the unity of all existence is called *Anubhava* or *Anubhūti*, So there is ultimately only one way of knowing and that is way of intuition, the expression of this knowledge in form of words is found in the *Upaniṣads* or *śrutis*. The *Upaniṣadic vākyas* in spite of their seeming conflict are uniformly and exceptionlessly oriented to the expression of one reality that is Brahman, e.g. *sarvam Khalu idam Brahma, Tattvamasi, Neti Neti,* etc. *Śruti* is the self-relevation of reality in form of words.

There is another possible source of knowledge also, i.e., reasoning or thought. Thought contemplates and reveals only that which is perceivable actually or possibly. Brahman being not perceivable either actually or possibly cannot be the object of thought-knowledge. No amount of thinking or reasoning can give us the knowledge of Brahman. Thought can know only the sensible, whereas Brahman is supersensible. So *prima facie*, Brahman cannot be the object of thought-knowledge. This is why in the second chapter of *Brahmasūtra Bhāṣya* Śaṅkara tells us that reasoning is '*apratiṣthita*'. It has been described as purely speculative in character (*utprekṣāmātra*). We have seen in the foregoing pages that there are two forms which reasoning can take:

(i) syllogistic, where there is smoke there is fire; there is smoke on the hill; therefore there is fire on the hill, and

(ii) analogical reasoning, e.g. we may say, just as there could be no pots without potter, we could say that this world must have for its cause an intelligent principle, an over all cosmic intelligence. The question is — is the application of reasoning to the sphere of the supersensible valid or not? Śaṅkara and the Advaita philosophers would say — reasoning left to itself could never establish the existence of Brahman. The Brahman being supersensible could not be established by reasoning. At best it could only be indicated as a probable existence in terms of which we might be able to account for the coming into being of the world. Analogical reasoning could at best remain merely probable. And someone could immediately object — well, have you seen Brahman? Have you knowledge of Brahman? If not, then what your reasoning points at is unverifiable and could at best be only probable and at worst merely fantastic and imaginary. It is true that every event has a cause in the phenomenal sense, but to extend the causal argument from the phenomenal realm to the transphenomenal realm looks like an unwarranted practice. It is a sort of philosophical smuggling which could be termed as transcendental illusion by Kant and *Adhyāsa* by Śaṅkara. The Brahman is translogical. Therefore Brahman is no object of thought-knowledge. The point at issue is — left to itself reasoning could not establish the existence of Brahman. But then Śaṅkara would say that aided by revelation the findings of reasoning could get a confirmation from the scripture. The Brahman being supersensible does not fall within the field of reasoning. Ordinary *pramāṇas* like *pratyakṣa*, *anumāna, arthāpatti*, *anupalabdhi,* could not establish the existence of Brahman. A super-*prāmāṇa* alone is needed to assure us of the reality of Brahman, This super-*prāmāṇa* is revelation or *Śruti*. So the existence and nature of Brahman can only be established by *Śruti* or revelation. The *Śruti* is more authoritative than *tarka* or reasoning because the *Śruti* is the direct expression in words of the vision of Brahman. It describes something immediately experienced. It seems to address us in this form — "If you had a knowledge of ultimate reality or Brahman, you would realize it as the unity of all existence, as the being of all beings, as the inner core of your own existence, as not this, not this – meaning the world of phenomenality, which is known to empirical consciousness and the *adhiṣthāna* of all the *bhūtas*". The *Śruti* is addressing a person like you and me in a purely impersonal style. It means that if there were a person to have a vision of ultimate reality (Brahman); he would know as such and such.

The question whether *Śruti* or revelation gives us a knowledge of Brahman or whether thought gives us a knowledge of Brahman is put in such a manner as denigrates the import of knowledge itself. In my opinion an authentic description or a probable reasoning do not constitute knowledge. To know Brahman means to experience Brahman, i.e. it means to become Brahman itself. The *Śruti* is helpful only in this that it prevents us from wandering aimlessly in the realm of mere *utprekṣā*. The knowledge of Brahman is not merely an information about something that we ultimately are. The knowledge of Brahman is an insight into our being. That is why it has been said that three things are necessary for the manifestation of the insight (i) *Śravaṇa* (hearing of the Vedāntic texts, (ii) *Manana* (thinking about the pros and cons of what they intend and (iii) *Nididdhyāsana* (meditating about what the final upshot of *Śravaṇa* and *manana* is). What is of central importance is this insight or integral experience (*anubhava* or *anubhūti*). Neither reasoning nor scripture gives us this *anubhūti.* Reasoning through becoming critical of its own deliverances testifies to the authentic character of our yearning for that which is beyond criticism. Scripture gives us an authentic description of the being beyond logic and reasoning. Both reasoning and scripture are simply exhortations to launch upon the spiritual journey. He alone will reach the destination who boards the train, not one who merely moves in the realm of one's thinking only or one who merely turns out the pages of the scripture (Time Table). The taste of a dish consists in eating it. So both scripture and reasoning have to be transcended in the knowledge of Brahman. No one can give us this knowledge. We have to have it for ourselves. Both scripture and reasoning will be helpful in rousing in me the vision of reality *par excellence.*

The most pertinent question in the present context is to ascertain whether Śaṅkara is a mystic or a theologian or a philosopher. Those who say that Śaṅkara is a mystic only are supposed to argue that he is not a philosopher because he condemns reasoning and is also critical of scripture. All that he is keen on is the intuitive experience of Brahman. Those who maintain that he is a theologian only extol Śaṅkara's orientation to *Śruti* to such an extent as to throw integral experience and reasoning into the back gear. Those who maintain that Śaṅkara is a philosopher consider his mysticism and theology as an eyewash. We have to be first very clear in our mind in respect of the connotation of the term mysticism, theology and philosophy and then examine their antagonistic or complementary character. I have the feeling that Śaṅkara and following him his disciples, should be primarily describable as mystics, but whose mysticism is authentically describable in the language of the scripture and is arguable at the level of reason. There is, I believe, in the philosophy of Śaṅkara a clear dovetailing of mysticism, theology and philosophy. Philosophy and theology complementing each other constitute in Śaṅkara's outlook the pathway to reality, which when known could be understood as knowable in mystic intuition. The only thing in this connection to be noted is that his intuition is not irrational and that his theological moorings are not dogmatic. His mysticism is not irrational because its *pros* and *cons* are arguable. It is a vision lighted up in reflective awareness. His mysticism has theological moorings in so far as the scripture in which it finds linguistic expression is the only authentic description of it. But both scripture and reasoning stand transcended in the intuition. He who knows Brahman need not reason or cite *Śruti* but he who does not know Brahman must seek acquaintance with Brahman through reasoning and *Śruti*. Reasoning has both a positive and a negative role to perform. It has to correct the *Śruti* aright by resolving the seeming conflict among the *Śrutis.* It has also to correct wrong reasoning. Besides it has to demonstrate the absurdity of the speculative systems of thought. But one great homage that Śaṅkara pays to reason is to declare non-contradiction as the criterion of reality. It goes to his credit to show that intuitive knowledge is the most adequate fulfilment of this criterion and that when the scriptures are rightly interpreted they indicate a *vastu* which is not likely to be contradicted by anything whatsoever. The *ekavākyatā* of the *Śrutis,* the unitive character of integral experience are the same as non-contradiction in knowledge and existence.

I do not doubt that Śaṅkara is a philosopher of the highest possible order, but his philosophy is ancillary to his mystical doctrine of the *Upaniṣads* — the reality of Brahman, the unity or identity of *jīva* with Brahman, and the religious fervour to envisage this unity of *jīva* and Brahman as an ideal, which has to be attained by ways and means adequate to it. If the philosopher means one who makes use of reasoning, Śaṅkara is a philosopher who has made use of reasoning. But the reasoning in question does not independently reach the truth advocated by him. He has the truth given to him or received as an intuition or vision. The truth is that Brahman alone is real. This means that the world is not of the status of Brahman, and the empirical individuals also should be having only sham individuality. How is one to fit the world and the individual into the scheme of Advaitic metaphysics of the only Brahman ? This is evidently done by reasoning. But the reasoning is merely a justification of what was given in the form of an original intuition, whose validity can neither be challenged nor tested by any reasoning. Reasoning has to accept this intuitive content as the criterion-concept. True and false refer simply to the coherence and consistency with which the intuitive content or the criterion-concept (Brahman) has been discursivized and worked out on the plane of reasoning, Śaṅkara has received the criterio-plasm from the *Śrutis* or the *Upaniṣads*. So the source of the knowledge of this criterio-plasm is revelation; the mode of its reception is intuition; only its explication is a logical process or a process of reasoning. If in order to be a philosopher one has to establish truth or discover truth through reasoning independently of any other source of knowledge, Śaṅkara is not a philosopher. But this conclusion does not look very much of a welcome order within the framework of revelation, he is philosophizing. Again if philosophy is considered merely as a critical undertaking, engaged in an examination of the pre-suppositions of all philosophies or some philosophies, Śaṅkara is not a philosopher. He does not engage himself in dialectic all for the sake of satisfaction of a theoretic, interest or curiosity. His main aim is to reiterate the doctrine of reality as Brahman or pure consciousness and to indicate that this is not merely a metaphysical doctrine. It envisages an ideal – an ideal existence, which has to be lived and practised.

While concluding our discussion I would like to make a very brief reference to revealed knowledge in Semitic traditions of revelation in order to throw some more light on the subject. Revealed knowledge there is a message which is received by a messenger and is transmitted by God. So three factors involved in revelation have made it a private message which differs from messenger to messenger. But such is not the case with Vedic revelation, which does not require three factors. Here the experiencer and the experience are the only two factors that are relevant. The Advaitic tradition, however, counts them as one and indivisible fact. Therefore it has more significantly highlighted revelation and invented a profound method of its verification. All those who have received revealed knowledge proclaim that it concerns the disclosure of the supreme reality which is one and without a second. They are sages, not messengers and their experiences are heard voices and not written scriptures, public and not private.

11

Logical Positivism and the Advaitic Metaphysics

S. Mishra

Kant made a distinction between transcendental knowledge and transcendent reality. Transcendental knowledge is the knowledge of the *a priori* conditions of knowledge. But the knowledge born of these conditions of knowledge (i.e. pure forms of understanding and pure forms of intuitions) is applicable and valid only in respect of the phenomenal world. Transcendental knowledge therefore according to Kant is nothing but the critical awareness of human reason of its application, validity and limits. This self-consciousness of reason provides the philosophical justification for the foundations of scientific knowledge on the one hand and on the other hand it makes the transcendent reality secure against the onslaughts of skeptical understanding. By restricting knowledge to the realm of the empirical and phenomenal, Kant denied the possibility of metaphysical knowledge without denying the value of metaphysics and reality of the transcendent entitles.[1]

However, Kant's caution in regard to the application of the pure concepts of understanding to the noumenal was completely disregarded by Hegel who equated the real with the rational and believed that the laws of logic were also the laws of the spirit. Thus arose an imposing superstructure of metaphysical knowledge in the Hegelian philosophy. The subjective and interpretative categories of Kant became objective and constitutive categories. The given manifold was conceived as an 'other' of the mind created by the mind itself.

Kant had silenced reason so that he could make room for faith regarding the noumenal realities. He had to silence reason and limit all theoretical knowledge to the realm of the phenomenal because no valid knowledge was possible in the absence of the manifold given through intuition. All efforts of reason to produce science of the noumenal realities are productive of transcendental illusion because such a science is based on pure concepts to which no corresponding intuitions are available. The logical positivists caught hold of this idea and converted it into the essential condition of the possibility of a meaningful discourse. Knowledge means any communication in the form of subject-predicate statement. Subject-predicate statements are meaningful only if either (a) the predicate states what is already unexplicitly stated in the subject itself. These are analytical statement which are tautological in character. Or, (b) the predicate says something about the subject which can be empirically verified. These are the statements of natural sciences. Metaphysical statements come under neither of these categories and so they are meaningless or nonsensical. Metaphysical knowledge only appears to be knowledge; it is not genuine knowledge. Thus the Kantian condition of the possibility of genuine scientific knowledge was converted by the logical positivists into an instrument of the refutation of all metaphysics much against the intentions of Kant. Kant, it must be noted, had rejected dogmatic metaphysics so that genuine metaphysics could be made secure.

II

Logical positivists' rejection of metaphysics has its reason in their motive of philosophizing. The motive, in its simplest form, is clarification of language. Philosopher is primarily a logician whose only function is to determine the precise meaning of words so that meaningless words could be eliminated from any meaningful discourse. Natural sciences are the realm of meaningful discourse and thc function of philosophy is to place at their disposal a list of words which is meaningful and unambiguous.

Philosophy is thus a mere caretaker of science. All utterances of meaningful form according to the logical positivists are public utterances. The private, the subjective and symbolic gestures fall outside the field of meaningful discourse as the principle of verification is inapplicable to them. The logical positivist is a mere 'logician' having no concern with the bigger, intimate and personal questions of life.

In opposition to Hegel as well as to positivism, phenomenlogical-existentialism believes that the public world of the natural sciences is far removed from reality because the status of the truth of the public and the natural is unexamined and unfounded. It needs examination and foundation. But before it can be examined and founded, the natural attitude must be rejected. A typical example of the naturalism is to be found in the empirical tradition from Locke to Russell that human consciousness is a 'container' of the already present sense-data. The function of philosophy, as phenomenology perceives, is to rid the mind of such gratuitous assumptions and discover through the methods of epoch and transcendental reductions the "originary and foundational" ego who is responsible for the structure of the world of our perception. Heideggar's exasperation against the natural, the scientific and the public is most forcefully expressed in his question "why are there things rather nothing?" We are so immersed in the things that we have forgotten to raise question about Being. Forgottenness of Being, according to Heideggar, is the mark of insensitive philosophical consciousness.

The logical, the explicit, the definite, therefore, is not

the primary truth; it is perceived as truth under the spell of the natural attitude or in a philosophically insensitive attitude. A similar thing was said by Śaṅkarācārya several hundred years ago. In the *adhyāsabhāṣya* he declares that all our life and conduct are characterized by ignorance.[2] *Pramāṇa-prameya vyavahāra* is the commonly accepted mode of life and thought and this is what Husserl possibly meant by the natural attitude. The consciousness glued to the conditions of *pramāṇa-prameya vyavahāra*, maintains Śaṅkarācārya, is unphilosophical and uncritical because such a consciousness lacks self-awareness.

III

Consciousness, only when it becomes reflective and critical, is capable of raising genuine philosophical problems. Only then it raises the questions of freedom, of value and of beauty; only then it raises the questions of ultimate reality and truth, of human choices and decisions, of human failures, despairs and disappointments, human bondage and liberation.

Logical positivism and its versions of analysis and language philosophy shut off these questions from the inquiring philosophical consciousness and deal only with what is commonplace and superficial. Logical positivism, therefore, cannot be an alternative to metaphysics in general and Indian and Advaitic metaphysics in particular because (i) its refutation of metaphysics does not and cannot apply to the Advaitic metaphysics and (ii) unconcerned as it is with the larger and real problems of life, it cannot serve as a basis of values and culture which the Advaitic metaphysics can.

Cognition for the logical positivists, as already pointed out, is meaningful only if it knows an object in such a manner that the knowledge of the object meant by it can be actually or possibly verified in sense-experience. This verification formula insists on the empirical presentation of the meant object. The Advaitic conception of knowledge is very comprehensive and also different from the positivistic one. Knowledge, according to the Advaitic, is neither necessarily knowledge of something given in sense experiences (a condition insisted on by the positivists) nor is it an awareness of something literally meant (a condition insisted on by Kant). Ultimately it is the *Ātman* that is to be known and the knowledge of the *Ātman* is the highest and the foundational knowledge because after having known the *Ātman* nothing else remains to be known and it is because of the knowledge of the *Ātman* that everything else becomes known.[3] The *Ātman* is not an object and therefore its knowledge transcends the limit of the verification principle which insists that knowledge can be verified only if its object can be presented before the scrutiny of verification principle like a natural object or event happening or supposed to have happened in space and time. The *Ātman* can never be known as an object yet it can never be said that the *Ātman* is unknowable.

Śaṅakarācārya authoritatively established the knowability of the *Ātman* in his analysis of illusion and error and also at several places. It is in the unreflective attitude that "everything, including the subject, is sought to be known as an object. In the reflective attitude there is necessarily the consciousness of reality other than the one that is objective".[4] This reality is none other than the *Ātman* which is the undeniable implicate of all experience in the reflective consciousness. When we come across the unreality of the objective and the other to consciousness, we are referred back to the reality of the *Ātman* as a being which is known as the only reality and knowledge *par excellence*. Here is a unique definition of knowledge. Knowledge in the objective attitude is subject to verification but the objective attitude is the breeding place for illusory knowledge because it is here that 'I' and 'thou' which are mutually opposed to each other are identified with each other. Genuine knowledge demands the suspension or transcendence of the objective attitude. On the reflective or critical plane, then, knowledge has to be "understood as an unmeant and unmeanable content". The unmeanability for a content means its unpresentability in experience; however it does not mean its unknowability in any manner whatsoever.[5]

It is in the light of this conception of knowledge that: the *Upaniṣadic mahāvākyas* have meaning. *Mahāvākyas* like '*tattvamasi'* are neither empirical propositions nor are they mathematical propositions. But they are meaningful propositions for a man seeking knowledge and freedom. Such statements are not to be understood as statements of ordinary experience or logic in which a content is presented as another to the knowing consciousness. What these statements indicate is beyond the spatio-temporal limit and also beyond the representational frame of knowledge-situation. They do not state a knowledge-situation which can be subjected to verification in sensuous experience. They are also not verbal or tautologous statements. The significance of these statements is "gestural".[6] The contents of these propositions "mark on an advancement in knowledge". They are illuminations in which ignorance and error are sublated and the fullness of immediate experience is realized as having been already possessed. That the phenomenon of linguistic expression means much more than the written and spoken words of expression has been very lucidly and forcefully pointed out by Husserl, Heidegger, Sartre and Merleau-Ponty in the twentieth century. Logical analysis "algebrizes" the meaning of words. It takes words as simple and atomic whose meanings can be exhaustively and adequately defined by use as "p's" "q's" in an algebrized syllogism. But words are world-phenomena. Man's being is the primary fact Knowledge comes after being and expression follows knowledge.[7]

IV

The sumum bonum of the Advaitic metaphysics is freedom—the spiritual freedom of man. The essence of this freedom consists in the inner realization of the unity of all beings and utter negation of all egoity. There are freedom of other sorts also, e.g., freedom of speech, freedom of association, freedom of worship and freedom from want, etc. These freedoms provide partial satisfaction to man but they are also likely to be abused. In order to attain freedom from want, the stronger men and nations have not only exploited weaker men and nations, they have exploited the nature around us and have thus created acute problems of environmental imbalance. The secular notion of freedom, therefore, unless grounded in spiritual freedom can lead to disastrous consequences and can create hatred between man and man, between nation and nation. Science, at whose service positivism pledges philosophy to place, has done a lot to make human life comfortable. But the questions remain to be asked: has it made human life happy? Has it been able to eliminate the possibility of war? Has it been able to provide a stable and sound foundation for values and a world-culture? It needs no proof to say that the answer to these questions is negative. No doubt the discoveries of science and the resultant technologies have reduced the distances of the physical world but the distances in the human world have increased. Man, particularly the western man, whose mind is caught in the positivistic frame has attained near mastery over nature but has no control over himself. His ability to control situations involving physical forces is matched by his corresponding inability to control situations involving human elements. Thus "we have gained the world but have lost our soul".[8] The material culture supported by positivism cannot get us out of the predicament. Material affluence by itself cannot result in the good of humanity because the basic principle underlying it is vicious. If material good of earthly life were the only good, then one would try to secure them as much as possible and by any means, fair or foul. The tendency to possess more and more cannot be eliminated though it can be kept under control by social and moral rules. The tendency can be conquered only by realizing the ultimate falsity of the earthly and transcending the standpoint of ego.[9] This is possible in the absolutism of the Advaitic metaphysics. It is the dualistic attitude which gives rise to difference and antagonisms; in non-dualistic attitude one sees the essential unity of all mankind. In the non-dualistic consciousness all the differences of ideologies and religions are annulled. On this point we have the authority of the Lord himself who declares that people ultimately attain me no matter what is the path they follow.[10] This metaphysical knowledge may be mysterious, unclear and inarticulate but in it lies a hope for a happy, harmonious and peaceful world. This knowiedge is not easy to attain. One may have to wait for one's whole life for this realization. But there is glory and hope even in this waiting. In an age of instant culture we have become impatient to wait. But it is better to wait in order to realize the fuller and deeper meaning of our being rather than let our lives be pushed along in a thoughtless, unreflective and medicore manner.

What we have said above is not because of an unquestioning reverence to the Vedic tradition. Impassionate and sensitive reflection on the nature of philosophy has led many thinkers to a similar conclusion. Heidegger for instance, who has no burden of tradition on his mind, conceives philosophy as an analysis of man's spiritual life which is marked by mystery and ambiguity. This makes the task of philosophy difficult and untimely in "an age which regards real as only what goes fast and can be clutched with both hands, which looks on questioning as remote from reality and as something that does not pay, whose benefits cannot be numbered". But he further remarks, "the essential is not number; the essential is the right time, i.e. the right moment, the right perserverence". And, finally he sumps up the essence of philosophical inquiry in the words of the poet Holderlin: "The mindful God abhors untimely growth".[11]

The *Upaniṣadic* wisdom contained in the parables of Naciketa and Yama, Indra, Virocana and Prajāpati, Maitreyi, Kātyāyinī and Yajnavalkya has underscored the same essence of waiting and preference of the ultimate over the instant.

Notes and References

1. Kant, *Critique of Pure Reason* (trans. N.K. Smith), London: Mac Millari & Co. Ltd., 1958, BXXV.
2. *—adhyāsam puraṣkṛtya sarve pramāṇprameyavyavahāra laukikā vaidikāśca pravṛttāh, Brahmasūtra*, *Śaṅkarabhāṣya* 1.1
3. "*Yaj jñātvā ne'ha bhūyo'nyaj jñātavyam avaśiṣyate", Bhagavad Gītā,* VII.2.
4. S.S. Roy, *The Heritage of Śaṅkara,* Allahabad: Udayan Publications, 1965, p. 171.
5. K.C. Bhattacarya, "The Concept of Philosophy" in the *Studies in Philosophy*, Calcutta: Progressive Publications, 1958, Vol. II, pp. 101 ff., also see, *The Heritage of Śaṅkara*, p. 179.
6. *The Heritage of Śaṅkara,* p. 181.
7. Thevenaz, *What is Phenomenology?* Chicago: Quadrangle Books, inc. 1962, p. 33.
8. T.R.V., Murti, *The Central Philosophy of Buddhism,* London: George Allen and Union Ltd., 1960, p. 338.
9. *Ibid.*, p. 339.
10. *Bhagavad Gītā,* 4.11.

Martin Heidegger, *An Introduction to Metaphysics* (trans. Ralph Manheim), New York: Doubledy & Co., 1959, p. 172.

12

Two Competing Interpretations of Śaṅkara : G. Misra and G.C. Nayak

Kalyan Kumar Bagchi

The late Prof. G. Misra gave an innovative interpretation of Śaṅkara's philosophy when he maintained that it is linguistic analysis in that it proposes a clarification of our ways of understanding the world of experience by introducing the concepts that it does introduce. For example, the concept of *adhyāsa* points to conceptual confusion in our experience which can be resolved by introducing the concept of Brahman. When the confusion is cleared, illumination takes place.

Prof. G. Misra's interpretation is questioned by Prof. G.C. Nayak. Nayak's plank of interpretation is the Vedānta idea of *Brahmānubhava*, Radhakrishnan translates *Brahmānubhava* as intuition. And Nayak seeks to derive the strength of his interpretation from Śaṅkara's statement regarding the relation of the analysis of Vedānta statements to the realization of Brahman. '*Vākyārtha Vicāraṇādhyvasānanivṛttā hi Brahmāvagatiḥ nānumānādi pramāṇātara nirvṛttā*'.[1]

Now, it must be admitted that any philosophy amounts to a critical review of our ways of understanding the world in which we move, to which we reach, within which we make appraisal of judgements and/or our conduct and so on. Such critical review may leave the world unaffected or may amount to a revision of our ways of thinking and talking about the world. So, critical review amounts either to a conceptual ordering or to a conceptual reordering of the world to which we are accustomed (in our thinking, responding, assessing or whatever).

Given this idea of philosophy as critical review of our thought or knowledge or talk of the world, we may no doubt say that in so far as Advaita Vedānta is a philosophical system, its fundamental concept, viz., the concept of Brahman is introduced by the philosopher, Śaṅkara to order our knowledge in a way that is different from, say a Vaiśeṣika or a Sāṁkhya way or an empiricist way or a realistic way or in any other way of looking the world. Advaita Vedānta, in other words, is a philosophical or conceptual reordering of our knowledge or thought reordering in this that it revises our ordinary, i.e. common sense and/or realistic way of thinking in relation to the world. In Strawson's idiom it is a kind of 'revisionary' metaphysics. But the point is whether it is a revisionary or 'descriptive' metaphysics— in Strawson's idiom again, it is a conceptual enterprise. And, from this point of view, man attains illumination not through *Brahmānubhava* or intuition but through correcting one's confusion, viz., the confusion that one labours under when one judges—rather misjudges—that the world as it appears is real. Illusion is wrong judgement and the clearing up of illusion is correcting the wrong judgement by the judgement that the world is Brahman. From this point of view, those who maintain that illumination is intuition of Brahman, take philosophy to consist in *anubhava* or vision, in *darśana* which, for them, is more than ratiocination.

Actually, the issue between Misra's interpretation and Nayak's interpretation of Śaṅkara's Advaita Vedānta boils down to the difference between philosophy and intuition, ratiocination and vision, analysis and *darśana*.

I think, however, that the foregoing alternatives are not exclusive or disjunctive, we may understand the issue not as that of conceptual analysis or ratiocination or logic or intellectual clarification and experience of Brahman but as that of a kind of analysis in which, with the progressive enrichment of one's conceptual baggage, one's initial knowledge of Brahman comes to be deepened. Advaita Vedānta, thus considered, is neither merely conceptual analysis nor merely a vision but a *phenomenology* of one's experience of Brahman.

What lends credence to such an interpretation is a rethinking that is needed of our illusion of the world-experience and the correction of it. Neither illusion nor correction should be understood as conceptual in nature. That is to say, illusion should not be taken as merely conceptual confusion and correction should not be taken as clarification of conceptual confusion.

For what, afterall, is an illusion? Illusion is not intellectual error. When the illusion is corrected, there still remains a wonder how what is not real was seen. The wonder remains as a fringe of the right knowledge of what is real. So there is a complete gap between the experience of illusion and the knowledge of what is real.

It is on this gap between our ordinary experience and the experience of Brahman that Śaṅkara builds his philosophy. One who experiences Brahman undergoes thereby a complete shift in one's outlook on the world. And it is only then, i.e. when one undergoes such shift that one reorganizes one's understanding in terms of the concept of Brahman in contrast to realistic (other kinds of) categories of interpretation. The concepts of Brahman, *adhyāsa,* etc., not only emerge out of Brahman-experience but also suggest a revision of our hitherto accepted realistic categories of interpretation. So the Advaita Philosophy of Śaṅkara is neither linguistic clarification nor a *darśana* or intuitive experience. It is, to use Prof. K.C. Bhattacharya's observation in a different context, self-evident elaboration of self-evident. There is, of course, a

and/or intellectual clarification most definitely is-but also-and this is of capital importance an existential shift in consciousness from its world-centric mentality to itself, to self, to itself as the subject: in such shift the world out there, the object *per se* lapses altogether. Remember: in the context of Śaṅkara's Advaita Vedānta illusion is wrong seeing and the dawn of Brahman—Consciousness is correcting the wrong seeing, no more linguistic or conceptual reordering of our experience in terms of the concept of Brahman. The concept is oriented to the realization of Brahman as the fact for the sake of *mukti* or liberation.

In the light of the foregoing understanding of the concept of Brahman *vis-à-vis* realization, it has to be said that Prof. Misra's interpretation of Śaṅkara's system despite of its impressive novelty does not do justice to Śaṅkara's phenomenology of Advaita concept/concepts. But then neither does Nayak's all too-intuitive interpretation of Śaṅkara's Vedānta do justice to the insight or existential shift that the seeker of *Brahmavidyā* undergoes through philosophy as the existential analytic of concepts.What is needed today in the way of situating Śaṅkara's Vedānta in the present day context, is to understand it may be indifferently as a hermeneutic of concepts or a hermeneutic of existence for which linguistic clarification or enrichment of (one's) conceptual baggage boils down to uncovering layers of (the) Consciousness (of Brahman).

I think it will be in order if, before closing, I make some general observation regarding the relationship between the introduction of a concept—which may be the ruling concept of a philosophical system and the generation of one's insight or deepening of one's perception. Actually concept introduction and insight generation are not two temporally different processes. The relation between the two may be understood in the light of the late Prof. K.C. Bhattacharya's observation viz., "Philosophy is the self-evident elaboration of the self-evident".

Notes and References

1. I have drawn upon Prof. G. Misra's book : *The Advaita Conception of Philosophy* and Prof. G.C. Nayak's, book : *Philosophical Reflections* in writing this paper.
2. Prof. K.C. Bhattacharya's statements referred to in this paper occur in his paper, "The Concept of Philosophy".

13

Śaṅkara and Vākyārthavicāraṇa : A Study of Prof. G.C. Nayak's Understanding of Advaita

S. Panneerselvam

Prof. G.C. Nayak's interesting paper, "Illumination Through Analysis: A Study in Vedāntic Conception *vis-à-vis* the Mādhyamika"[1] deals with an important issue regarding the role of analysis in Advaita. Generally scholars argue that Advaitins who are interested in liberation of the individual are concerned with the intuitive experience of Brahman. This means that illumination is possible though *Brahmānubhāva.* But Nayak talks about illumination though analysis. This analysis is made on the basis of the understanding of the nature of Brahman and not by inference, or by any other means.[2] Different means of knowledge though are important, they cannot help us in the realization of Brahman and hence Śaṅkara shows the limitations of the *pramāṇas.* Perception and other means of knowledge cannot give us the immediate knowledge of the Self. It is because the scope of such means of knowledge is limited to empirical knowledge. The nature of the Self as identical with Brahman can be known only through the *śruti* texts and not through inference or any other *pramāṇas.* The knowledge of Brahman is something which cannot be reduced to empirical knowledge. The immediate knowledge according to the Advaitins is conveyed by the *Vedānta-āgama-vākyas.* The Vedāntic texts, which are sentences by themselves, are valid on their own.

Nayak argues how the *vākyārthavicāraṇa* or analysis of the meaning of statements plays an important role in the methodology of Śaṅkara. Thus analysis of meaning is not something alien to Śaṅkara. But the analysis, which he speaks of, is different from that of the ordinary one because for Śaṅkara mere analysis of statement is not important for the realization of Brahman. It means only the analysis of statement dealing with the *mahāvākyas* will lead us to Brahman. It is because of the main reason that ordinary sentences are secular and hence cannot help us in any way in the attainment of liberation. Ultimately, it is the understanding of the *mahāvākyas,* which gives us enlightenment, "...it is not merely the understanding of the explicit meaning of any sentence that gives enlightenment", says Nayak.[3] Without understanding the meaning of the Vedāntic statements one cannot realize the ultimate unity between the Ātman and Brahman; it is only through these statements that one can gain access to Brahman. "The Knowledge of being eternally free comes from Vedāntic statements, not from anything else," says Śaṅkara.[4] Vedāntic statements, which occupy a different realm and status, will lead to enlightenment. This means the texts, which deal with identity alone help us in realization. Freedom or illumination here means freeing oneself from the bondage and once this is attained realization is possible. Freedom from bondage is possible by the knowledge of the *mahāvākyas.* Śaṅkara shows an analogy between the *mahāvākya, tattvamasi,* and statements like "The horse is dark" where there is a mutual restriction existing between each of the terms, "horse" excluding everything that is non-horse from the sense of the word "dark", and the word "dark" excluding everything that is non-black from the sense of the word "horse".[5] The word *tvam* by being brought into conjunction with the word *tat,* which expresses the sense of being free from suffering *(nirduḥkha),* has the sense of being the sufferer *(duḥkhin)* excluded from it, and similarly the word *tat* by coming into conjunction with the expressed sense of the word *tvam,* which is the inward self in its immediateness, has the sense of what is not the inward self or non-immediacy excluded from it. Śaṅkara does not consider the statements such as *tat tvam asi* and *neti neti* as operating on different levels, because according to him both are taken to explain the fact that for the understanding of Brahman one has to negate what Brahman is not.[6]

The Vedāntic texts like, *tat tvam asi,* convey the knowledge which is direct, immediate and non-relational. In interpreting the *mahāvākya* like, *tat tvam asi,* we must take into account the following: (1) the grammar of words, (2) the semantics of words and, (3) the logic of the relation of the implication and the implied in construing the sentential import of the text, *tat tvam asi.* The grammatical coordination between the two words *tat* and *tvam*, convey the meaning which are not synonymous. The word *tat* means Brahman, which is infinite and non-dual. Similarly the word *tvam* refers to the individual self. When we consider the mutual qualification of the two terms, i.e., the qualification of the meaning of *tat* by *tvam* and the qualification of the meaning of *tvam* by *tat* we find that a simple and direct identification of the same with the other outwardly conveyed by the sentence is not possible.[7] Since the two terms are mutually incompatible, it is incorrect to identify the terms, *tat* and *tvam.* To avoid this problem, we depend on the implied meaning or *lakṣyārtha* of the sentence. By removing the determinants of each term, which are incompatible with those of the other term, and by retaining the common element, it is explained that the text, *tat tvam asi* conveys the sense of identity. This means that ultimately it is *śruti,* which conveys the direct and immediate knowledge of Brahman-Ātman, and the knowledge is non-sentential and non-relational. The purport of the Vedānta texts is ascertained by the application of six marks *(ṣaḍliṅga)*.[8] (1) the harmony of the initial and concluding passages *(upakrama-upasaṁhāra)*, (2) repetition *(abhyāsa)*, (3) novelty *(apūrvatā)*, (4) fruitfulness *(phala)*, (5) glorification by eulogistic passages or condemnation by deprecatory passages *(arthavāda)* and (6) intelligibility in the light of reasoning *(upapatti)*. Since the purport of the text is based on the above marks, they are different from that of the ordinary sentences.

The analysis of meaning of the *mahāvākyas* removes ignorance. "When we get rid of the multiple forms created by *avidyā* or ignorance through an analysis of the meaning of the *mahāvākyas* like *tattvamasi*, we realize the Advaita or non-duality, the unity of all existence", says Nayak.[9] Here Nayak analyses the approach made by Ganeswar Misra who argues that for Śaṅkara, everything is linguistic analysis. *Adyāsa* or *avidyā* for Misra is nothing but linguistic confusion, and consequently, *Brahmajñāna* is reduced to nothing but a linguistic illumination through linguistic analysis. For Misra, even *avidyā* is a linguistic error. This made Nayak to argue that the position of Misra will lead to the fallacy of reductionism. I am in full agreement with Nayak.[10] Nayak's arguments to substantiate the point, namely that Misra's position will lead to the fallacy of reductionism, are extremely good. I have also two points to offer on this.

Firstly, it must be admitted that analysis is not something new to Indian tradition. It is also to be noted that the term "analysis" is used in Indian tradition in a broader perspective and special importance is given to reasoning and valid argumentation. It is often said that Indian philosophy is analytical on its own independent footing and in certain cases the analytical rigour presented by classical Indian thinkers seem more profound in nature. Śaṅkara in his interpretation of the *prasthānatraya* adopts the analytical method. The *prasthānatraya* is the source for Advaita, which rests on *śruti, smṛti,* and *tarka.* The *Upanisads* represent *śruti-prasthāna,* the *Brahmasūtra* represents *tarka-prasthāna* and the *Bhagavad Gītā* represents *smṛti-prasthāna.* The texts are connected with the commentaries or interpretation. The texts are expository and they are to be commented. The role of interpreter starts here. The commentaries are as important as the texts. In fact, the commentaries do much work than the texts, because sometimes the texts are not only brief, but also elliptical in nature. The interpreter, as a way of his commentary, explicitly analyses what the text says and interprets according to the need and the historical conditions. Thus it is not a mere interpretation but an interpretation mingled with historicity. It is inevitable for the interpreter or commentator to take into account of his historical conditions and other factors. Thus the text when it is written may have one goal or intention, but the commentator has to interpret the text taking into consideration various factors. Actually speaking these factors which play a dominant role in interpretation, are implicit in interpretation. The interpreter need not wait or search for the historicity to operate on him, while interpreting a text. It is automatic. It is because historicity simply operates on and the interpreter simply exists in it. The interpreter not only understands the texts, but also presents in a different way so that more people can have easy access to it. The text written by the author is not always elaborate and hence cannot pass the message to the reader; whereas the interpreter, who has a better understanding of the text, interprets and presents in a better way than that of the author. Thus the interpreter has a more important role to play than the author does. Here the author is transcended but not the text. In other words, the text becomes more meaningful in the hands of the interpreter. I feel that Misra considers that the writings of Śaṅkara as mere synthesis or combination of words and sentences which must be analysed to know the meaning. Śaṅkara's interpretation has a deep inner meaning, which cannot be neglected so easily. Linguistic understanding might have been important for Śaṅkara, but metaphysics has deeper and inner significance and hence everything in him cannot be merely reduced to linguistic analysis. It is also necessary, to discover the intention of the author. In the interpretation of the text, the intention of the author plays an important role. Śaṅkara while interpreting the texts, definitely had an intention, which cannot be neglected so easily.

Secondly, it is through proper understanding and interpretation of the *mahāvākyas* that one can know the nature of Brahman. All understanding is interpretation. Understanding includes always an element of application. Understanding, interpretation and application is a triunity. Ultimately, understanding and interpretation are the same. This is what is implied in the hermeneutical understanding of Advaita. The identity of Brahman with the individual self can be known if one knows the correct understanding of the *mahāvākyas.* Śaṅkara's way of doing philosophy emerges out of a definite presupposition of Being or Brahman which may be taken to be either *a priori* or a matter of inner experiential truth, and from this presupposition, he deduces the nature and significance of human existence and the world. The interpreter makes use of *lakṣaṇā vṛtti* for interpreting the scripture. It is the intention of the sentence rather than the logical connection between words that is important.

Nayak examines the role of *śruti* to explain how the *mahāvākyas* help us in the realization of Brahman. He says that it could not be understood as the logical analysis of meaning and *śabda* as linguistic category. For Nayak, some passages of *śruti* are not conducive to illumination. *Śruti* cannot be mere logical analysis of meaning. He says: "...some of the passages which are regarded as *śabda* or *śruti* no less than others are regarded as either not being conducive to illumination or possessing only figurative or secondary significance".[11] Śaṅkara considers *śruti* or *śabda* as a *pramāṇa.* But some scholars like Misra are of the view that *āgama, śruti, śabda* and *śāstra* stand for logical analysis of the propositional symbolism.[12] He further says that *śabda* and *śruti* univocally signify language and linguistic forms and nothing else.[13] But for Śaṅkara, *śabda* as a means of valid knowledge has a two-fold capacity: it can communicate the facts of the sensible universe, and can also enlighten us on suprasensible truths because it is the only vehicle of suprasensuous knowledge. In the empirical usage, the testimony of a trustworthy person makes known truth; in the sphere of the suprasensuous, scripture is of use as the revelation of what is true. This means that verbal testimony can convey the knowledge of the sensible and also the suprasensible. In his commentary to the *Brahmasūtras,*[14] Śaṅkara says that the scripture is the only source of knowledge of the truths regarding the suprasensible. In all empirical matters the verbal testimony of a trustworthy person is valid, but the knowledge of Brahman cannot be known through the testimony of a person because Brahman is trans-empirical and hence the Advaitins hold the view that Brahman can be known only through *śruti* or verbal testimony. It is the only source of knowledge of the existent Brahman. Hence Misra's contention that *śabda* does not stand for authority but for critique of language cannot be acceptable.

Brahman is inaccessible to the senses and therefore has no connection with the *pramāṇas* dependent on them and *śruti* and *anubhava* are the means to *brahmavidyā.* The true purport of *śruti* is to show that Brahman as the eternal subject is never an object, and thereby to remove the distinction of objects known, knows and acts of knowledge which is fictitiously created by ignorance. The function of *śruti* is to bring out knowledge, which is inaccessible through other *pramāṇas. Bṛhadāraṇyakopaniṣadbhāṣya* says:

> It does not create anything. Nor can a scriptural statement impart any power to a thing, for it is an accepted principle that scriptures are only informative, not creative.[15]

Śaṅkara rejects the Mīmāṁsakas position according to which *śruti* is a body of injunctions and prohibitions. But for Śaṅkara by concentrating on the Vedāntic statements, Brahman can be realized. Nayak very well stresses this point. He probes into question of what sort of analysis would lead to *mokṣa.* He says:

> Certainly, one cannot say that illumination, according to Śaṅkara, would follow from an analysis by itself of the meaning of any referring expression of any identity statement *vis-à-vis* descriptive or prescriptive statements.[16]

This means that for Nayak it is not mere analysis that would lead to illumination. Illumination is possible only when statements are analysed in the context of *mahāvākyas.* Very rightly Nayak says:

> Even an analysis of secular statements like 'Thou art the tenth' or 'This is that Devadatta' can lead to illumination, provided they are considered alongside *tattvamasi,* etc. found in Vedāntic literature, which alone are regarded as *mahāvākyas.*[17]

Thus Nayak makes it clear that illumination is possible only when the secular sentences are discussed in relation to the *mahāvākyas.* Two things are emphasized by him. (1) When the Advaitins talk of analysis for illumination it is not the ordinary analysis and (2) the secular sentences are to be considered only in the context of the *mahāvākyas* because analysis of the *mahāvākyas* is essential for illumination.

An objection may be raised here. It may be argued that in the case of the *mahāvākyas,* while interpreting them, we are assigning some additional value to it by constructing an ontology, which they do not possess. For example, it may be argued that in the case of the *mahāvākyas,* we take the meaning of these words too further so as to show that they have some transcendental value. In other words, the empirical meanings that are found in the words like, *tat, tvam* and *asi* are replaced by some other meaning, which cannot fit in with our language structure. It may further be argued that we are trying to take the language out of its context, then assign some meaning, which is different from that of the ordinary one. We use language to refer to empirical things. A word denotes an object or a thing that has some physical existence in the empirical reality. But how are we to understand the word "Brahman"? What meaning should we assign to this word? It is neither an object nor a thing which can be pointed out by means of language. How can the ordinary sentences have as their object, Brahman, which is said to be eternal? Thus one can question the meaning that is assigned to the word "Brahman". But Śaṅkara answers this question by saying that the *Upaniṣads* do not indicate Brahman as the "this" or "that"—an object to be known by us. According to the *Upaniṣads,* Brahman is not an object *(aviṣaya),* because it is the inner self *(pratyagātmā).* Vācaspati says that if a man who knows words, meanings, and the principles of testimony, studies the *Upaniṣads,* then he knows Brahman as the Self, on account of the capacity of scriptural testimony to give such knowledge. If the principles of testimony and the meanings of the words are not known, then Brahman is not known even though *Upaniṣadic* sentences are studied. Śaṅkara in all his commentaries tries to drive home the point that Brahman can never be *described,* but can only be *shown* somehow approximately *(adūraviprakarṣeṇa).* At least two methods are suggested for this purpose—(1) the method of *adhyāropa* and *apavāda* and (2) the method of *lakṣaṇa.* In the commentary to the *Bhagavad Gītā,* Śaṅkara says : "Brahman is not said to be *sat* or *asat.*[18] Brahman cannot be described by the word "is" or by the word "is not", for, it is not the object of knowledge in the form of "is" or "is not". An object of knowledge is known through the means of knowledge and is defined as "such and such". But Brahman cannot be described by any word, not even by the word, *sat* for a word can denote a thing if that object is associated with a genus *(jāti)* or an act *(kriyā)* or a quality *(guṇa)* or relation *(sambandha)*.[19] For example, cow and horse imply genera, cook and teacher imply acts, white and black imply qualities, wealthy and cattle-owner imply possession. But Brahman belongs to no genus and cannot be denoted by such words as *sat*. Being devoid of attributes, it possesses no qualities. If it were possessed of qualities, then it could be denoted by a word, implying a quality. Being actionless, it cannot be indicated by a word implying an act. It is not related to anything else; for it is one. It is one without a second. It is no object (of any sense). It is the very Self. Therefore, it is but right to say that it cannot be denoted by any word at all.

In this context, it is important to discuss what modern scholars like Daya Krishna and others have to say on this. Daya Krishna asks the question whether *tat tvam asi* is the same type of identity statement as the Fregean statement, "The morning star is the evening star".[20] He is interested in knowing whether both are meaningful in the same way. "Both the statements share a common problematic as they point to two seemingly different entities which are regarded as totally different from each other and yet which are really identical in a fundamental sense that is not known to those who see them as different", says Daya Krishna.[21] He argues that the identity of the morning star and the evening star is realized in empirical experience whereas the identity of Ātman and Brahman is not something, which can be directly experienced and they need a special spiritual praxis for their existential realization in experience. There are some difficulties with regard to Daya Krishna's position especially when he says that identity of Brahman and Ātman is not something, which one cannot directly experience, but he is correct when he says that both the statements cannot be treated in the same way. One finds it difficult to accept Daya Krishna's argument that the identity of Ātman and Brahman cannot be directly experienced. The *anubhava* plays an important role in Śaṅkara. Some other scholars like Bokil argue that *tat tvam asi* is a metaphysical hypothesis. He claims that though this statement is grammatically correct it is misleading because Brahman is not an expression belonging to natural language. For him, Ātman is Brahman is a case of pseudo-identity. He asks the question whether there is identity at all between the empirical and transcendental selves. To substantiate this point, Bokil says that the demonstrative *tat* can refer only to a material object and as such no empirical self can be sensibly asked to identify itself with a material object.[22] Thus Bokil questioned the identity of Brahman and Ātman. But it should be noted that the principle of identity is the cornerstone of Advaita. Commenting on this Dravid very correctly says: "... to question the identity of the empirical and the transcendental self is to question the very fundamental basis of Advaita".[23] Further he says:

> ...the Fregean sentence, 'The morning star is the evening star' is intended to serve quite a different purpose than that of the *mahāvākyas.* Frege is concerned to show that if the sense and the reference of words are not distinguished from each other the sentence would be reduced to the tautology, 'The morning star is the morning star' or 'The evening star is the evening star'...In the *mahāvākya* on the other hand the situation is diametrical opposite of this.[24]

When the Advaitins talk of the interpretation of the *mahāvākyas,* they have a different message to convey. The identity statements cannot be understood in the same way as we understand the ordinary sentences. The ontological status of these statements is different The *mahāvākyas* come under the category of coordinate relation or *sāmānādhikaraṇya.* It speaks of the grammatical coordinate relation that exists between words. It is the application to one thing, of several words having the same case, for the application of each of which there is different reason.[25] In the *sāmānādhikaraṇya,* (1) the words used are in the same case, (2) they are not synonyms, (3) they refer to the one and the same entity and (4) there is a reason for the use of each word. The relation of *sāmānādhikaraṇya* is of two kinds, the *mukhya* and *bādhāyāṁ.* In the former, the objects denoted by the words of a sentence will have equal ontological status, will be identical in nature, and will not be really different from each other. For instance, when we say, "The pot-ether is but the great-ether" *(ghaṭākāśa mahākāśa eva)* the words, "pot-ether" *(ghaṭākāśa)* and "great ether" *(mahākāśa)* are in *mukhya sāmānādhikaraṇya.* The ether enclosed by the pot and the ether outside it has the same ontological status. Both are empirically real. Also both of them have the same nature and are not different from each other. If the words of a sentence, which have the same case-ending, denote objects which have different ontological status, and if they purport to convey only one idea, then they are in *bādhāyāṁ sāmānādhikaraṇya.* For example, in the sentence, "This post is a man" *(ayaṁ sthāṇuḥ puruṣaḥ)* the objects denoted by the words "post" *(sthāṇuḥ)* and "man" *(puruṣaḥ)* have different ontological status. Since what exists really is a man and not a post, "man" is empirically real, whereas "post" is apparently real. A person due to distance and other factors, first of all perceives a man as a post, but subsequently corrects the mistake when he knows that the object seen by him is not a post, but a man, and utters: "The post is a man". It is absurd to say on the basis of a superficial reading of the sentence that he identifies the post and the man. What he intends to convey by this sentence is that the object which he cognized as a post is, indeed, a man. Here, the subsequent cognition of the object as a man sublates the earlier cognition of it as a post; and it does not take place without canceling the earlier cognition, which is erroneous. The object referred to by the sentence is only one; and the sentence achieves its objective through the sublation of one cognition by another cognition. The *mahāvākya,* "I am Brahman" *(aham brahmāsmi),* can be interpreted in the same way in which the sentence "This post is a man" has been interpreted. When a person realizes that he is Brahman as a result of the hearing of the *śruti* text, the right cognition which he has attained sublated the wrong cognition he had earlier, i.e. cognition such as "I am a man" "I am blind" etc. It is incorrect to argue that the words *aham* and *brahmāsmi* because of their grammatical co-ordination are identical. The purport of the grammatical co-ordination here is not to convey the identity of "I" and Brahman, but to deny it.[26]

Nayak emphasizes the importance of *śruti* or verbal testimony. He explains how *śruti* is not a mere logical analysis of meaning. Advaita holds the view that Brahman can be known only though *śruti* or Vedic testimony. Verbal testimony which is of two kinds, namely that which is personal *(pauruṣeya)* and that which is impersonal *(apauruṣeya)* Brahman or Ātman which is the absolute reality is trans-empirical and can be known through *śruti* or Vedic testimony. This has been questioned by the Mīmāṁsakas. For them action is the import of all sentences including the scriptural sentences. The meaning of words are known only when they occur in injunctive sentences which have their import in action. The Vedic sentences are not exception to this. The Veda is a book of commandments according to the Mīmāṁsakas. It consists of injunctions and prohibitions *(vidhi-niṣeda).* They say that the assertive sentences in the Veda are significant only when they are construed in accordance with the injunctive texts. Hence the entire Veda has its purport only in action. The Absolute or Brahman is ever existent. It is not something, which is to be accomplished by action. Since the Vedic sentences have no significance in respect of the existent Brahman which is not related to action, the Mīmāṁsakas are of the view that Vedic sentences cannot give us the knowledge of Brahman. The above contention of the Mīmāṁsakas cannot be acceptable for the reason that it is incorrect to say that the purport of entire Vedic sentences is in action. For example, a text like, "Brahman is real, knowledge, and bliss" only explains the nature of the existent Brahman. Sentences of this kind are significant in and by themselves. Moreover, action cannot be import of all secular sentences. Some sentences give only information about something. For example, a person mistakes a rope for a snake, and is frightened. In order to remove his fear, we do not subject him to an injunction, "Don't be afraid", but we give him the information that the object in front is only a rope and not a snake. The import of the assertive sentence "This is a rope" is not in any action to be done. But the sentence is not without significance.[27]

The Mīmāṁsakas put forth another argument to say that *śruti* or Vedic testimony cannot explain the nature of Brahman. According to them, if Brahman is already known through any means of valid knowledge other than *śruti,* then *śruti* is only a restatement of it and hence has no validity. On the other hand, if Brahman is not known through any other means other than *śruti,* then *śruti* cannot explain the nature of Brahman for the main reason that words are significant and denote objects only when they occur in injunctive sentences that lead to action. Brahman is ever existent and cannot be accomplished by means of action; it cannot fall within the scope of *śruti*.[28] The argument is also not acceptable to the Advaitins because for them the nature of Brahman is trans-empirical and the various means of valid knowledge other than *śruti* cannot explain the nature of Brahman. It is only through the Vedic sentences that one can know the nature of Brahman.

A sentence must be admitted to be a source of knowledge if it conveys a sense not already known, through words whose meanings are already known. The validity of the *Upaniṣads* can be justified in the same way, because they intimate Brahman, which is otherwise not known, through words whose meanings are already known to us in empirical discourse.[29]

Here one has to see the ontological status of *śruti*. According to Advaita, Brahman alone is real and everything other than Brahman is illusory or *mithyā*. This means *śruti* which is different from Brahman also is illusory. Moreover, all the means of knowledge, including *śruti* are valid only within the empirical framework, *śruti*, which functions only at the empirical level, it is valid to one who is ignorant of Brahman. For the one who has realized the Self, there is no need for *śruti* because it is no more a *pramāṇa* to him.

Since *śruti* along with the entire empirical realm suffers sublation at the dawn of knowledge, it is said to be *mithyā* in respect of its ontological status. The ontological status *śruti* does not in any way jeopardize the functioning of *śruti* as a *pramāṇa*.[30]

Let us see how the Advaitins approach the nature of the *Vedānta-vākyas*. According to them, the *brāhmaṇa* part of the *Veda* is divided into: (1) *vidhi*, (2) *arthavāda* and (3) *Vedānta-vākyas*. The *arthavādas* are divided into three kinds: *guṇa vāda*, *anuvāda* and *bhūtārthavāda*. A *guṇa vāda* is a sentence, which contradicts what is known from the other *pramāṇas*. For example, the sentence, "The sacrificial post is the sun" is a *guṇavāda*. An *anuvāda* is something already known through other *pramāṇas* as e.g., "Fire is the antidote for cold". A *bhūtārthavāda* states something, which is neither contradicted, nor confirmed by other *pramāṇas* e.g., "Indra raised his weapon against Vṛtra".

The Mīmāṁsakas argue that the purport of the *Vedas* lies in action. The Prābhākaras maintain that only injunctive sentences of the *Veda* have validity and informative sentences which occur in the *Veda* such as *sātyam jñānam anantam Brahma*" which describe the nature of Brahman are not valid on their own, since they are not injunctive. But these texts form part of the *Veda* and hence cannot be ignored either. They have to be accommodated by making them subsidiary to the injunctive texts, which are principal. The *arthavādas* in order to be valid, must be construed as subsidiary to the injunctive texts *(vidhi-śeṣa)*. A secular sentence like, "There are fruits (in the trees) on the river bank" which is existential has to depend on another *pramāṇa* or means of valid knowledge for what it conveys and hence has no validity. If a sentence is injunctive, what it enjoins cannot be within the range of another *pramāṇa;* and hence it will have independent validity. Applying the same principle to the *śruti* texts, which are existential, the Mīmāṁsakas argue that they should be treated as injunctive or construed with injunctive texts for preserving their independent validity. Thus for the Mīmāṁsakas, all *arthavādas* are not authoritative in themselves and they serve as auxiliaries to injunctive statements *(vidhi-vākyas)*. This view is rejected by the Advaitins on two grounds: First, it should be noted that dependence on another *pramāṇa* is not due to a sentence being existential, because there is such dependence even in the injunctive sentence like "Bring a cow". The reason for dependence on another *pramāṇa* is elsewhere. A sentence uttered by a human being will have to depend on another *pramāṇa* for what it conveys, of whether it is existential or injunctive. Only sentences of human origin have this dependent nature. In the case of *śruti* texts like, "That thou art", there is no difficulty since they are *apauruṣeya*. If the Mīmāṁsakas say that the *arthavādas* do not have any independent validity and hence should be treated as subsidiary to injunctive texts, then the injunctive texts *(vidhi-vākyas)* can also be rejected on the same basis. Secondly, knowledge has intrinsic validity *(svtaḥprāmāṇya)* both in respect of its origin *(utpattu)* and ascertainment *(jñaptau)*. First of all, the very conditions under which it arises account for its validity. Secondly, even as it arises, it is believed to be valid without requiring verification by some other knowledge. It means that all knowledge is presumably valid, whatever be the *pramāṇa* from which it arises. If so, then the Mīmāṁsakas contention that all informative sentences which occur in the *Veda* are not valid on their own and hence must be construed as subsidiary to injunctive texts is not correct. All sentences are meaningful and valid by themselves and need not be construed to other sentences. Thus the Advaitins argue that all the *Vedānta-vākyas* are purportful because the identity of Brahman and the individual self is realized from them. These sentences are not subsidiaries to any ritualistic actions as conceived by the Mīmāṁsakas. When the identity is realized, then there is no necessity for us to practise the ritualistic actions.

Another significant contribution of Nayak in this paper is his analysis of the concept of *adhyāsa* or *avidyā*. He very correctly says that the problem is not merely a linguistic one but an ontological one. "Distinctionlesss non-dual reality has an ontic status in Advaita Vedānta, and the error is, therefore an ontological one... "[31] Analysis according to him is a means to eradicate error. For him one has to make a distinction between (a) mere understanding of the linguistic forms through analysis and (b) the eradication of ignorance and consequent realization of advaita which is effected through analysis.

Brahman of Śaṅkara was not meant to be identified with a mere logical subject...there is a peculiar ontic reference in Śaṅkara which cannot be eliminated, and this ontic reference cannot be brought out by pointing out the role of logical subject in language. Such exclusive talks of logical subject, logical predicate distinctions in advaita would not only involve the fallacy of reductionism, but it would also amount to a sort of philosophical anachronism.[32]

According to Nayak, there is some sort of absolutistic ontology embedded in the very structure of Śaṅkara's philosophical enterprise.[33] It is not clear what Nayak means by the "absolutistic ontology". No doubt, Śaṅkara speaks of an ontology which is operative within the empirical sphere but it looses its significance in the higher level. What does Nayak mean by "absolutistic ontology"? One does not know whether this term has a special significance in his Advaitic understanding. I maintain the view that Advaita is not only trans-empirical, but also trans-ontological for the main reason that it transcends everything and there is no place for any ontology. Śaṅkara would question any ontological status that is assigned to Brahman because it is beyond everything.

Notes and References

1. G.C. Nayak, *Philosophical Reflections,* New Delhi: Indian Council of Philosophical Research, 1987, pp. 1-14.
2. Śaṅkara's Commentary on the *Brahmasūtras,* I.i.2.
3. Nayak, *op. cit.,* p. 1.
4. *Upadeśasahasri,* xviii, 188.
5. *Ibid.,* xviii, 169.
6. *Ibid.,* xviii, 194-95.
7. R. Balasubramanian (ed. & tr.), *The Naiṣkarmyasiddhi of Sureśvara,* Madras: Radhakrishnan Institute for Advanced Study in Philosophy, University of Madras, Introduction, p. xxxviii.
8. T.M.P. Mahadeven, *The Philosophy of Advaita,* New Delhi: Arnold-Heinemann Publishers (India), 1976, p. 57.
9. Nayak, *op. cit.,* p. 2.
10. See my paper (unpublished), "An Analysis of Prof. Ganeswar Misra's Understanding of Advaita", paper

presented in the ICPR National Seminar on "The Philosophy of Prof. Ganeswar Misra", held at ICPR Academic Centre, Lucknow, from 20-22 February, 2001.

11. Nayak, *op cit.*, p. 3.
12. Ganeswar Misra, *The Advaita Conception of Philosophy,* Bhubaneswar: Utkal University, 1976, p. 9.
13. *Ibid.*
14. Śaṅkara's Commentary on the *Brahmasūtras,* II, i, 27.
15. *Bṛhadāraṇyakopaniṣadbhāṣya* I, iv, 10.
16. Nayak, *op. cit.*, p. 4.
17. *Ibid.*
18. *Bhagavad Gītā,* xiii, 12.
19. *Ibid.*, xiii, 13.
20. *IPQ,* January 1998, pp. 1-15.
21. *Ibid.*
22. *IPQ,* July 1999, pp. 425-434.
23. *IPQ,* January-April, 2000, p. 335.
24. *Ibid.*, p. 337.
25. George Thibaut (tr.), *The Vedānta-sūtras – With the Commentary of Rāmānuja,* Delhi : Motilal Banarsidass, 1962, p. 79.
26. R. Balasubramanian (ed. & tr.), *The Naiṣkarmyasiddhi of Sureśvara, op. cit.*, p. 136
27. R. Balasubramanian, *Advaita Vedanta,* Madras: Centre for Advanced Study in Philosophy, 1976, p. 10.
28. *Ibid.*, p. 12.
29. *Ibid.*, p. 14.
30. R. Balasubramanian (ed. & tr.), *The Naiṣkarmyasiddhi of Sureśvara, op. cit.*, p. 212.
31. Nayak, *op. cit.*, p. 5.
32. *Ibid.*
33. *Ibid.*, p. 11.

14

Dharma : Rules, Virtues and Paradigmatic Individuals

S.S. Rama Rao Pappu

In the past two decades, Western Ethics has taken what we may call a "Virtue Turn". In 1981, Prof. Elizabeth Anscombe has published a very influential paper entitled "Modern Moral Philosophy"[1] where she criticizes modern Western philosophers for developing a legalistic model of ethics which revolves around the concepts of "duty" and "obligation". This preoccupation with a duty-ethic is, in her view, rests on a mistake and she suggests that moral philosophers adopt the Greek/Aristotelian conception of virtue which has its source in the idea of human flourishing. The virtue turn that Prof. Anscombe has launched is variously described as a shift from "Quandary ethics" to an ethics of Virtue (Edmond Pincoff), from Nietzscheanism to Aristotleanism (MacIntyre), from ethics of duty to ethics of aspiration (Lon Fuller and Richard Taylore), etc. Because of the Indian philosophers' close association with Western philosophers and their study of Western philosophy in the past two centuries, the paradigm for understanding Indian ethics was, like the West, an ethic of duty or obligation. Like Western moral philosophers, the key concepts that were used to interpret Indian ethics were deontology and utilitarianism. Thus, there were lively disputes and book-length studies whether the ethics of the *Bhagavad Gītā* is deontological or utilitarian and how similar the Gītā ethics is to Kantian ethics.[2] I would like to dispute the duty paradigm of Indian ethics and will explore the virtue-ethics paradigm. By doing so, I would suggest Indian ethics may be viewed more like Confucian ethics than Biblical or Kantian ethics.

I shall do the following in this paper. First, I shall show that unlike the obligation ethics (also called the ethic of oughtness) which separates the "ought" from the "is", *dharma*-ethic has never separated the "is" from the "ought". *Dharma*-ethic traditionally was both a normative and naturalistic ethic. It does not merely ask: "What ought I to do?" but also "What by nature *(svabhāva)* will I be doing?" Second, I would like to show that when we examine the list of dharmas given in Indian classics like the *Rāmāyaṇa* and the *Bhagavad Gītā* or those *dharmas* contained in the *Dharmaśāstras,* it becomes clear that most of the *dharmas* in the list cannot be interpreted as "duties" but as virtues. The catalogue of *dharmas* presented by Indian thinkers is an exhortation to lead a virtuous life rather than an obedience to a set of moral rules. Third, Hindu texts and Hindu lawgivers recognize that an important source of *dharma* is conduct of "dharmic individuals" *(mahātmā, dharmarāja,* etc.*). Dharma*, in other words is embodied in paradigmatic individuals like Śri Rāmā or Gandhi. They are the sources of *dharma*, not because these *Mahātmās* have commanded us to do our moral duties nor because they have promulgated moral rules. They are the sources of *dharma* because *they* have lived a virtuous life and have set an example for others to emulate.

I

Indian ethics revolve around *puruṣārthas,* of which *dharma* is the most important *puruṣārtha.* The *puruṣārthas* (lit. human aims) are said to be four : viz. *dharma, artha* (wealth, power), *kāma* (desire, esp. sexual desire) and *mokṣa* or liberation. Though, for purposes of classification, *dharma* looks like other *puruṣārthas,* it is in fact given a much higher status than the rest. The other *puruṣārthas* have been subsumed under *dharma*, for the Indian thinkers maintain that *artha, mokṣa,* etc., are also *dharmas*, i.e. there is the *artha-dharma*, *mokṣa-dharma* etc. implying thereby that *dharma* is THE key concept around which everything revolves. As a concept, *dharma* signifies religion, law, morality, equity, usage, custom, tradition, merit, virtue, righteousness, justice, propriety, disposition, essential property or attribute, resemblance, devotion, duty, etc. *Dharma* is, to use Gilbert Ryle's expression, a "polymorphous" concept like "work" or "thinking". Despite the myriad meanings of *dharma*, there is a central meaning which is that it is an Eternal Law. The important thing to note here is that it is a "law" but as a "law," it is both Natural Law and Moral Law. *Dharma* is both descriptive and prescriptive, an "is" and an "ought. In order to explain how the "is-ought" distinction collapses in Indian thought, I shall explain five conceptions of *dharma*.

Dharma as a Cosmic Impersonal Law

As a cosmic impersonal law, *dharma* is derived from the Vedic concept *Ṛta. Ṛta* literally means "the course of things". The Vedic Indians understood *Ṛta* as the principle of harmony and orderliness of the universe, but also gave it a moral status. For example, in the language of the Vedic Indians, to say that "it is because of *Ṛta* water flows downwards" means not only that it in the cosmic order of things, it is not only a law of nature but also that "it is RIGHT (morally) for water to flow downwards". *Dharma*, as a conceptual successor to *Ṛta,* not only retained the full meaning of *Ṛta* but also acquired additional meanings in the course of history.

Dharma as Laws of Nature

When used to connote laws of nature, *dharma* refers to the whole spectrum of natural laws and includes "what *necessarily* happens", "what *regularly* happens" and even "what *ought* to happen".

Dharma as an Essential Property or Disposition

Dharma also means "the nature of a thing". By the "nature of a thing" we may mean either (a) its 'essential property' or (b) "disposition" *(svabhāva)* depending on whether we are referring to inanimate or animate objects. Thus when we say that the *dharma* of a river is to flow downwards *(pravāha-dharma),* we are attributing an essential property to the river. Likewise when it is said that the *kṣatriya-dharma* is to fight for and protect the people, we are stating that kṣatriyas are disposed to, temperamentally suited to, fight and protect.

Dharma as Social Norm

Dharma is a social norm, which includes all the rules which govern an individual's life in society like the moral, legal, customary, traditional, religion and even rules of etiquette and propriety. Thus, it is one's *dharma* to tell the truth (moral rule), to obey the king (legal rule), to perform morning ablutions (religious rule), to greet a friend (propriety), etc. Though social rules are primarily prescriptive, there is a descriptive element to them. When we say for example that the *dharma* of the kṣatriya clan is to fight, or that the *dharma* of a *grihastha* (householder) is to be hospitable to guests, *dharma* is used in the sense of "what is recognized as one's *dharma*" which is a descriptive meaning.

Dharma as Duty or Obligation

A common use of "dharma" is in the context of "duty" or "obligation". Duties and obligations arise out of rules and roles people play. We have a duty, for example, to keep our promises because there is a moral rule that "everyone ought to keep his/her promises". It should also be noted here that *dharma* refers not only to rules but also to duties which arise from rules. Rules create duties sometimes directly and sometimes indirectly. Indirectly rules create duties via roles. Duties arising out of positions of trust like a judge *(dharmamahāmantra)* or out of recognized social roles like that of a father or a mother *(pitṛdharma* or *mātṛdharma)* are of this nature. Obligations, on the other hand, are created or incurred voluntarily by individuals. We "assume" or "get into" a pre-existing social role. From the above analysis, it is clear that *unlike* the "duty ethic" or "moral oughtness" of Western ethics, *dharma* has built into it a naturalistic element. As applied to human beings, it means "the nature of a person" and the "moral psychology of humans," and it is clear that naturalism (which includes dispositions, *(saṁskāras),* attitudes, etc.) play a very important role in virtue ethics. From the above discussion, it becomes clear that *dharma* is more than pure "moral oughtness", and therefore it cannot be identified with a normative ethic, answering the question "What ought I to do?"

II

In this section, I shall discuss why *dharma* should be interpreted as virtue. I have stated earlier *puruṣārthas* are the foundation for Indian ethics. *Puruṣārthas* or "the aims of humans" are traditionally considered to be four, viz. *dharma*, *artha*, *kāma* and *mokṣa*. *Puruṣārthas* are not duties and therefore the doctrine of *puruṣārthas* should not be interpreted as an ethic "duty" or an "obligation". In fact, any interpretation of *puruṣārthas* as duties leads us to some interesting conclusions. For example, if *puruṣārthas* are duties, then *dharma* being a *puruṣārtha,* we have a duty to discharge our duties. Likewise, the state of *mokṣa* is traditionally considered to be a state beyond *dharma*, beyond duties. If *Mokṣa* is said to be one of our duties, we men have a duty to go beyond duties. *Dharma* and *mokṣa* should not therefore be interpreted as merely "duties", without getting into the awkward position that "we have a *dharma* (duty) to discharge our duties" (*dharmas*) and we have a (*dharma*) duty to go beyond duties *(mokṣa).*

Artha and *kāma* fare no better. *Puruṣārtha* literally means "that which is sought by humans" or "human aims". The expression "human aim" may mean "what in fact humans aim at" or "what humans ought to aim at". This ambiguity led Karl Potter, in a very influential paper, to translate *puruṣārtha* as "attitudes", "orientations", "capacities for doing things in a certain way". In his influential book *Presuppositions of India's Philosophies,* he argues:

> I do not see what else these terms (*puruṣārthas*) can mean if they do not refer to attitudes. They do not refer to states, in any commonly recognized sense of the term: states are the sorts of things people are IN,; and one is never in a state of *artha* rather than *kāma*, instead he takes *artha* attitudes towards some things in his environment and *kāma* attitudes towards other things. They do not refer to objects, or classes of objects, or relations or classes of relations. They are "aims of life" I conclude just in the sense that they represent capacities for taking things in a certain way. This is what I have in mind in calling them attitudes.[3]

Even if we do not accept Potter's translation of *puruṣārtha* as human attitudes, and keep the traditional meaning "human aim", the vocabulary of "aim" and "attitude" share many characteristics. Both are sometimes known behaviouristically—we come to know what a person's aim or attitude is by what he or she tells us and by what they do. People "have", "develop", "adopt", or "give up" aims and attitudes. Sometimes, however, aims determine attitudes and attitudes determine aims. A's aim to become rich is a consequence of his miserly attitude to money; and B's friendly attitude to his mother-in-law is a consequence of his aim to get her estate. (Linguistically, we can say: "What is A's attitude *to (or towards) B* not What is A's Aim to B? But we can say, "What is A's aim in doing B?").

If *puruṣārthas* are interpreted as "attitudes," to act according to *dharma* is not to act according to rules, or out of a sense of duty or obligation, but to adopt an appropriate attitude for doing X. Rules, duties, etc., are all or nothing; but attitudes are complex. Though compassion *(karuṇā)* is a *dharma*, it cannot be specified by a set of rules, because it is an attitude, a disposition *(saṁskāra).* A *karuṇāmayī* or a compassionate person is not only who does occasional acts of compassion, but is one who is "filled with compassion". It is because he is "filled with compassion" that we can specify his acts as compassionate.

Like the Greek texts, Indian texts also list a number of virtues. As early as the *Taittirīya Upaniṣad*, a "Convocation Address" by the Teacher, having taught the Veda to the student, exhorts him as follows: "Speak the truth: Follow *dharma*. Be one to whom mother and father are 'gods'... One should give with *faith;* one should give with *modesty;* one should give with sympathy *(sam-vid),* etc." (*Taittirīya Upaniṣad*, 1.11.2 eleventh *anuvaka).* Now this exhortation to be truthful, to respect elders, to live a life of modesty, humility, sympathy, etc., are not duties or obligations, but are virtues.

In the *Bhagavad Gītā,* likewise, while describing the *varṇa-dharmas* of different *varṇas*, Śrī Kṛṣṇa says:

Calm, (self) control, austerities, purity
Patience, and uprightness.
Theoretical and practical knowledge, and
religious faith,
Are the natural-born actions of brahmins

Heroism, majesty, firmness, skill,
and not fleeing in battle also,
Generosity, and lordly nature,
are the natural-born actions of warriors.

Agriculture, cattle-tending, and commerce
Are the natural-born actions of artisans;
Action that consists of service
Is likewise natural-born to a serf...
(XVIII. 41-43. Edgarton translation)

Kṛṣṇa emphasizes above not so much the duties of different *varṇas* but the (natural-born) virtues of different *varṇas*. This is akin to the moral psychology that contemporary virtue ethicists are interested in.

The *Rāmāyaṇa,* again, contains its own list of virtues. In the *Ayodhyā Kāṇḍa*, a list of virtues is given, which Śrī Rāma typically exemplifies. These are: "Truth, righteousness, prowess, kindness to creatures, smart speech, worship of the twice-born, gods and guests, these are the ways to go to heaven as told by the pious people" (*Satyarn, sadharmam ca parakramam ca; Bhutatanujkampam privaditam ca; Dviojatithidevatithi-pujanam ca; Panthanamahutrridivasya santaḥ). Ayodhyā Kāṇḍa 38-39.*

Manu, the great Hindu lawgiver distinguishes between *Viśeṣa dharma* or *dharmas* relative to one's station in life, and *Sādhāraṇa dharma* or *dharmas* for everyone. According to him, the common *dharmas* are ten in number. They are:

1. *Dhairya* or *Dhṛti* (patience or steadfastness)
2. *Kṣmā* (forgiveness)
3. *Dama* (application)

4. *Asteya* (non-appropriation or non-stealing)
5. *Saucha* (cleanliness or purity)
6. *Indriya-nigraha* (restraint of sense-organs)
7. *Dhī* (wisdom)
8. *Vidyā* (learning or knowledge of the sacred texts)
9. *Satya* (veracity)
10. *Akrodha* (freedom from anger).

Like Manu, other lawgivers like Prasasthapāda, Patanjali, etc., have their own list of *dharmas* or virtues which I need not elaborate here. I hope I have made my point with quotations from these texts that *Dharma*-ethic in the Indian tradition is primarily a virtue ethic. In passing, we should also note that an important implication of our interpretation of *dharma* as virtue is that Manu and other *Dharmaśāstra* writers will not be the "whipping boy" for all the ills of Hindu society. Sure, Manu had said that wives should be subservient to their husbands and śūdras should obey the twice-born. At the same time, Manu's list of virtues contain pursuit of wisdom, development of self-restraint, which are *sādhāraṇa dharmas*. Have people pursued these virtues? Manu, or any other lawgiver, also cannot command people to be virtuous. Virtues cannot be promulgated into law. We cannot pass ordinances demanding people to pursue wisdom or develop self-restraint.

Is *dharma* then a virtue ethic or a duty ethic? We may say it is both, though *dharma* is primarily a virtue ethic. A virtue ethic need not necessarily reject rules, duties, obligations. Take for example self-restraint as a virtue. A virtuous person who practices self-restraint may adopt *Brahmacharya* or sexual abstinence as a rule. On the other hand, the non-virtuous persons may also follow the path of *Brahmacharya*: when he does so, he does not become a virtuous person. He is of course doing the right thing, but it does not entitle him to the ranks of virtuous persons.

conception of perfection. The Moral Exemplar *(puruṣottama)* in the *Bhagavad Gītā* is a desireless person. That this is a new notion of virtue will be clear if we compare this notion of perfection with the Vedic and *Upaniṣadic* thought. The Moral Exemplar in the *Bhagavad Gītā* is variously described as one who is free from wishes (IV.21), whose "undertakings are free from desires and purpose" (IV. 19), who is not attached to objects of senses nor to actions. He is "indifferent to success and failure" (IV.22), he "neither delights nor loathes" (XVII. 17), "neither grieves nor craves for anything" (XII.17), and neither rejoices on attaining the pleasant nor repines on attaining the unpleasant (V.20). He has the same mental attitude to "foe and friend, also to honour and disgrace" (XII.18). His supreme self remains concentrated in absorption and his mind is tranquil "as a lamp stationed in a windless place flickers not" (VI.9).

B. *Rāma:* Like the *Bhagavad Gītā*, Śrī Rāma also does not question the eternal *dharma*. In fact, he is said to personify it. But his attitude in the performance of what is his *dharma* is different from the spirit of the *Bhagavad Gītā*. Instead of taking a cold, unemotional attitude (which the *Gītā's* conception of paradigmatic individuals imply), Rāma puts his heart in doing his *dharma*. He maintains his cheerfulness even when his expectations according to *dharma* are frustrated. As per *dharma*, Rāma had the expectation that he will succeed Daśaratha to the throne, but when his father had ordered his exile, to keep the promise he had made to Rāma's stepmother, Rāma did not forsake his cheerfulness. Rāma as a moral hero is one who rises above the conflict between duty and inclination by inclining, always with a smile, to do what is his duty.

One also notices in Indian thought a unique virtue that paradigmatic individuals have, viz., their beauty or "physical excellence". In the *Rāmāyaṇa,* not only Rāma's moral virtues but also his physical virtues are emphasized.

He is described as *mahābāhu* (having long arms), *vipulaṁṣaḥ* or broad shouldered, *ratapavan,* majestic, *ṣuci* or clean, etc.

C. *Mahātmā Gandhi:* The very title *Mahātmā* given to M.K. Gandhi means that he is a "Great Soul", a paradigmatic individual. Gandhi's source book in ethics is the *Bhagavad Gītā* and Rāma was his moral exemplar. Gandhi considered himself to be a Sanātanist or a "traditionalist", but in his interpretation of the Hindu tradition, he was the most radical. Thus, Gandhi reinterpreted traditional notions like *Satya* and *Ahiṁsā* and *Tapas*, and gave them new meanings. According to him to follow *Satya* and *Ahiṁsā*, one must undertake an active life *(pravṛtti-mārga),* not a contemplative life *(nivṛtti-mārga).* Gandhi's concepts of Satyāgraha, Civil Disobedience, etc., have no Indian precedents but he somehow derives them from the Indian tradition. Likewise, Gandhi's reading of the *Bhagavad Gītā* as a philosophy of non-violence is a creative rather than a literal interpretation of the text. Though Gandhi accepts the four sources of *dharma*, he reverses the order and makes *sadāchāra,* like the lives of "Hariśchandra, Prahlād, Rāmachandra" the most important source of *dharma.* By leading a life of *Satya* and *Ahiṁṣā*, Gandhi made these virtues, not merely obligations.

Notes and References

1. G.E.M. Anscombe, "Modern Moral Philosophy," originally appeared in *Philosophy, 33 (1958);* reprinted in *Collected Papers of G.E.M. Anscombe,* iii, *Ethics, Religion and Politics,* Oxford: Basil Blackwell, 1981.
2. See, for example, B.S. Gauchhwal, *The Concept of Perfection in the Teachings of Kant and the Gītā,* Delhi: Motilal Banarsidass, 1967; and G.W. Kaveeshwar, *The Ethics of the Gītā,* Delhi: Motilal Banarsidass, 1971.
3. Karl H. Potter, *Presuppositions of India's Philosophies,* Englewood Cliffs, New Jersey: Prentice-Hall, 1963.

15

Rethinking the Two Faces of Svarāja : Pre-Independence and Post-Independence

Rajendra Prasad

Thinking and Rethinking

We can think of anything whatsoever, with the only restriction that we cannot think of a thing the thought of which involves a contradiction. But we cannot rethink of everything which is not self-contradictory because rethinking presupposes prior thinking. To rethink is to think again. We can rethink, or rethink of, a thing at any time only if we had thought, or thought of, it sometime earlier than it. When we think again of a thing, we normally think of it in a more careful, serious, or critical manner, and almost invariably in a revaluative manner. Speaking in a little more earthly manner, the rethinking of or about a phenomenon has the following structure. We first think of it as having such and such features, plan a scheme of actions in accordance with this thought, and bring the phenomenon into existence. But living with it for some time we find that it does not have all, or most, of the features which we had thought of it as having, or required of it to have; or, that some of the features it has are undesirable, or not very desirable, and some of those it does not have more desirable than some of those it has. We then naturally feel the need to rethink of it.

The seriousness or urgency of our rethinkinhg of a thing would be determined by a number of factors some of which are the following: Our valuing some of the features it is missing, our disvaluing some of the features it actually has acquired, our disposition or attitude to take seriously, or lethargically, what we consider desirable or undesirable, our intellectual maturity and ability to rightly distinguish between the desirable and the undesirable, our moral maturity to move us to take steps to make the phenomenon get rid of what we consider its undesirable features and acquire those which we consider desirable, our self-confidence, or lack of it, to produce the change or changes in the phenomenon we consider worth producing, etc.

The Reason for Rethinking *Svarāja*

It is a historical truth that, before getting political independence, we had thought, or formed a picture in our imagination, of the kind of thing or self-rule, or, *svarāja* would or should be. By *svarāja* then we did mean and even today mean political independence, self-rule, or self-government, i.e. emancipation of India from the foreign rule and putting it under the rule or governance of its own citizens. But we did not, and do not even today, mean by *svarāja* only this, i.e. change of the ruler. We had also thought of its having a set of some other features in order to be the *svarāja* we were struggling to have. It can also be asserted as equally historically true that the *svarāja* we now have—and *we* have *svarāja* in the sense that our rulers are some of our own men and women, i.e. some Indians lack some of the features which we wanted it to have when we first thought of it and which we still very greatly value, and has come to acquire some other features which, as per its original conception, it was required *not* to have, i.e. to be free from. A large number of people, imbued with the original conception, still consider the latter undesirable. This is why we think it necessary to rethink of the *svarāja* we have. Therefore, the reason, for rethinking of *svarāja,* basically, is that the post-independence *svarāja* we are living, or living with, has become importantly different from what we had thought of it in our pre-independence conception of it.

On which lines the rethinking should be carried would depend on our reading of the lines on, or the aspects in which, the existing form of *svarāja* has faulted, or gone away *vis-à-vis* the original, the pre-independence, conception. The reading of these lines, I admit, can be done in more than one way. Someone may also not accept the original conception in toto and still think that the *svarāja* we have has gone awry. It is also possible that another person thinks in a way drastically different. For example, he may think that to be viable it should go still further on the lines, or at least on some of the lines, on which it has gone, or is going.

What I will do here is the following: I will first state the original conception of *svarāja* which would be a reconstructed, and not a reproduced, account out of some of the ideas of M.K. Gandhi about *svarāja* which he held while guiding the struggle for freedom or even after it. Then I will state, as per my perception, the ways in which the *svarāja* we have has gone astray, and finally suggest, in a revaluative manner, how to bring it back on the right rails. In the latter task the role which intellectuals can meaningfully play would also be touched upon. It will not be discussed in any great detail because it belongs, properly speaking, to another topic, namely, the social responsibilities of Indian intellectuals, and not so obviously to that of rethinking *svarāja.* But, all along, I will be presenting a substantive 'rethinking', and not just a formal, one. It would very likely be a personal one, but one with which I hope, many would agree. There is nothing unfair in one's giving a personal rethinking if he admits, as I do, that there can also be some other different rethinkings of this matter. In reaching it I have tried to keep myself, as far as possible, behind the veil of ignorance and therefore expect it to be the least idiosyncratic or biased, if not completely unidiosyncratic or unbiased.

Pre-independence Conception of *Svarāja ā la* Gandhi

During the struggle for freedom Gandhi evolved a *comprehensive* concept of freedom or *svarāja* which did include freedom from foreign rule or domination as a basic component, but was not exhausted by it. It was a comprehensive concept of self-rule because it touched all the corners of an Indian's life and of the Indian society. In characterizing it he did use ideas obtained from his reflection on the nature of other societies and from his experience while living in other societies, but he claims, as he puts it in a picturesque way, to have written it on 'the Indian state'.[1] By writing it on the Indian state he means that he has drawn the picture of *svarāja* in the setting of the ethico-socio-cultural infrastructure of the Indian society as it has developed from the classical to the time he is passing through. In dilating, or building, on it I may not go completely on the lines he would have approved of. But I have no reason to think that he would have disapproved of it. In any case, the way I go gives a perspective to rethink of the *svarāja* we got, or have, in a manner very relevant to the prevailing social and societal situation, and this is a good justification for my going that way.

Gandhi says:

> Let there be no doubt about my conception of *svarāj*. It is complete independence of alien control and complete economic independence. So at one end we have political independence, at the other the economic. It has two other ends. One of them

is moral and social, the corresponding end is dharma, i.e. religion in the highest sense of the term. It includes Hinduism, Islam, Christianity, etc., but is superior to them all. Let us call this square the square of *Svarāj*, which will be out of shape if any of its angles is untrue.[2]

At another place he asserts that, "The essence of our civilization is that we give a paramount place to morality in all our affairs, public or private".[3] Since he describes what *svarāja* is on the Indian slate, it means that in India's *svarāja* morality has to occupy a paramount place. And, this *svarāja* would not be the *svarāja* of any particular class or group of people but that of each and every Indian. "*Svarāj* or a people means", he says, "the sum total of the *svarāj* (self-rule) of individuals".[4] He is very emphatic about the dignity of the individual as, according to him, "Ultimately, it is the individual who is the unit",[5] whose *svarāja* is the basic brick of the *svarāja* of the people, or country, he belongs to.

Gandhi's Conception Elaborated and Reconstructed

When we organize the above ideas to get with them as its constituent's a picture of *svarāja* on Gandhi's lines, it is obvious that a country, say India, can be said to have *svarāja* in the true sense of the term if and only if it satisfies all of the following conditions:

(a) It is politically independent, i.e. not under the domination of any foreign, non-Indian, country, directly or indirectly. Since the *svarāja* of a country is the sum-total or aggregation of the *svarāja* of each and every citizen of it, it is also necessary that no citizen of it is under the domination of any foreign power, it may be said that when a country is free, every citizen of it is free. In a sense it is true, but only in a sense. A politically free citizen of a politically free country may be mentally servile to, or under the domination of, a foreign culture. To be truly free, he should be a free thinker, one with the ability to make his own decisions, and not chained, or sold, to an alien agency or culture. That is, he must have the rational maturity to make a proper decision, using his own mental resources, or have the potentiality to acquire such an ability. The duty of the state, in this regard, would be to provide to its citizens all the facilities, as far as possible, he needs in order to acquire this ability. One of the major, or the most important factors in this connection would be the right sort of education which enables the educatee to develop his creative and critical potentialities.

An individual can be enslaved not only to a foreign culture, but also to some undesirable components of his own, and thereby cease to be a free agent. For example, a Hindu may be so much glued to his institution of caste that he may find it abhoring for a member of one caste marrying a member of another caste, or think that caste differences are unbreakable because they have been created by God. Therefore, to be a free individual one has to have the ability to protect his individuality not only from being dominated by an alien culture, but also from being dominated by his own. This is necessary because every culture may have some components which have become dead wood, or which obstruct free thinking. It is more difficult to emancipate oneself from the domination of some undesirable components of one's indigenous culture than to emancipate from that of an alien culture. The grip of the former on his mind is much tighter than that of the latter. It is more difficult to be critical of one's own culture than to be of an alien one, and it is particularly so if his culture is an old one. This is so because there is a strong feeling in the mind of many that the old is good simply because it is old. Age no doubt deserves respect, but not always. As Kālidāsa says in the very beginning of his *Mālavikāgnimitram,* the old is not good simply because it is old, nor the new bad simply because it is new; wise men consider anything good or bad only after properly assessing its worth, while dullards go by the judgement of others, or follow the traditional rating. Therefore to function as a free agent, to be a really free individual, one has to be not only critical of alien influences impinging on his style of life, but also of those which are rooted in his own culture. That is, he has to be self-critical. The ability to be self-critical, like the one to be self-respecting, is to be cultivated with circumspection because not only it is, like the latter, a difficult thing to do, but also because if overdone, it may make one a self-diffident cynic, as the latter, if overdone, may make him a bloated egoist.

(b) A country is, as a country, economically independent if it does not need economic assistance from any alien agency (i) to sustain the welfare of its people and (ii) to provide every physically and mentally fit citizen of it, if he is willing to have an occupation yielding him a wage sufficient to enable him to attain his well-being, (iii) In addition, for all those of its citizens, who are not physically or mentally fit to earn their living, it must have such economic arrangements which enable them to live a worthwhile life. That is, in an economically independent country, it must be possible for every person, who is fit and willing to earn his living, to earn it in a manner compatible with self-respect and self-dignity. This is important because, in the Gandhian picture of the good life, an individual is the unit of his society, and a country's *svarāja* the aggregation of the *svarāja* of its citizens. If any citizen, fit and willing to earn his living, needs a dole from any agency, indigenous, or foreign, in order to survive, the country he belongs to is not really economically independent; or, if the country itself is economically independent, its political or economic arrangements are lop-sided on account of which an individual is to depend on a dole for his survival. This would be true if the country is affluent but still has a citizen who is below the poverty line. But the country, or its political-economic arrangements, would be called faulty only if the latter is not himself totally responsible for his being below the poverty line.

(c) The third component of *svarāja* is moral and social. Morality is a social phenomenon because to be moral is basically to have a concern for the welfare of the other. Therefore, a moral order would essentially contribute to social cohesion. In a pluralistic society social cohesion is extremely important, and the way to have it in a stable way is to give to morality a paramount place. Neither political, nor economic, independence of an individual can be maintained in a worthwhile manner if morality is not honoured. Therefore, any commendable political, or, economic, system has to be based on morality. This means that the primacy of the moral has to be maintained in private and public arrangements. This means that when there is a conflict between a non-moral, for example a political, or economic, consideration and a moral consideration, the moral consideration has to be given the overriding position. It is legitimate for the moral to override the political, or the economic, but not for the latter to override the former. It may temporarily seem that it is more advantageous to adopt a politically, or economically, expedient policy or measure even if it is morally unjustified but in the long run such a step is bound to be injurious or self-defeating.

(d) The fourth component of *svarāja* is dharma which

is not religion in a particularist sense, in which it means Hinduism, Islam, etc., but in a more basic sense in which it is compatible with all particular religions. If we take dharma in this sense, i.e. in the sense of something basic, or common to all religions, again we find that it is nothing but the moral core of all religions. Only morality is inter-religious; in other respects, religions may differ among themselves. This means the primacy of the moral has to be accepted even in relation to the religion. That is, if a religious consideration conflicts with a moral consideration, then the moral is to be preferred, and not the religious. If a choice is to be made between constructing a place of worship to increase religiousity among the adherents of a religion and constructing a hospital to provide healthcare to the indigent, one who holds the primacy of the moral would say that there is a moral, and therefore a conclusive, overriding, reason for constructing the hospital, and for not constructing the place of worship.

All of (a), (b), (c) and (d) components are to hold good in a country in order that it may be credited with having *svarāja.* Even if the above is not a cent per cent correct characterization of the Gandhian notion of *svarāja* it is a fair enough characterization of the kind of *svarāja* Indians were, under Gandhi's leadership, aiming at in their struggle for freedom, or were hoping to have after emancipating the country from the British rule.

Rethinking *Svarāja* : Revaluating the Received in the Light of the Conceived

It is some such thought of *svarāja* which at least the thinking type of Indians, unsold to a political party, still entertain. It is this thought which generates in them the need to rethink of the *svarāja* they have enjoyed, or suffered, for a little more than half a century. At the moment we have *svarāja* of some sort which does not seem to many of us the realization of the thought of *svarāja,* outlined above, which we originally had, or still have. Therefore, some rethinking is necessary. And, one who rethinks of it must not rethink of it in the light of the benefits India's *svarāja* has given to him, or of the deprivations it has inflicted on him. Let us, then, try to place ourselves imaginatively at an Archimedean point, i.e. occupy, as far as possible, a spot outside the social system to which we belong and which is living the existing *svarāja.* In course of detecting or diagonising the latter's deviation from our earlier thought of *svarāja,* we must also be ready to rethink even of the Gandhian model, if we find it necessary.

The Received *Svarāja* Infringing the Two Principles of the Primacy of the Moral and of the Dignity of the Individual

For a non-political, or politically non-committal thinking, type of Indian, his actual experience of India's *svarāja* does not compare very favourably with the thought of *svarāja* outlined above, in some very important respects. Two of them are the primacy of the moral and the dignity of the individual. *Svarāja* is a necessary institutional, or political, condition for leading a good life, for any citizen of any country. A good life may mean morally good life or a non-morally good life. The latter would mean a happy life led at any cost, even at the cost of some moral principles or values. Without defending it, since doing that would take me too far afield, I would simply assert that a morally good life is better than a non-morally good life howsoever happy the latter may be, and it is better simply because it is *morally* good. It is this truth which Hanumāna gives expression to when, seeing Rāvaṇa sleeping majestically on his golden bed in his golden palace, he exclaims that had morality been given its rightful place in Rāvaṇa's style of life, private and public, his kingdom would have shone with greater brilliance than that of Indra. When I say that *svarāja* self-rule, is an institutional condition for leading a good life, I mean a morally good life. A morally good life does not have to be a life made miserable by the ravages of poverty because poverty itself is a moral, and not just economic evil. And, since equity is an important moral requirement, a morally good life has to be a life which ensures the well-being of all concerned, and enables each one to flourish as best as he can, or as his desert entitles him to.

In any democracy, power lies in the hands of elected representatives who generally belong, declaredly, or undeclaredly, to some political party or organization. Political power, in a democracy, is to be used to enable the people, who elect the ruling elite, to flourish in desirable, morally permissible, ways, keeping in view not only their flourishing but also equity and justice in the distribution of benefits and burdens. To fulfil these goals, the politician, the ruling elite, has to be fair to all concerned, and therefore he has to give primacy to moral considerations in whatever decision he takes, or whatever political, social, or economic, arrangements he plans to be, or gets, brought about. This means that he may have to initiate a measure which, though beneficial in the long run, or better than the other available alternative, is not so considered by his electrorate. This the ruling elite can do only if he adheres to the principle that a moral consideration has the right to override any political consideration, for example, one which motivates him to do anything to please his electorate in order to be returned to power in the next election. In present-day political life, by and large, a political consideration overrules a moral one in the relation of the ruling elite to the ruled people, as well as in the relation exising among different political groups. Political practice primarily involves manipulative bargaining and adjustments and all sorts of compromises, including moral compromises.

It may be said that the principle of the primacy of the moral is a too purist, fanatical, principle, one which cannot always be adhered to in any political practice. Therefore, those, who believe in the theory of dirty hands, would say that political life is a life in which howsoever hard one may try to keep his hands clean, on some occasions he would have to dirty them. Perhaps this is true, and therefore the primacy of the moral has to be taken in a slightly liberal, or unrestrictive, way. Whenever the morally best is not obtainable, it may be urged, we have to be satisfied with what is morally good enough. Therefore, to the politician it can be said that some specks of dirt on his hands are condonable. But no one would condone if they are soiled more often than not. What has happened is that political practice has become permeated with a pervasive climate of moral relaxation, or, amorality. A general consensus seems to have emerged among political parties that it is out of date, or too academic, to raise a moral issue in settling an intra-party or inter-party political dispute, or even in taking a political decision, or formulating a political policy. Some immorality in political affairs an otherwise healthy policy can digest, as some infected good healthy stomach can digest. But there is a limit to this kind of tolerance, and it seems the amorality, or neglect of morality, in Indian politics, has exceeded the limit of Indian polity's tolerance, or power of digestion. Since political power is at the top, the consensus about indifference to morality has percolated from top to bottom. It was to prevent this sort of percolation that Jai Prakash Narayan used to emphasize that it is most important to keep Gangotrī clean. It may be that the consensus about amorality, or neglect of morality, is the result of moral apathy travelling from the

It would be unfair to say that the Gandhian model is too utopian and therefore that those who are discontented with the *svarāja* we are living with are either obstinate utopians or incurable cynics. The Gandhian model is not even too idealistic, what to speak of being too utopian. It is much humbler than the later model of a highly industrialised, internationally competitive India. In fact, even the later model cannot be realized in a manner felicific for at the least the majority of the Indian population by ignoring any of the four sides of the Gandhian square of *svarāja*.

Before concluding this essay I will say a few things more about the two components I have discussed above while discussing what intellectuals can do in the direction of getting them honoured more than they presently are in political behaviour, or rather in the behaviour of the Indian people, and thereby in realizing the original thought of *svarāja*.

Role of Intellectuals

It may be said that to properly rehabilitate the primacy of the moral and dignity of the individual (and do a lot more), we need to change the prevailing pattern of political functioning in the country. It is something like this which, Gandhi felt, needed to be done immediately after gaining political independence. He seems to have had a foreboding that Indian politics would shape in the coming years the way it has actually shaped. His draft[6] of a new constitution for the Indian National Congress, which he made on 29 January 1948, just a day before his death, very clearly shows which way he wanted the politics of the country to go. But that draft has become only a document stored in the annals of Indian history. Jai Prakash Narayan tried to change Indian politics by leading a people's movement to get introduced the provision of giving to an electorate the right to de-elect an elected represeintive if found errant and to get political power replaced by people's power. The result of his struggle is well known to any student of modern Indian history. Therefore, 'change the polities' is easier said than done. But it is also true that politics of the country has to be changed.

An intellectual is not, or need not, rather better not, be a politician, or sold to a political ideology or party. If he is, then he cannot play the role which only an intellectual can, and therefore should, play in striking at the amorality, or, moral apathy, of the Indian politician. He can strike at it only by doing well what he, as an intellectual, can do, i.e. by doing well his own calling, by doing constructive, objective, criticism of political plans, projects, and policies, in brief, the functioning of the political parties which are, as well as of those which are not, in power. This is his limit, but not a frustrating limit. Assuming that education is in the hands of intellectuals, intellectuals can do a lot by helping an educatee develop a critical, assessive, bent of mind, a habit of mind which enables him to see things as they really are. Proper education is the most potent agent of making a people capable of making right decisions and choices.

But who is an intellectual? Any one, I would say, who can make a creative use of his intellect, his thinking ability. He does not have to be a professor. Only, he must not be a parrot, not even a parrot who has learnt to utter some Vedic mantras, and Mandana Mishra's parrot cannot be called a logician even though he had learnt to utter the question whether the validity of a piece of knowledge is intrinsic, or extrinsic, to it. Criticizing a national polity, or even an age-old cultural practice, is not impatriotic, as some people may think. Those who do they do that because they slur over the distinction between patriotism and nationalism. A patriot is he who examines a stand taken by his country, or a stand approved of by his culture, and accepts or rejects it on its merits, whereas a nationalist accepts whatever his country or culture approves of, or considers commendable, even if it is not defensible. Patriotism is, whereas nationalism is not, in tune with the intellectual temper. Therefore, in criticizing a policy, or plan, prepared by the ruling elite of his country, an intellectual would not become impatriotic. He would not even if he criticizes a tenet held to be sacrosanct in his classical culture. At the present moment many intellectuals have developed some sort of a political apathy which to me seems to be a symptom of pessimism or frustration. Their thinking seems to run as follows: Politics of the country has become incurable. The *svarāja* we had thought of and fought for, and the *svarāja* we are suffering from, are two kinds of animals. To replace the latter by the former is impossible. Therefore, better lock ourselves inside our laboratory or library and let the politicians play their game as they want to. The fatalists among them say: There would some day be a nemesis; after all, the depth of the pit is limited; some day it is bound to be full, and further falling down into it to stop. But being fatalists, even they too are politically apathetic. This apathy has first to be jolted, and then only intellectuals can play their role of the critic of social, including political, plans, policies, and practices, with care, caution and confidence, as a step in the direction of potentializing, what Jai Prakash Narayan called, people's power, which alone, in a democracy can replace an anaemic *svarāja* with a full-blooded one.

In saying all that I have said here and admitting that the number of sayable things left unsaid is much larger than the things said—I have all along been assuming that there are in the country some free-thinking, unsold, or uncommitted, creative, and fearless intellectuals, and some people, even in the arena of politics, who honour the primacy of the moral and the dignity of the individual.

I hope it is not a totally unfounded assumption. Moreover, if we do not have it, we cannot even think of rethinking *svarāja.*

Notes and References

A revised version of the keynote address, under the title on the 'Why and How of Rethinking *Svarāja*', to the National Seminar on 'Rethinking *Svarāja*' delivered on January 24, 2000, at the Indian International Centre, New Delhi.

1. M.K. Gandhi, *India of My Dreams,* Compiled by R.K. Prabhu, Navajivan, 1947, p. 8.
2. *Ibid.,* p. 10.
3. *Ibid.,* p. 9.
4. *Ibid.,* p. 11.
5. *Ibid.,* p. 99.
6. *Ibid.,* pp. 290-93.

16

Equality : Slogan and Utopia

Arun K. Mookerjee

Social Philosophy for me is in a major sense applied philosophy. The philosopher looks at the social phenomena or statements about them together with the sociologist. There is no social philosophy without sociological studies. Theories in sociology and social philosophy are results of this joint endeavour. There is hardly any sociological theory, not to count statistical statements, without philosophizing. Thus the social philosopher knows that "equality" is a slogan for socio-political (economic included) action, while inequality and discrimination are socio-political facts so far as felt to be so by the unprivileged unequals. If there is no feeling of inequality then there is no inequality as a matter of fact. Individual differences, as we say in psychology, is the only inequality with any sense. Felt-inequality in social life is of interest to the sociologist and the social philosopher. Once upon a time a brother felt discriminated against another because his oblations were ignored by the "Authority" and so he went into action against the Authority and the privileged or favoured. Call it man's second sin and first crime of murder (in only two generations of life on earth), call it a revolt. May be the fellow became envious in Robert Nozick's sense, or suffered from a loss of honour and respect in Bernard William's sense. Nevertheless the fellow went into action in anger, affront causes by the inequality of treatment. However, he was ultimately tamed and his sense of ineqality was metamorphosed into a sense of guilt against the Authority and the norms of life set by the Authority. The fellow believed eventually that he had committed a retributively punishable guilt. The feeling of inequality was thus erased out of his consciousness by the Authority, the embodiment of Power. The protest was not heard again, for the agony melted away and took the shape of remorse. Point one is that only a felt inequality moves individuals and groups to socio-political action for equality, whether it is a divine regime or a mortal one, whether man is acting in a divine power system or a human power system. Point two is that the thought structure and conscience is moulded by the power structure suitably to its purpose. Thus did live a *wise* Socrates and his slave (wise or idiot) in a harmonious system where the unfelt inequality raised no ripples, intellectual or material. So was the case with the *Varṇa* system in India. The Brahmin had "legitimate" demands upon the *Kṣatriya, Vaiśya* and *Śūdra.* So had the *Kṣatriya* upon the other two, and the *Vaiśya* upon the *Śūdra,* and the *Śūdra* upon none. The *Śūdra* was made to believe that servility was his element, his given nature. Any breach of this privilege in inequality, in this structure of inclusive hierarchy of status, was regarded as a sin against good and in law a punishable crime. Thus has lived our society for centuries without any seriously felt inequality. At least, equality as a slogan was not loud enough to be heard by the members of the social polity until modern times. The system worked not by any miracle. The inequality was not felt as adversity, deprivation, because the power system could successfully induce a sense of belongingness to the religious-polity, belonging with a sense of duty and obligation. The *Śūdra* felt himself as a person needed in the religious polity. In some version of the *Mahābhārata* the coronation ceremony of Yudhiṣthira is described — along with the other three *Varṇas*, the *Śūdra* is also bathing the King. It is just a little example to explain how the power-system worked by not alienating even the most unequal, the most unprivileged section of the people. It was exploitation without alienation. History tells us of the patricians and plebeians in ancient Roman empire, and the revolution. History gives us another example of an intense feeling of inequality that flared up into a revolt against the authority, pulled down the royal power and replaced it by another, but at the same time saved the system, a religious belief system, called Islam. I am talking of the revolt against the Arab aristocracy and the Umayyads in Iran.

It is obvious that demand for changes, social political economic, are not the characteristics of modern societies alone. Stress and strain in social relations are common social phenomena that constructively, more often than not, have been inducing change for a better living adjustments. Anodyne "drug" is very important in such circumstances. How the power brokers use it to lull the feelings of inequality and dishonour is the point. One lesson of history is that conflicts over inequalities, positively stated — the demand for equality, even if defeated, never dies. It survives at least in the form of an anarchist protest to disturb the conscience through ages. True, in the face of "Individual difference" equality has become a broken concept. Individual difference, merit, power system that rules an era of history, the urge for liberty and creativity, have helped in the process of breaking the unitary meaning of equality, if indeed it had any. In modern democracy, equality is understood in terms of civil rights. It means, equality before law, equality of opportunity. It intends to provide a level ground for the citizens at the starting point. Beyond the starting point, it is merit, manipulative capacity, relations social and political, power equations, private property both inherited and acquired, determine what equality should mean *vis-à-vis* liberty.

French Revolution has given us a lesson. The slogan of the revolution was "liberty equality *fraternity*". It is this slogan that set a savage pace for the revolution in spite of the divergent pulls within the *third estate* which brought about the revolution. It was a mixed population of peasants, traders, professionals, intellectuals, workers, and small factory owners. All the peasants were not landless and all the workers were not such as having only the chain to lose. During the revolution a bulk of the confiscated property of the Church and feudal holdings were grabbed by the well-off amongst the peasants in the villages and the professionals, traders, factory owners in the cities who could buy. The third estate wanted to be equal with the two estates above it. Thus bourgeoisie as a class was born in the French social polity. With them the meaning of the slogan changed. They looked away from *equality* to press instead for *liberty* in the sense of civil rights. The poor in the cities and the villages were left behind. Gradually *equality* acquired new meanings, one for the liberal world, and quite another for the socialist world, in relation to respective power structures created and ruled by a politico-economic aristocracy and a politico-military oligarchy respectively. In India we have coined a word to designate these people of power, namely, Very Important Person. Has "equality" then any unitary meaning for us 'social philosophers and the people at large'? It has. It means "tolerable inequality" in status, power, living condition, honour, etc.

One may cherish a hope that with the diminishing state-power, as proposed by philosophy of Liberalism, men shall become truly equal to each other in respect of need and supply, social status, political power sharing, personal honour, and protection and privacy. In this connection I may refer to Robert Nozick and Bernard Williams again. Nozick thinks that individual liberty being the ultimate social and moral value and a fact, it is only in the "minimal state" that the individual rights could be preserved and advanced. The question of inequality and equality would become irrelevant. Irrelevant because in a minimal state man would find his fulfilment as it would respect rights and freedom to choose and realize one's own conception of life. Minimal state would treat persons as "inviolate individuals", never used as a means.

Precisely the argument is that if every individual can live up to himself, without any interference by the State in the form of "greatest good for greatest number" or Welfare State, then such individuals would agree either to co-operate or at least not to meddle in other's affairs. Thus liberty with fraternal co-operation would reduce the equality-inequality question into empty words. Bernard Williams, on the other hand is not prepared to become an inspired visonary of the Utopia of minimal State. He thinks that individual differences being a fact, a practical solution can be tried by combining as far as practicable, equality in the sense of "equality of opportunity" with equality in the sense of "quality of respect". While explaining "equality of respect" he invokes the Kantian idea of "Kingdom of ends". If no individual is used as a means to an end then, his respect preserved, he will co-operate with others, inequality of merit being no obstacle. Distribution of goods could then be made according to need obviating the competitive character of distribution of goods according to merit. In other words, under such circumstance the individual would not demand according to merit and the unequal would remain satisfied with distribution of goods according to needs. Admittedly he thinks this the best way of eating and having as much cake as possible.

I need not repeat Nozick's argument against such a meaning of equality as equality of rights or equality of opportunity. What is of interest to me is that all the three present advocates of liberalism, Nozick, Williams and

Rawls, however, differ from each other, have taken into serious consideration the idea of fraternity as they talk of voluntary co-operation. Can Nozick's minimal state, a practicable Utopia he claims, survive with free individuals living in respective islands, not in a society? Mutual co-operation, even in a minimal State would not be casual as he would have us believe. What passes my understanding is how the equality-inequality question could become irrelevant? It will become more acute as a large number of people would fall behind a few meritorious, moneyed, powerful people. Moreover, Nozick seems to be brave with the idea of "co-operation". In his minimal state it is not all that needed. Bernard William's honest dream is of having the cake and eating it too, that too as much as possible. It may be said that an honest belief that in some State man would agree not to exploit another man is an Utopian idea. All that he can practically hope is that in a Welfare State with such means as distributive justice, the inequalities could be softened psychologically, reduced and kept at a tolerable level by political action. He is quite candid in his admission that with any "noble" political ideal there are difficulties that cannot be fully overcome, can only be softened. Why not then Williams say that tolerance and fraternity as cultivated values could only preserve a society. Otherwise the tension of individual differences in a society shall keep the society perpetually disturbed. Thus societies and cultures die.

History shows us that at every age a power-system rises and thrives by exploitation of a section of people by another. A value system evolves therein only to keep things within a limit. Thus only is preserved the jargon of liberty equality fraternity, the first two being conflicting rational concepts, the third one is an emotional relation. The jargon becomes a slogan as soon as the inequality is felt acutely by the adversely affected population in a social polity, certainly a well-meaning slogan for socio-political action. Equality as a round full concept is a myth. The equalitarian, like the libertarian, is deemed as a visonary of an Utopia or pretenders with honest look. Even if equality is defined like "equality before law", "equality of opportunity" it will have broken edges. Even in suffering there is no equality. Equality as a practicable idea can only mean, tolerable inequality accepted by the larger number of affected people. Otherwise equality is a slogan, an Utopia, an ever unrealisable idea. An inspiration for the "lesser people"?

Our concepts are all of broken edge. Thus they play in a power-system of which we all are prisoners, the ruler and the ruled alike. Minimizing suffering must be the aim of all socio-political actions. If "honesty" has any meaning then only Fraternity can cut through the individual differences, merit and meritocracy, pride of power and pains of life. How this fraternity, the emotive in man, could be preserved in its pristine nature, not exploited by politicians and other privileged people, I do not know.

Fraternity is the cement of the society. Only amongst a free people it can find its natural expression. Lest we forget, the word "free" etymologically comes from the root *pri*, to love. Co-operation as an expression of fraternity and love pours itself into the cleavages in a society. In such a society, expectedly free from power game, "individual difference" is creatively employed for the social progress. Is it again another Utopian thinking? If so then the alternative is the conflict theory of social change. But then it is said that the stain of blood does not wash easily.

17

Commonism : An Analytical Review

Bijayananda Kar

Prof. Nayak, in recent past,[1] has made a sincere effort in evolving a novel point of view which he terms: Commonism and he considers it relevant for religion as well as philosophy. He firmly hopes "in any case it is the commonistic element in religion or commonistic religion backed by a commonistic philosophy which is likely to play the most significant role at present and also in future".[2] His view-point has provoked response among the philosophic community of the country.[3] Prof. Bhupendra Nath agrees with him in holding that there is "the widespread religious crisis which has gripped the modern" but differs from him on what is termed by him as "the commonist elements in Hinduism". He, on the contrary, maintains "the hold of the mystical" is the distinctive feature of the Hindu outlook. According to him "the Indian emphasis on a direct experience, i.e. the mystical experience, which supplies vitality to her religion and emancipates the religion from dogmas and blind ritualism".[4] He seems to have not so much opposition for a commonistic outlook in the context of Hinduism but strongly holds that it should not "mean a type of secularization which seeks to demolish all that is associated with the ancient conceptions of spiritual or transcendental".[5]

Prof. K.P. Mishra objects to the commonistic rendering of religion on the ground that true religious consciousness, according to him, is transcendental to the dichotomy of rich and poor, elitist and non-elitist, common and uncommon. Essentially the religious consciousness, to him, is nothing but 'God-realization'. This is primary whereas temple, church and monastery are all of mere secondary significance.[6] Hence, if in the present day setting there is less sincerity in attending to church and temple etc., in West that need not belittle the importance of religion and one should not be led to the conclusion that there is *dharma-saṅkata*. Referring to the situations prevailing in Iran, Iraq, Pakistan and India, Prof. Mishra has suggested that the Western model of formulating crisis in religion is never applicable in these countries and specifically the term : *dharma-saṅkata* has notably a different connotation in the classical dharmic tradition of India.

Prof. Nayak, in his later writings on the same issue, has however made certain significant point of clarification. To him, philosophic reflection stands for exposing as well as exploring the real meaning of any issue by means of logical analysis. Here logical analysis need not suggest a formal, technical, symbolic exercise. It only means a sound rational investigation of an issue in its own framework. So philosophy, according to him, cannot afford to dismiss the tract of reason and logic. While trying to expose the meaningful basis of religion, it has to highlight and focus those elements which can be rationally sustained and at the same time can meet the demands of the social condition. Prof. Nayak presents a significant clarification by pointing out that his emphasis on common need not mean that he finds everything good and noble from religious point of view *only* in ordinary, common and non-elitist. Dawn of religious consciousness can be traced anywhere irrespective of caste, creed or social or economic status. But because there has been an age-old unreasonable supremacy of the elitist over the non-elitist in the human history, it is not worthless to point out that *even* the commoner, the poorest of the most neglected is in no way inferior to attain the religious awareness.[7] In another context, he too emphasizes that in case of a true devotee there is no consideration of family, or creed.[8]

Prof. Nayak's point of view and some reactions advanced on his standpoint have created an interesting situation in the intellectual field. It arouses a scope for further discussion which is quite in tune with the healthy philosophical tradition. It seems to me that Prof. Nayak views religion with a pro-attitude. He seems to have seriously noted the growing tendency of casting doubt on the rational justification of religion. And, in this sense, he fully shares with the view that there is now definitely some form of religious crisis. Whether one prefers to use the term : crisis in this context or some other term, it does not seem to affect his basic viewpoint. For, according to him, if religion is accepted as the continuing source of inspiration to the mankind in invigorating spiritual excellence then there is of course the need for reviewing the concept of religion. Taking into consideration of the present day social situations which, undoubtedly, have strong impact of science and technology, religion must be reconsidered and re-evaluated. There must be both sincere and serious attempts to expose that element in religion which can stand to the test of the present day and at the same time it can well preserve the perennial religious consciousness that has been the source of inspiration throughout the ages. Prof. Nayak finds commonistic element as the most significant one within the Hindu dharmic framework which, if effectively understood as well as put into practice, can satisfactorily meet the challange of the present religious crisis.

Now it may be noted that so far as spiritual background of religious framework is concerned, the views expressed by all these three thinkers seem to have no opposition. They all agree that religion, in some way or other, must aim at spiritual upliftment. But they seem to differ considerably on the point what is to be meant by spiritualization and where it needs to be emphasized. While Prof. Nayak finds the human basis of the commoners, non-elitist and downtrodden as the most suitable one for the growth and sustenance of spiritual element in religious consciousness, Prof. Bhupendra Nath insists for the mystical and transcendental background of religious spiritualization and in this sense opposes any form of secular rendering of religion specially of Hindu dharma. Prof. Mishra prefers to take religious spiritualization as nothing but 'God-realization'. It is obvious that all the three views indicated here are not descriptive in the full sense of the term; these are rather considerably prescriptive in their own ways. If one is to investigate the actual uses of the concept of religion, one will surely come across of multiple uses in such magnitude that perhaps one has to give up the idea of formulating one single definition as *the* definition of the term : religion and also on the same ground of the term : spirit. Here lexicographers' account surely is not futile. But it only helps one to have a manageable or working idea about the use of such concept without ever suggesting that what it supplies is absolutely precise and perfect without demanding any revision or modification. So there is nothing improper at the outset if one makes a move for a new formulation in understanding the spiritual element in religion and thereby offering certain prescription. To that extent any move, in this direction, is laudable at least in the intellectual setting.

But difficulty starts when one insists one's own prescription as the valid one as against other. Here there is the necessity for adducing some reason in support of one's claim of superiority over other. It is precisely here, one finds the need of philosophizing. For philosophical enquiry has been committed to analyse different views and conceptions at the background of rational plausibility and thereby to arrive at a sound conclusion. Now the attempt of understanding spiritual element of religion at the human basis is, no doubt, a notable as well as encouraging venture. Humanistic interpretation of religion has been taken up with great enthusiasm not only by some distinguished Western thinkers like Leo Tolstoy and Martin Luther but also by the famous Indian thinkers like Gandhi and Tagore. Not only that, Prof. Nayak has supplied number of instances in his writings from the classical dharmic sources as to how in the Indian context service to humanity is given great importance. Even God is depicted in the tradition as *Dīnabandhu.* All these go a long way in emphasizing the point that religious spiritualization cannot be meaningfully carried on without the basis of human touch. Transhuman rendering of religion is thus not only undesirable but surely defeats the very spirit of religious consciousness. Hence instead of emphasizing on the transcendental, mystical and dehumanised formulation of religious/ dharmic consciousness, more emphasis need be given on the humanistic version of spiritualism. For spiritual excellence cannot at any level reasonably bypass and overlook the human needs and aspirations.

Of course, that spiritual awareness in a sense does point at 'God-realization', has been asserted in certain quarters. The concept of God, no doubt, has spiritual significance. But it is also to be considered whether in a religious formulation the acceptance of God is indispensable. There are many established world religions which are explicitly nontheistic, if not atheistic. In the context of Hinduism too, the acceptance of God-realization is perhaps not so much insisted upon. True, there is the acceptance of temples, rituals, dogmas and various sacred practices. But, side by side, there is also the recognition of a person as attaining dharmic *siddhi* or religious excellence even if he keeps himself away from all such practices and guides fellowmen in attaining moral refinement and illumination that sustain the well being of human society. Buddha, Śaṅkara, Kabir and Gandhi are adored and respected in this tradition not because they have the theistic vision and they have been able to inculcate theistic outlook among the mass but primarily because they have been successful enough to arouse the significant sense of human value among the fellowmen and thereby have played important role in well shaping the development of human society at large.

In this sense, religion has a secular responsibility and this has been well noted even in the Vedic and *Upaniṣadic* sources. Spark of divinity is not expected at the cost of human welfare; rather, on the contrary, it is accommodated only when it is assured that spiritualization becomes a boosting factor in promulgating human unity, solidarity and good will. To ignore the secular basis of dharma and to emphasize on the mystical, obscure transcendence with all such dogmas, rituals and blind authoritarian beliefs will, perhaps, shake the very moral and spiritual foundation of dharma as such. Dharma, from this point of view, can be understood and appreciated as having distinct ethical rather than theological significance. This, at least, puts dharma not as opposed to science but as quite complementary to the growth of scientific temper and progress. In this sense dharma is profoundly human, this-worldly and secular. This version of religion is not untraditional. The emphasis of *śreyaḥ* over *preyaḥ* is not for any mystical theological attainment but is distinctly aimed at comprehending moral excellence at the human plane by way of disparaging rigid egoism shrouded with passions and emotions.

It therefore seems to me that Prof. Nayak's appeal for reviewing religious outlook at the background of a human, secular perspective is quite reasonably convincing.

This sort of outlook towards religion in general and Hindu dharma in particular is not necessarily unconventional.[9] *Nowadays*, even in the Western circle, one finds the religious protagonists moving more enthusiastically in the fields of social reform and human welfare than confining themselves merely with the propagation of theological obscurant dogmatic ideas and practices. Perhaps religion, in recent times, is perceptibly more human and Humanism is now more accommodative of spiritual and moral values at the human setting than before. It is rather least based upon a rigid materialistic foundation which perhaps considerably neglects human values.[10]

But, nevertheless, Prof. Nayak seems to have not stopped at this human secular basis as such. He has a distinct soft corner for a particular section of human society. For his Commonism "is a doctrine which is essentially anti-elitist in its outlook".[11] He again and again emphasizes that the poor, socially neglected and non-elitist person is no less important in the moral and religious framework. Even at times he may be found to be far more ahead in this noble journey. Prof. Nayak seems to have a great concern over the so-called moral and spiritual supremacy of the elitist group. In this context he seems to have been somewhat impatient (perhaps it is natural) in creating an impression that religion must finally be traced in the common mass. The view held by the non-elitist and also which becomes desirable within the common framework is never unimportant and must be regarded as the core of religious view of life. To him 'commonistic element' must be accepted as intrinsic to religion which again is backed by a commonistic philosophy.

But it should be observed here with due regard to the sincerity of Prof. Nayak's point of view that any person, whether belonging to elitist or to non-elitist group is regarded with high esteem if he is successful in becoming an examplary figure in the socio-moral plane having full respect for human values. He is respected not because he is either a commoner or an elitist but because he shows certain examplary form of noble character which is definitely uncommon and extraordinary. No doubt, the *mahāpuruṣas* (ideal men) are not just dropped from heaven. Any such mythological sources depicting great men and their activities have obviously no factual but valuational significance. Such stories concerning great men become instructive only when one gets message which is highly relevant in the human valuational set up. It is true that not only Rāma but also Hanumāna are given due respect in the tradition and both are designated as *Bhagavān* because of certain examplary uncommon featuers. Any person who has shown sincere as well as serious attention for the preservation and propagation of human values at the ethical plane is accepted as the moral and spiritual mentor.

So it is neither elitist nor anti-elitist framework which in any way helps us to properly understand and appreciate the sense of dharma. Dharma, in itself, is clearly above all such class distinction. It is, as a matter of fact, framed by man for his well being. That again is not necessarily at the cost of other beings and objects. Ecologically well balanced human outlook seems to be the most important message of secular based humanistic religion. That is why perhaps the classical Vedic dharma aspires for *mahāpurṣa* or *mahāmānava* who is to guide the human race for the proper inclucation of socio-moral values. In *Gītā,* it is therefore said of Kṛṣṇa that he clearly reminds Arjuna that he is never a mystical superman but his *sakhā* (bosom friend) alone. Here the moral implication seems to be that nobility is never without the human touch. There is nothing mystical about *puruṣottama.* He is clearly a man of flesh and blood, quite ordinary and common. But he is able to display the high noble sense of human values and becomes a fit person to guide the humanity.

Prof. Nayak, however, concedes that moral refinement can be noticed anywhere irrespective of caste and creed. But he views the difference between commoner and uncommoner on the basis of status symbol and feels disturbed by that. He pleads that "the uncommon is only because of the common" and "the excellence of the uncommon in the common".[12] But it can be noted here that the distinction between the uncommon and common can very well be held not on status symbol but on the actual exhibition and vindication of certain accepted forms of strength and courage at the human setting. Any body who shows sign of greatness on this account is adored as uncommon. From this point of view, uncommon need not be understood either in terms of rich/poor or elitist/anti-elitist. It is therefore not perhaps convincing to hold "the uncommon in the common" (that would be rather logically imprecise) but uncommon is to be realized only in the *human plane* and any trans-human or mystical rendering of uncommon remains only vague and obscure.

So it is the presence and growth of the very uncommon qualities and features in men which make them examplary and great. Here there is no need to remain confined either in the elitist or in the non-elitist camp. Human values clearly transcend the *class framework.* In this sense, it seems to me that the reading of religion or dharma as commonistic needs definitely reconsideration. Prof. Nayak's point of view surely becomes more plausible if it is not named as Commonism. For by that the significant point which it otherwise aims at emphasizing seems to have been adversly affected. It would be perhaps better to characterise his view-point as some form of Humanistic Uncommonism. Here the moral and spiritual values at the human plane are intelligible only when we identify such rare examplary persons who move beyond the common, ordinary limit and exhibit certain social norms and standard that becomes positive source of inspiration and encouragement in the realm of socio-empiric plane.

Notes and References

1. See Prof. Nayak's article "Religious Crisis, Hinduism and Common Ism" published in *Philosophica,* Vol. X, Nos. 1-4, January 1981, December 1981; His Oriya book: *Dārśhanika Cintana,* Upagupta Publications, Berhampur, 1984; His another Oriya article "Janatā Darshana-eka spaṣṭīkaraṇa" published in the *Dharitrī,* 24. 2. 85 and his article "A plea for Commonism" published in his book, *Philosophical Reflections,* Delhi: Motilal Banarasidass, 1987.
2. Vide "Religious Crisis, Hinduism and Common Ism", *op. cit.,* p. 35.
3. Vide, in this connection, article "Religious Crisis: Some Comments" by Prof. Bhupendra Nath in the same *Philosophica,* Vols. 11-14 combined, 1982-1985 and "Janatā Darshana" an Oriya article by Prof. Krushna Prasad Mishra in the same *Dharitrī,* 17. 2. 1985.
4. "Religious Crisis : Some Comments" *op. cit.,* pp. 116-117.
5. *Ibid.,* pp. 119-120.
6. "Janatā Darshana" *op. cit.,* p. 4.
7. "Janatā Darshana : Eka Spaṣṭīkaraṇa" *op. cit.,* p. 4.
8. Vide his Oriya article "Orissāra Dharma Dhārāre Śrī Caitanya" published in the *Samāj* I. 4. 1989.
9. Despite procedural and other differences, Prof. Nayak's approach here is found to be strikingly close with the secularistic view-point expressed by Late Prof. Ganeswar Misra. Vide his book, *Vaidica Dharma Cetanā : Eka Dārshanika Vicāra* (in Oriya), Cuttack: Santosh publications, 1985.
10. Vide, in this connection, A.J. Ayer (ed.), *The Humanist Outlook,* London : Pemberton in association with Barrie & Rockliff, 1968.
11. "Religious Crisis, Hinduism and Commonlsm", *op. cit.,* p. 35.
12. *Ibid.,* p. 33.

Index

Page numbers in *italics* refer to notes